NOT ADDED BY
UNIVERSITY OF MICHIGAN LIBRARY

KILCLIEF
&
OTHER ESSAYS

About the Author

Patricia Craig was born and grew up in Belfast. She spent many years in London and returned to live in Northern Ireland in 1999. A highly distinguished critic and reviewer, she is the author of two biographies, three memoirs, and (with Mary Cadogan) three critical studies. She has edited many anthologies, including *The Oxford Book of Ireland, The Belfast Anthology* and the *Ulster Anthology*. Volume Three of her memoir and trilogy, *Asking for Trouble,* is forthcoming.

KILCLIEF
&
OTHER ESSAYS

PATRICIA CRAIG

THE IRISH PAGES PRESS
2021

Kilclief & Other Essays
is first published in hardback
on 18 January 2021.

The Irish Pages Press
129 Ormeau Road
Belfast BT7 1SH
Ireland

www.irishpages.org

Copyright © Patricia Craig & The Irish Pages Press

All rights reserved. No part of this book may be reproduced,
stored in a retrieval system, or transmitted in any form,
or by any means, electronic, mechanical, photocopying or otherwise,
without prior written permission from The Irish Pages Press.

Typeset in 14/18 pt Monotype Perpetua
Designed and composed by RV, Belfast. Printed by Bell & Bain, Glasgow.

A CIP catalogue record for this book
is available from The British Library.

Dust jacket photographs courtesy of Jeffrey Morgan (front)
and Rachel Brown (back).

ISBN: 978-1-8382018-1-4

This book has been generously supported by
The Arts Council of Northern Ireland.

Also by Patricia Craig

Elizabeth Bowen
(1986)

Brian Moore: a Biography
(2002)

Asking for Trouble
(2007)

A Twisted Root
(2012)

Bookworm
(2015)

WITH MARY CADOGAN

You're a Brick, Angela!
· (1976)

Women and Children First
(1978)

The Lady Investigates
(1982)

AS EDITOR

The Oxford Book of English Detective Stories
(1990)

The Penguin Book of British Comic Stories

(1990)

The Penguin Book of British Comic Writing
(1992)

The Rattle of the North
(1992)

Julian Symons at Eighty
(1992)

The Oxford Book of Modern Women's Stories
(1994)

The Oxford Book of Schooldays
(1994)

The Oxford Book of Travel Stories
(1996)

Twelve Irish Ghost Stories
(1998)

The Oxford Book of Ireland
(1998)

The Belfast Anthology
(1999)

The Oxford Book of Detective Stories
(2000)

The Ulster Anthology
(2006)

In memory of my parents
Nora and Andy Craig

CONTENTS

PIOUS GIRLS AND SWEARING FATHERS

(Women and Children)

FIDDLESTICKS!

(Miscellaneous)

PROLOGUE

KILCLIEF

The word "Kilclief" first impinged on my consciousness when I heard it spoken by the poet John Hewitt. I had gone to visit him at his Stockman's Lane home in Belfast and we were discussing Ulster literature, as was our wont. It was the mid-1970s, the Troubles raging and horrors a stone's throw away. "Kilclief" came up because Hewitt was telling me about an artless author whom he found especially diverting. The Reverend Samuel Burdy (c. 1760-1820), Perpetual Curate of Kilclief during the early part of the nineteenth century. (Before that, Burdy was attached to Ardglass.) Burdy's most celebrated work is his *Life of the Late Revd. Philip Skelton* (1792), which abounds in exigencies and eccentricities. The lives of the two fellow clerics overlapped by six years, during which time they became friends. When Skelton died in 1787, Burdy undertook his biography. The resulting book presents a very curious and striking figure: impatient, impetuous, learned, charitable and subject to "the hips", that is, hypochondria. Frequently believing himself to be at death's door, the Revd. Skelton would rouse his parishioners out of their beds in the middle of the night to pray for his soul. In his youth, he had a trick of running up turf-stacks "like a cat", which amazed lookers-on. Twice, in times of famine, he sold his library and with the proceeds bought great quantities of oatmeal to distribute among the starving. Burdy, in his book, does full justice to Skelton's peculiarities. Like the "aslant" Tommy Cran, in Elizabeth Bowen's story "The Tommy Crans", the older cleric is an enormous presence.

Samuel Burdy had peculiarities of his own. In his long topographical poem, "Ardglass, or, The Ruined Castles" (in his sole collection, *Ardglass and Other Poems*), he describes in the following manner a clatter of tinkers encountered along a Co Down road:

> There have I seen them with their wives and lasses,
> Their smiling babies, and their little asses;
> Each ass then carried on its useful back
> Two pretty babies sticking in a sack.

These lines brought on an outbreak of merriment in Hewitt and myself as we pored over Burdy's innocent pages. And others in the same poem were not behindhand in raising a snort of laughter. For example, "Three lofty towers these antique walls defend, / One in the midst, and one at every end". Or: "Herring's the food of Mona's greedy sons, / Who eat them up as fast as butter'd buns". ("Mona" being the Isle of Man, the solitary place outside Ireland to which Burdy had travelled.) You have to admire the Kilclief curate's self-possession and chutzpah. It is tempting to endow him with the appearance of Sir Henry Raeburn's "Skating Minister", though we know it's the Revd. Robert Walker in that painting putting his best foot forward. A sportive or absurd element seems common to both. What's interesting about *Ardglass and Other Poems*, though, is the way it incorporates some local place-names, Ballyhornan, Killard Point, Strangford, Struell Wells. Many of these are names of villages and townlands along a particular stretch of the Co Down coast, from Strangford to Ardglass and beyond. They include Kilclief, where Burdy's Church-of-Ireland church, St Caolan's, was situated just beyond the Norman castle, "on an elevated spot near the sea-shore" (as an ancient guidebook has it). The present church on the site dates from 1839. It is small, sturdy and picturesque, but probably larger than the one that existed in Burdy's day. Burdy, in his will, specified "the north side of the church of Kilclief" as his burial place, but nothing now remains to mark the spot.

John Hewitt pronounced "Kilclief" as it is spelt, and correctly in my view, since it comes from the Irish "Cill Cléithe", which can be translated as "Church of the Wattles", or Wattle – though I wonder about "Cill Claimhe", i.e. "Church of the Lepers", since it's known that a Leper Colony was once located there. In the seventeenth century it was spelt Killcleefe and considered itself an ancient place even then, with associations stretching back to Saint Patrick. Locals today have somehow managed to drop the "c" and call it "Kil'lief". It has grown into quite a large village set well back from the shore, whereas in the past it would have consisted of nothing more than a scattering of cottages, farms and outbuildings. Its two consistent features are the church and the castle, and about the latter John Hewitt was quite informative too. He recounted with a certain glee the story concerning its original occupant, a Bishop Cely, or Sely, Bishop of Down, whose dalliance with a married woman named Lettice Savage got him into a lot of hot water and eventually cost him the See. Demoted "for crimes and excesses" in the year 1443, the unfortunate ex-bishop would have had to leave the tower-house where he and she had engaged in immorality. A fifteenth-century clerical sex scandal, an ancient fragment of ecclesiastical and domestic drama, has the power to hold one's attention for a moment, even though the details are sparse. About Lettice Savage all we know — or all I know — concerns her collector's instinct: it seems she was devoted to rare ceramics. Where did she find them, and what would have been considered "rare" in the mid-1400s? How did she go about amassing her collection? Glazed pottery was made at Downpatrick, not too far away, "where the only mediaeval kiln has been found in Ireland" (I'm quoting from Jonathan Bardon's *History of Ulster* here), but I imagine the stuff produced there would have been contemporary and therefore not of interest to a collector. I'm intrigued by this detail, as a collector of antique spongeware myself. I am also intrigued by castles and have been ever since I read Enid Blyton's *The Castle of Adventure* at the age of eight. I'll get back to the one at Kilclief in a minute. So far, my knowledge of the townland is confined to its existence as a setting for those two clerics and their doings, separated from me by more than two centuries: one wayward and notorious, the other waggish and orthodox. Certainly, as I sat in John Hewitt's book enriched room listening avidly to his anecdotes — Belfast-bred, London-domiciled as I was — I had no reason to think that "Kilclief" would shortly assume a considerable importance in my own life. But that's what happened.

I had left Belfast in the mid-1960s and moved to London to attend the Central School of Arts and Crafts and defer for a few years longer the necessity to earn a living. It was a heady time, and I soon succumbed to the charms and derestrictions of the era. But I never relinquished Belfast as a sobering and assuaging hinterland. It was where I was from, and even when it fell apart it never lost its hold on me. Three times a year I'd make the journey home, by plane or boat, and sink back gratefully into warmth and familiarity. There were the chairs and sofas, the flocked wallpaper, the blue satin eiderdown, the plane trees along St James's Avenue, all unchanged since 1950. But other things were changing. By the early 1970s, Belfast could no longer be regarded as a place of safety or recuperation. It was on a course towards disaster. Its old, untroubled, dull, decorous atmosphere was a thing of the past. In its place you had near-anarchy in the streets, enormity piled on atrocity. Something was rotten, the times were out of joint.

I was well out of it in S.E. London, but the news from the North brought incessant alarm and despair. Sometimes it came very close to home – or what had once been home. A particular school friend, once a kindred spirit and fellow poetry enthusiast, was shot in the head during an ambush of soldiers in Andersonstown and nearly died. Another, whom I remember from Form 4A as a lively and playful fifteen-year-old, was tarred and feathered for consorting with soldiers. I think of the three of us in our innocent classroom, conspiring to pull the wool over some tyrannical teacher's eyes. But that was before – in the words of the poet Ciaran Carson – Belfast "tore itself apart and patched things up again". The city, in its newest incarnation, had become indeed a thing of shreds and patches.

I'm not sure when the idea first took hold in my parents' heads that they had to turn their backs on Belfast, but by 1976 they had had enough of fear and loathing in the Falls, Ballymurphy, Andersonstown, St James's Road. They had come to crave tranquillity. They were sick of the sight of boarded-up shops, bomb damage, a burning bus against the backdrop of Divis Mountain. It would not be especially convenient for them to relocate themselves, since their respective places of work were close at hand. But as it happened, my school-teacher mother hadn't long to go before she reached retiring age, and my father with his job as store-keeper at Eastwood's Scrap Yard on the Andersonstown Road, professed himself willing and eager to drive to work each day from wherever they ended up.

Where they ended up was Kilclief, after a couple of summers spent driving round the Ards and Lecale ("Lecale", from the Irish *Leath Cathail*, meaning Cathal's share of the country, is the name of the whole district of which Kilclief is a tiny part), in search of a suitable habitation. They had never heard of it either, before chance deposited them along the rocky shore of Strangford Lough, looking across to the southern end of the Ards Peninsula with its straggle of white houses just discernible in the distance. Further away to the right was the open sea, with the Angus Rock Lighthouse presiding over the entrance to the Narrows. The new house was a 1950s bungalow, built on the site of something much older. It was a final choice after numerous other possibilities had been considered. It would not have been my choice, though I kept my reservations to myself and feigned enthusiasm. All right, the setting was lovely, but the house was nondescript. I had no emotional attachment to it and never would have, though I suppose I got used to it. I first stayed there in December 1976, and between that date and my mother's death in 2001, there must have been more than seventy occasions when it became, for me, a zone of comfort if not bliss. My actual home, between 1972 and 1999, was in Blackheath, South-East London, where I lived with my husband the painter Jeffrey Morgan, and two enchanting cats. From the early '80s on, Jeff too would spend a part of each summer in Kilclief, where he grew to relish its pure clear air, its ever-changing sea – one minute azure, the next stone-grey – its birds and butterflies and profuse vegetation, its gorse and montbretia along the roadside, the crooked apple tree in the back garden, the beach before the house, the rocks commandeered by lolling seals. The house itself never seemed to bother Jeff, even though his aesthetic sense is more highly developed than mine. The beauties of the place overrode the bungalow's shortcomings.

My parents' bungalow had no history, or none that I was aware of. But as I've indicated, the district was steeped in history. And a mile or two along the road into Strangford was a house that offered everything I could wish for in the way of atmosphere and fraught decrepitude. Isle O'Valla. "Do you know that house", some friends who were staying at nearby Castle Ward had asked, "just outside Strangford, set well back from the road, hidden by all the trees that have sprung up in front of it, on what must once have been a lawn?" (Saplings having rooted away, as in the Yeats poem.) Like something out of Jane Austen, they added. I didn't know the house, but, thus alerted, I quickly found it. Filled with curiosity, Jeff and I made our way up the lane that separated Isle O'Valla from the fields running on towards Strangford Village. We squeezed through a rusty iron gate and into the overgrown meadow where cattle sometimes grazed between the trees, and there in front of us was the house with its Georgian doorway and fanlight still intact – beautiful, spooky and utterly unreclaimable (though we didn't realise it at first). Like the House of Usher, it sported an enormous crack running the entire length of its south-facing side.

For a few crazy months, we thought we could save it. We found the farmer who owned it (solely for the land), and he agreed to sell us the house for £50,000. This was in the late eighties or early nineties, and Isle O'Valla at the time had been lying derelict for more than 30 years. We were very happy living in Blackheath, but our thoughts were already turning towards Northern Ireland. What had started as a vague idea, a possibility for the future, suddenly looked as though it might come to pass. To leave London would be a wrench, but we had my ageing parents to consider; also, the prospect of somehow rescuing an endangered house was very attractive. Both of us were mad about pre-twentieth-century architecture, and conscious of how precarious its survival was in the benighted North. It was dreadful to contemplate the losses in this area, due to bombing, redevelopment, or, more frequently, cold indifference and neglect. If – when – we came to live in Ireland, we had decided, it would be with the aim of saving some historic building on the verge of obliteration. Whatever the merits of a tainted house's "returning to the clay", as in the William Trevor story "The News from Ireland", we took a different view.

It wasn't long before we had infiltrated Isle O'Valla. Though it was warped and swollen with damp, the impressive front door could be pushed ajar sufficiently to enable a person of reasonable girth to slither through. (Later, with the door secured uselessly against miscreants and vagrants, we gained an entry – as they would – by scrambling through a ground-floor window.) The interior, at first glance, was chilling in its creepiness and blight. We stood, holding our breaths, in a house broken up and dishevelled. To the right was a room we never saw because it languished in darkness, but we had an impression that its floor had collapsed. It was easy to visualise trolls or ghouls rising out of its blackness like an emanation of menace – or, more cheerfully, with a comic-book formlessness. From Isle O'Valla's once-grand entrance hall an imposing staircase swept up to the first floor; it was still negotiable, though you had to be careful to avoid the corpses of crows which littered every tread. Along the first-floor landing was a succession of doors, mostly closed, causing a frisson of almost pleasurable dread as I thought of Eel Marsh House in Susan Hill's great ghost story "The Woman in Black" with its empty chair behind a locked door rocking back and forth. Unlike Eel Marsh, though, with its copious fusty furnishings, Isle O'Valla House was empty of everyday accoutrements, disconsolate and stripped to the bone. There was light enough up here, partly due to the holes in the roof. I was drawn to the place, no doubt about it, but also overwhelmed by its murk and melancholy.

At the back of the house lay a warren of unspeakably gloomy and decaying rooms – probably once servants' quarters – and a narrow staircase, up which I declined to venture. God knows what extremes of rot and infestation might wait to assault you at the top. This part of the building was even more filthy, more woebegone than the rest. Wherever you stood in Isle O'Valla, though, the house closed in around you and at the same time induced a sensation I associate with agoraphobia, a sort of diffused trepidation, or shrinking feeling. We succeeded in taking a look at most of the rooms on the first and second floors, but very warily, on my part at least, very much aware of perils both physical and metaphysical. The rules of Health and Safety were unknown to these precincts. And the house was surely haunted by *something*, if only a miasma of abandonment, or only in the realm of the imagination. Some sinister residue remained in place.

And yet. If you stood by the door of Isle O'Valla on a summery afternoon, with flothering roses and trampled grasses burgeoning around you, you could almost imagine a very different scene. Here is the house in its palmy days, order and comfort within, and people in Victorian dress taking tea on the lawn. Not quite Jane Austen's era, but embodying an Austen-like decorum none the less. (There is an actual connection between Jane Austen and Isle O'Valla House which I will get to in a minute.) And not an inauthentic vision either. But before it became attached to aristocratic Ulster, Isle O'Valla had a darker past. While our interest in the place was at its height, we began to piece together aspects of its history, bit by bit.

We learnt that Isle O'Valla was built as a Charter School in 1817. But is this true? Nothing about it suggests an institution. The sweeping staircase, the handsome ground-floor rooms and other features are more in keeping with a Georgian family home. According to the records, there *was* a charter school in Strangford from the mid-1700s, but whether or not this was replaced by Isle O'Valla I have no idea. The charter movement in Ireland had a proselytising purpose, which doesn't sit well with ecumenical imperatives of the present. The schools catered solely for Catholic pupils, charity children, with the aim of turning them into Protestants. The movement didn't – doesn't – have a good reputation, and Isle O'Valla is not enhanced by the connection; but I suppose we have to accept that during the early nineteenth century a school of this sort existed on the spot. It seems it was visited in 1818 by an inspector who declared the current master to be "a giddy man, and not fit for such responsibility". For this reason, or some other, the charter was withdrawn around 1830, whereupon a local minister named Samuel Livingstone promptly set up another school at Isle O'Valla. But that doesn't seem to have prospered either.

The next time Isle O'Valla comes into focus is during the Famine in Co Down, when local people infected with typhus or cholera were brought to the house to be tended by volunteer nurses. Most of the famine victims quickly died, and were carried out in makeshift coffins, through the front door and down the long stretch of garden, to a burial place on a kind of island facing the house in Strangford Lough, and connected to the mainland at low tide by an isthmus. No doubt the grim processions took place in the dead of night, the coffin-bearers in black frock coats, and others, similarly dressed, carrying flaming torches to light the way. Or so I envisaged it, in daylight, looking towards the stony, gorse-strewn burial spot from a first-floor window of Isle O'Valla (not that I could see the spot, with trees blocking the view), and letting the ancient imagined charnel atmosphere go to my head.

In 1847, then, Isle O'Valla functioned as a kind of supplementary workhouse. 12 years later, all trace of disease and calamity cleared away, it became at last what it had seemed always destined to be: a family home. In 1859, Captain the Honourable Somerset Ward of nearby Castle Ward (an historic mansion on a very much grander scale) married Norah Mary Elizabeth Hill, eldest daughter of Lord George Hill of *Facts from*

Gweedore fame, and brought his bride to a refurbished Isle O'Valla House. Norah's mother, Cassandra, who died in childbirth in 1842 when Norah was just seven, was a niece of Jane Austen, the daughter of Austen's brother Edward (who had changed his name to Knight). These remarkable facts only came to my attention in 2011, when our interest in Isle O'Valla House had long waned. In that year was published a fascinating account, by Sophia Hillan, of Jane Austen's nieces in Ireland, *May, Lou & Cass.*

So the friends who described Isle O'Valla, back in the 1980s, as resembling "something out of Jane Austen" had got it right. (In acknowledgement of this, I sent them a copy of Sophia Hillan's marvellous book.) Norah Ward, in fact, was Austen's great-niece; her three children were born at Isle O'Valla, and her unmarried aunt Marianne Knight – the "May" of Hillan's title – often visited her there, travelling by sea from Stranraer to Belfast, and then on to Downpatrick, "where a fly waited for me and deposited me ... quite safely here [Isle O'Valla] at 4 o'clock", Marianne assured her nephew Montague Knight at Chawton in Hampshire, writing in 1884 when she, Marianne, was in her eighty-fourth year. She was in Ireland again when Somerset Ward sustained an accident five years later. He was dragged along the ground by a runaway horse and suffered a concussion of the brain. He must have recovered, however, for he lived on until 1912. His wife Norah died in 1920. When or why the Somerset Wards left Isle O'Valla I do not know, but in 1910 the house was sold to a family named McCausland, hoteliers from Downpatrick. They, or their descendants, lived there, as far as I can tell, until the 1950s when the last of them died. Then a farmer named Lowe acquired the property and presided over its long decline. His cattle occupied the outhouses and grazed the land. The house itself – described in architectural surveys as "a very tall, austere Georgian house with three bays, three storeys, quoins and a large fanlight above the front door" – was merely a white elephant in Farmer Lowe's view. Over the years, some attempts were made to take it over and restore dignity to it (including ours), but nothing came of these. It still stands – just – but ivy grips not only the steps but the entire facade, windows and all. It has died from neglect and is steadily decomposing.

It dawned on us gradually (and especially, on me) that the restoration of Isle O'Valla would be an unworkable undertaking. We hadn't the resources, of time or money. But the house continued for some time to draw us towards it like addicts to an opium den. Whenever I stayed at Kilclief I'd invite friends down from Belfast and introduce them to the drear delights of Isle O'Valla House. The wonderful American photographer Rachel

Brown (Rachel Guise), who was then based in Ireland, came with me to Isle O'Valla and captured on film its stark fascination. She set her camera on a tripod and photographed the two of us, incongruous intruders, larking before the grey facade, the cracked and broken window-panes, the ominous interior looming beyond the half-open door. Like the entrance to burnt Danielstown, in Elizabeth Bowen's novel *The Last September*, the door at that point "stood open hospitably" – not upon a furnace, indeed, but upon an ultimate darkness and desolation.

Derek Mahon, Paul Muldoon, Douglas and Marie Carson, some old friends from school and art school, all arrived at Kilclief at one time or another, and had the enigmatic hidden house pointed out to them as a local feature. The poet Michael Longley came more than once, and on one occasion he brought with him his friend Michael Allen who was then a lecturer in the English Department of Queen's University. The three of us, unlikely delinquents, broke into Isle O'Valla House and proceeded gingerly to the top floor, where we entered a room and encountered a sight that made our "flesh to creep the day an' [our] hair to stan' on end" (to quote a line from the opening verse of Mrs Alexander's grisly ballad "Stumpie's Brae"). In a corner of the otherwise empty room was a table on which reposed a candle in a candlestick. A rickety chair was drawn up to the table, and leaning against the chair was a single crutch.

We were brought up short by the eerie tableau. To the aura of emptiness and neglect was added a qualm of the unearthly. Nobody spoke. An impulse came over me to beat a hasty retreat, but I didn't altogether give in to it – just backed away slightly, thankful that I wasn't alone. I don't know what direful presence I thought I was sensing in the vacant upper room. The ghost of a cripple? A Famine victim? Had we stumbled into an offshoot of *Nightmare Abbey?* A flesh-and-blood tramp was a rather more likely candidate for the role of trespasser. I'm sure it *was* a tramp. But a question arises: why would a disabled vagrant stomp all the way up to the second floor? And why, unless he needed to leave in a hurry, would he then abandon his crutch? Did some unspeakable alarm occur in the dead of night, causing him to flee for his life? Safe and snug in my bed at 119 Shore Road, I would sometimes waken in the small hours and think of nearby Isle O'Valla, a candle burning, an occupied chair, wafts of dust and decay, and some supernatural element added to chill the blood.

These are the kinds of imagining that flow into one's head in the hours of darkness. But even in sober daylight, Isle O'Valla House has a singular power to provoke disquiet. Even the seals disporting themselves in the choppy Lough waters nearby partake of its palpable foreboding. There is of course a vibrant lore connected with seals. "It is the end of a bad summer for all but the seals", wrote the poet Damian Smyth in his 2012 collection *Market Street*, "those souls of the dead turning themselves over in the waves / as though they cannot sleep ...". Souls of the dead: local nineteenth-century victims of drowning or cholera. The house, Isle O'Valla, is awash in malign associations. So I was grateful, again, to *May, Lou & Cass* for painting a different picture, one composed largely of tranquillity and domesticity. (The main Irish locale of Jane Austen's nieces was Donegal and the Inishowen Peninsula, where they are buried, but Isle O'Valla makes an intriguing sideline to the story.) Sophia Hillan deserves great credit for uncovering it. But it's not her only connection to the locality. Leaving Isle O'Valla House and continuing along the road by the shore, you reach the castle, then a bungalow known as "the Judge's house", another recently built, my parents' home, and further along the road towards Ballyhornan, the holiday home of the Belfast novelist Michael McLaverty, to which a blue plaque was affixed in 2009, in the presence of Seamus Heaney, Michael Longley, Sophia Hillan and others.

McLaverty deserves his plaque, but to my mind, only just. As I see it, his reputation rests on his first two novels and a handful of stories. Sophia Hillan, our premier McLaverty scholar, does not agree. Her study of 1992, *The Silken Twine*, treats with subtlety and sympathy his entire body of work, and the reasons for the change which overtook it in the 1940s. She notes the cost to himself, and to his dismayed readership, of the decision he took at that time. "His novels, after the first two, caused severe strain on a nature finely attuned to delicacy and lyricism, as though a painter of miniature water-colours had set himself to cover a vast canvas in oils." Certainly McLaverty turned his back on delicacy and lyricism, but the mould into which he forced himself, I would argue, was more akin to an oleograph of the Sacred Heart. After the charm and lucidity of *Call My Brother Back* (1939) – as fresh as a raindrop – and the invigorating Falls Road realism of *Lost Fields* (1942), a terrible distorting element got into McLaverty's fiction. A Catholic element. Rather than continuing to write as someone profoundly attuned to the rituals and routines of an Ulster Catholic world, he chose instead to present himself as a writer imbued with Catholic values: piety, pusillanimity, priest-adulation, anti-feminism and all. It played havoc with his literary impulse. Out went insight and sensitivity, and in came unction and sentimentality.

All right, I'm being too hard on the later McLaverty, who became a friend of my parents, and to a lesser extent, of myself. We found him an accomplished raconteur and an intriguing neighbour. But I can't deny the distaste I felt for his suite of Catholic family romances, starting with *In This Thy Day* (1945). They seemed to me to encompass a stupefying banality, with their priests for ever uttering platitudes, their dreary courtships going awry, and their unfortunate women characters getting it in the neck for failing to be enthralled by the simplicities of cottage life. "[S]omehow a girl was made for one spot", he wrote. "When she starts the roaming she's like a dog that goes after sheep – never contented." Observations such as this (there are many) make you wish he had stuck to his miniature water-colours.

But there he was in the 1980s, his literary activity a thing of the past, cycling gamely past my parents' house wearing his trademark black beret. He was heading towards his bungalow opposite Killard Point with its exhilarating walks, its wild orchids, bees and butterflies and zestful sea breezes. And a bit further along the Lough shore, Ballyhornan, immortalised in jingly homespun verse by Samuel Burdy, who had occasion to lament a culinary scarcity:

No sweet milk in Ballyhornan,
In the evenin' or the mornin',
For the curate, honest, civil.
No! They'd send him to the divil.

The day was saved, the poem goes on, by a local woman who supplied the doleful cleric with the milk he craved for his tea. It's a pretty paltry placement for Ballyhornan on the literary map of Lecale, but that was about the sum of it until Michael McLaverty took up residence in the area. (One of his stories alludes specifically to "Kilclief National Schools, 1880".) Seamus Heaney, who unveiled the plaque and attended the later celebratory gathering at Down Arts Centre in Downpatrick, has often recorded his admiration for the novelist – who was, incidentally, headmaster of the school in West Belfast at which Heaney taught for a brief period in the 1960s. The early poem "Fosterage" pays tribute to McLaverty and his bracing advice: "Go your own way"; "... to hell with overstating it". And Heaney goes all out to extol "the precision with which [McLaverty] recreates the life of Belfast streets or Rathlin shores or County Down fields, and the authenticity of the speech he hears in all those places."

All McLaverty's work, even – or especially – the novels drenched in holy water, has a flavour of times past, a rural or an urban spareness of feeling, a state of low expectation or a faraway unworldliness. (The impulse connected with this modus operandi can lead to an outcome either rewarding or dismaying.) The shore road between Strangford and Ballyhornan is intimately tied up with Michael McLaverty's particular way of seeing the world, his devotion to minutiae and propriety and tradition. "The soil softened, wet mist lay in the folds of the land, and in the evenings there was the smell of growing things."

Other, more recent, writers have drawn inspiration from the place. Damian Smyth's most characteristic work, for instance, is full of the landscapes and inscapes of this part of coastal and inland Lecale. Kilclief, Strangford, Ardglass, Struell Wells, Downpatrick, the Quoile River … these are places where the actual and imaginative worlds of this poet strike sparks off one another. They are densely and mysteriously present, even in his city poems. "And then the rain falls", he writes in Section X111 of his long elegy for a young schoolteacher murdered in Belfast in 1984 by IRA gunmen. "Losing Mary Travers" continues:

> … and I know that if
> it's raining in the town it's dry out there,
> along the coast, by Strangford and Kilclief …

Over the topographical features – back roads, the back gate of Castle Ward, beech trees along the River Quoile – is superimposed a vibrant sense of history and melancholy: the pungency and melancholy of history, especially local history with its obscure tragedies, its dead struck by lightning, drowned, murdered, lost in some forgotten battle or other. And always, the sombre coast as a haunt of seals.

I would like to think, as well, that Michael Longley's seals – "Head and shoulders above seal-grey water" – are the seals of Kilclief, which are often to be spotted basking on rocks along the rugged shoreline; though I know they are just as likely to be denizens of Carrigskeewaun, Longley's home from home on the other side of Ireland. In a different mode, and coming at it from a different direction (Ardglass), you get "Richard Rowley", too, rejoicing in the weatherbeaten coast and its seasonal glories:

> Oh, there by many a loaning,
> Past farms that I could name,
> Thro' Sheeplands to Gun Island,
> The whins are all aflame.

The whins are generally aflame around Easter, a time of the year when I could be found at Kilclief, getting on with whatever project was currently engaging my attention. Part of my Brian Moore biography was written here, along with my MI5 book *One Girl's War* (ghostwritten for Joan Miller) and introductions to various anthologies. The house close to the sea where my parents lived had a separate wing which was allocated to me. Well, "wing" is too grand a term: what it was was a bed-sitting-room and bathroom. The old pine table on which we ate our meals at 551 Donegall Road, Belfast, now stood in front of a window facing the side garden and the sea beyond. The view from the window was rather restricted, even without the streams of rainwater which frequently drenched it, but the sea was visible out there, on stormy days and sunny days, between the side wall of the house and the two large trees and overgrown hedge which separated us from the neighbouring field. You couldn't see the lighthouse from my sitting-room window, but often its lonesome fog-horn hooting would sound through the night. Gradually, the place established a tentative and easily dissolvable hold on me, remote though it was from my urban requirements. The rocks, the shore, the castle, Burdy, Isle O'Valla, the sea wall, the seals, the whins, the exorbitant weather, all somehow coalesced into an image beyond the commonplace, and beyond gainsaying.

RED HANDS
AND DANCING FEET

A MASTER OF THE UPROAR

Barbara Hayley (ed.), *Carleton's Traits and Stories and the 19th-Century Anglo-Irish Tradition*

William Carleton (1794–1869) received the greater part of his education in a barn in County Tyrone, and thereafter had a good deal to say on the subject of poor scholars and the standard means of social betterment available to them: recruitment to the priesthood. Carleton himself came close to following this traditional course. He was saved for literature by going on a pilgrimage to St Patrick's Purgatory in Lough Derg, in his late teens, and afterwards succumbing to apostasy as his eyes were opened to what he deemed malpractices and defects infesting Irish Catholicism. The church edifice fell apart in front of him, revealing nothing at its centre but shoddiness, inanity and barbarism.

Carleton's revised religious views made a favourable impression on the Revd Caesar Otway, editor of the anti-Catholic *Christian Examiner*. When the two men met in the late 1820s and discovered a common repugnance for Catholic noxiousness and chicanery, Otway invited Carleton to set out in writing his recollections of the degrading pilgrimage, with particular reference to its enlightening effect on the mind of an observant young Catholic. "The Lough Derg Pilgrim" was the result.

This was Carleton's first published work, but it wasn't included among the *Traits and Stories of the Irish Peasantry* until the new edition of 1842, when it appeared with the bulk of its anti-Catholic observations intact. Barbara Hayley, who has noted and recorded every tiny textual alteration carried out by Carleton between 1830, when *Traits and Stories* (first series) was originally published in book form, and 1842, when the "definitive edition" came out, as well as tracking down every deletion and every addition to the stories, restores to Carleton sole responsibility for certain extreme views expressed in his works. Earlier critics, such as W.B. Yeats and Alice Curtayne, had preferred to attribute these to Otway's influence, or even to Otway himself, on the grounds that no Catholic, even a renegade one, would turn on his hereditary church in such a heated way ("It is strange to reflect how many ordinances of the Romish religion are on the side of man's depravity ...", Carleton wrote in "The Station", an early *Christian Examiner* piece included in the first series of *Traits and Stories*). Actually, Carleton's opinions – like Otway's own – are the product of an impulse towards social criticism, rather than bigotry, which he deplored as much as anyone. The Catholic Church is by no means the only institution at the mercy of his considerable oratorical powers. No source of hardship or disaffection in the Irish countryside escapes his attention.

The scope for his invective was pretty wide. "Merciful God!" he exclaimed in his unfinished autobiography, "In what a frightful condition was the country at that time. I speak now of the North of Ireland." The Orange Order fostered sectarianism and the abuse of power; the Ribbonmen (a secret agrarian society) retaliated by means of cattle-maiming, arson and other traditional terrorist expedients. Pressure to align oneself with one or other of these bodies was extreme. "I have never entertained any ill-feeling against the people on either side; it is their accursed systems which I detest", Carleton declared with feeling, dissociating himself from the lot of them. His novel *Valentine M'Clutchy* stands as an indictment of Orangeism; and he tackled the Ribbon Movement in a similar spirit of antagonism in *Rody the Rover*.

You could say that Carleton's most spectacular achievement was to turn peasant discontents and disabilities into the stuff of melodrama. His story "Tubber Derg", for example, contains a worthy Catholic family whose fortunes are followed from prosperity to poverty and back again; and this vicissitude motif recurs in a number of his novels. Bad landlords and bad agents are to blame for the families' misfortunes; Carleton, temporarily diverted from his strictures on Catholicism, called them "the two great curses of Ireland". Valentine M'Clutchy, in the novel of that name, is an agent of the most deplorable type (and an Orangeman to boot), and the novelist makes his origins as hideous as possible to underline the point: he's the bastard son of a gaoler's daughter and a lustful squire. The anti-Ribbon piece in *Traits and Stories*, "Wildgoose Lodge", with its fearful descriptions of burning and slaughter, has its roots in an actual historical event: in October 1816 a midnight attack was carried out on the home of a man named Lynch who had fallen foul of the local Ribbon gang. Both parties were Catholic; Carleton is careful to distinguish between sectarian rampages and "faction fights" involving members of the same sect.

It was a time when the countryside was studded with gibbets, as Carleton recorded; murder, evictions, beggary and starvation were other features of a particularly colourful era. In "The Poor Scholar" Carleton alludes to a desperate practice of the starving, the bleeding of bullocks and calves. This, in fact, was a common resort: a celebrated work of 1792, the Revd Samuel Burdy's *Life of Skelton*, mentions the typical famine diet of boiled weeds and blood stolen from cattle. Carleton's feelings about this matter occasionally erupted in ferociously satiric comment. "Abstinence from food is the national diversion", he avers, in *The Squanders of Castle Squander*. His outrage, however, is more often expressed in conventionally dramatic terms. We have *The Black Prophet*, for example, a romance of destitution written during the great famine and referring back to a lesser one, which makes its point about the effects of hunger in a series of intemperate evocations.

Without an exacting readership – as Yeats pointed out – Carleton was under no obligation to differentiate in his fiction between drama and melodrama. On the evidence of certain passages in his works, it is possible to surmise that his earliest literary models included the first historical novel to emerge from Ulster, James McHenry's engagingly artless *O'Halloran; or The Insurgent Chief* (1820), with its wild contrivances and startling diction. But Carleton's remarkable fluency, assurance and recklessness soon carried him beyond such an elementary narrative technique as we find in McHenry. He's perhaps the most thoroughly riproaring of the nineteenth-century Irish novelists; characteristically, his stories proceed in an atmosphere of incessant animation and agitation. He gets the fullest theatrical effect from every incident he depicts. Extraordinary physical signals accompany the strong emotions of his characters. Veins bulge, lips froth and eyes blaze. At one point a defrocked cleric, in a passion, tears the hair from his head and flings it on a table (in "The Lianhan Shee").

The language of his tales is equally extravagant. Barbara Hayley's excellent study documents the way in which Carleton kept tinkering with his *Traits and Stories*, striving over and over to reproduce the authentic speech-pattern of Clogher Valley peasants in the first half of the nineteenth century. The result, it's true, is often pretty florid and tiresome: "No, in troth, Alick, wudn't they; but maybe if you wor, the promise ye broke to Sally Mitchell might throuble ye a bit; at any rate, I've a prayer, an' if I only repeated it wanst, I mightn't be afeard iv all the divils in hell." Carleton thickens his peasant voices almost to the point of impenetrability, and at the same time he runs the risk of making his more noble characters appear as buffoons. It is hard to take seriously the activities of someone who constantly broadens "easy" to "aisy", adds an extra consonant to words like "order" ("ordher"), and speaks obsequiously of "gintlemen". These dialect peculiarities, in conjunction with the unrelenting volubility of all the characters, are almost totally overwhelming.

Carleton, however, deserves credit for his attempts to transcribe an Irish country vernacular, roughness, unruliness and all; with a little more circumspection he might have brought it off. His fiction, as a number of critics have pointed out, contains three types of English: standard, colloquial and "tall". The last, which denotes affectation in Carleton's characters, goes in for malapropism on a large scale – "Would you feel a delectability in my superscriptionizing the epistolary correspondence, ma'am, that I'm about to adopt?" The effect of this is meant to be comic, but it also reminds us that English wasn't the indigenous language of the locality, and that in many instances it was only imperfectly acquired. Carleton's store of Gaelic expressions contributes pungency to his fiction, though his annoying habit of transliteration has produced some very peculiar renderings of them.

Traits and Stories is full of stock ingredients which were later elaborated in the novels: the temporary frustration of an innocent romantic attachment, an obsessive desire for revenge on the part of a villain, prodigious injustice, demented meanderings and comic roguery of every kind. "Authenticity" was the one merit Carleton claimed for himself, and you find it over and over in his details of social life; it didn't, however, extend to his plots, which owe a great deal too much to the popular "sensationalist" fiction of the day.

He suffered, too, from a serious inhibition in his treatment of "immaculate" women characters, turning out, among a welter of minor female nonentities, two of the least appealing heroines in Victorian fiction. These are Kathleen Cavanagh in *The Emigrants of Ahadarra*, and Mary M'Loughlin in *Valentine M'Clutchy* – one a prig and the other a ninny. Only his servant girls, like Nanny Peety in the former novel, are ever forthright or witty.

And yet. The energy and resourcefulness of his narratives are disarming; and occasionally he surprises us with the sharpness of his observations and their relevance to the present time. Bigotry and its consequences affronted him, but he remained alive to its absurdity none the less. There's a marvellous set-piece in *Valentine M'Clutchy* in which a Protestant convert comes face to face with his Catholic counterpart. Both men start off by defending their new religions, but before long a subtle shift in positions occurs. By the end of the argument each has reverted, willy nilly, to his original faith. The ex-Orangeman proceeds atavistically to curse the pope, while the ex-Catholic vehemently retrieves his discarded Papism. The two men come to blows. By this point a crowd of supporters has gathered, an equal number of Catholics and Protestants, and, Carleton tells us, "the Catholics, ignorant of the turn which the controversy had taken, supported Bob and Protestantism; while the Protestants, owing to a similar mistake, fought like devils for Darby and the Pope." It's hard to think of a more telling indictment, or one more economically expressed.

Belligerents on both sides still exist, some of them no less ludicrously misled, but many of Carleton's other standard types were already becoming obsolete when he took on the task of recording their traits and customs. The project endeared him to the Young Irelander Thomas Davis, who believed the work would enrich the understanding of future social historians. Carleton marshalled an array of hedge schoolmasters, Ribbonmen, barefoot scholars, corrupt agents, sanctimonious attorneys, industrious peasants, greedy clerics and so on, putting them through their paces with elan and enthusiasm, and, in the process, making himself a master of the Irish uproar.

Times Literary Supplement, 1983

GREEN MARTYRS

Thomas Kinsella (ed.),
The New Oxford Book of Irish Verse
Paul Muldoon (ed.),
The Faber Book of Contemporary Irish Poetry
Dillon Johnston, *Irish Poetry After Joyce*

Each of these books – two anthologies and a critical
study – is notable for its exclusions, among other things;
each takes a strong line over questions of definition and
evaluation; and each contains much to applaud. Thomas
Kinsella's *New Oxford Book* goes right back to the beginning, to a rath in front of an oak wood singled out for
comment by some anonymous poet of the sixth century,
and cherished as a survival from an even more distant
past, while the Faber book takes as its starting point
(as the blurb has it) the death of Yeats. The American
publisher and critic Dillon Johnston plumps for Joyce
rather than Yeats in his title: not on a whim, he tells us,

but in acknowledgement of certain literary procedures sanctioned by Joyce, and thereafter available to poets no less than prose writers. The lofty tone perfected by Yeats didn't do at all when it came to the bleakness and piecemeal quality of the post-Yeats world: so many poets found. Joyce's more variable manner showed a way to take in every aspect of current social conditions, and keep the end result tricksy.

With the death of Yeats, in other words, came something like a full stop, and then with the death of Joyce a new beginning, as back after back was turned on all approaches to poetry not in keeping with the realities of the day. In that year, 1941, Patrick Kavanagh was composing a 757-line poem on the charmlessness of Irish country life, which nevertheless manages to encompass a good deal of its pungency:

> The potato-gatherers like mechanised
> scarecrows move
> Along the side-fall of the hill ...

Austin Clarke was moving on from the kind of social criticism, lyrically expressed, which we get in "The Straying Student" (say), to a knottier and more derisive manifestation of the same drive (though it took him 17 years to get together a volume of poetry in the new mode: *Ancient Lights* came out in 1955, while 1938 was the date of its predecessor, *Night and Morning*). Social criticism: this is one of the two major preoccupations of Irish writers in the twentieth century, whether the tone is glum, angry, ironic or ebullient.

The other notable enterprise in contemporary Irish writing is the retrieval, or acknowledgement, of some facet of the past, generally for the purpose of savouring the sense of national distinctiveness. Such a past needn't be beyond one's own recall, as we find in Louis MacNeice's enumeration of the egregious inheritances of Ulster:

> The linen mills, the long wet grass, the ragged
> hawthorn,
> And one read black where the other read white,
> his hope
> The other man's damnation:
> Up the Rebels, to Hell with the Pope,
> And God Save — as you prefer —
> the King or Ireland.

However, one of the most important reclamations of recent years is the group of translations by Thomas Kinsella of poems assembled by Seán Ó Tuama, brought out in a dual-language anthology called *An Duanaire 1600-1900: Poems of the Dispossessed* (1981). During the three centuries covered in this collection, the destruction of Gaelic Ireland was deplored as it was taking place, in the mordant verses of poets like Ó Bruadair and Ó Rathaillle, and also in the more mellifluous *aislingí* (vision poems) which proliferated in the eighteenth century. Kinsella has included a good supply of *Duanaire* translations in his *New Oxford Book*. Some are more felicitous than others – Ó Rathaille's lovely *"Gile na Gile"* ("Brightness most Bright"), which defeated Mangan in the nineteenth century and Frank O'Connor in the twentieth, doesn't prove manipulable by Thomas Kinsella either – but all are of the utmost interest and significance in denoting the cultural resources of the unregenerate Irish.

As literature in Irish dwindled virtually to a handful of songs scattered throughout the countryside, the note most frequently sounded was a plaintive one. At the same time, while the Gaelic tradition was all but eradicated, another was forging ahead, as various confident and sagacious Anglo-Irish voices were raised in deliberation or mockery. Swift, Goldsmith, Sheridan: these turn up in the Oxford anthology, alongside the anonymous authors of such demotic verses as "Lilliburlero". Incidentally, the title and refrain of this Orange song is surely the transliteration of an Irish phrase, *An lile ba léir é, ba linn an lá*, which means "The lily [the Orange lily] was triumphant, we won the day" – and not, as Kinsella asserts in a note, "a nonsense parody of the Irish language". For another line on the Williamite Wars, Kinsella – who, in the interests of consistency, sticks by and large to his own translations – might with profit have included the Frank O'Connor version of the anonymous *"Slán Chum Pádraic Sáirséal"* ("Farewell to Patrick Sarsfield"), a tribute to the vanquished Lord Lucan written after the Siege of Limerick in 1691, and among the earliest utterances of an untutored Gaelic voice:

At the Boyne Bridge we took our first beating,
From the bridge at Slane we were soon retreating,
And then we were beaten at Aughrim too –
Ah, fragrant Ireland, that was goodbye to you.

However, Kinsella doesn't overlook the fact that, as he has it, "the Irish tradition has always presented an intimate fusion of literature and history", or that the pattern thereby created is continually being adapted to accommodate contemporary feelings about past events, along with items extracted from one context to enrich another. "Rapparees, whiteboys, volunteers, ribbonmen ...": so runs a line in Richard Murphy's poem "Green Martyrs" (one of Kinsella's choices), naming bands of disaffected countrymen from the seventeenth century to the nineteenth, and getting the fullest flavour from these historical allusions. In a

similar way, the phrase "hedge school", with its connotations of deprivation and resilience, crops up in
the work of Heaney and Montague, recharged. And
when Patrick Kavanagh writes about carting dung to
an outlying farm, he remembers a casual labourer and
Gaelic poet of the 1750s or thereabouts, who, with
his mind inappropriately engaged by literary matters,
forgot to empty a cart-load of manure at the top of a
hill and trundled the whole lot down again – and calls
his poem "Art McCooey".

Kavanagh, testy and disgruntled and lyrical, marks
the middle stage in the rural Irish mode. Before his
hardy approach, in the twentieth century, comes the
work of many minor poets who succumbed too readily
to wistfulness and associated emotions – hankering
after a cottage in a bog or an epiphany on a heathery
hill – and in his wake we get the urbanities superimposed over country themes by such accomplished
writers as Heaney and Muldoon. Neither innocent
pastoralism nor innocent republicanism, to be sure, was
a tenable sentiment in Irish writing from about 1910
on (though these modes didn't altogether die out), as
the ironic way of looking at things, and its attendant
complexities, supervened. Once we reach the present,
and the resourceful imaginations of poets like Muldoon, various new and memorable configurations are
obtained by means of an outrageous and productive

rifling of standard verse forms like the *aisling*. John Montague, a poet much given to the perusal of the past, has a blunter, if no less telling method of setting out his historical material:

> a shattered procession
> of anonymous suffering
> files through the brain:
> burnt houses, pillaged farms,
> a province in flames.

The province laid waste in this way is Ulster, whose historical assets are suppressed and fragmented. "All around", Montague writes elsewhere, "shards of a lost tradition" – some of which reside in Gaelic place-names like *Glanchuill*, Glen of the Hazels, and names commemorating bygone emergencies. These shards are recoverable, if not restorable, like the devices of Gaelic literature – for example, Austin Clarke's most celebrated recovery, as Dillon Johnston points out, consisted of "certain assonant effects adapted from Irish poetry". What else do we find among the special bequests of Irish writers? Well, there are always those potent emblems, discredited or not, like the harp sighed over so copiously by Thomas Moore.

Moore of "Moore's Maladies" as Joyce called them, is well represented in the part of Kinsella's anthology devoted to the nineteenth century, and many other standard works of the era get a showing: Mangan's "Dark Rosaleen", Thomas Davis's "A Nation Once Again", Samuel Ferguson's "Lament for Thomas Davis". It is good to find some lesser known, more inspiriting works by Ferguson included too – "At the Polo-Ground", for instance, a blank-verse monologue "in the manner of Browning", according to the author's wife and biographer Lady Ferguson, which imagines the musings and misgivings of an Invincible recruit and participant in the Phoenix Park murders of 1882. From this point, we come up pretty swiftly to the modern age, via Yeats, Synge, Francis Ledwidge, Padraig Colum and one or two others; no Joyce, James Stephens, Joseph Campbell, F.R. Higgins, Donagh MacDonagh or W.R. Rodgers. It's hard not to feel that John Montague's *Faber Book of Irish Verse* of 1974 offers a rather more satisfactory selection from the middle part of the century.

Kinsella is at pains to repudiate any idea of a "Northern Irish Renaissance", claiming those Northerners whose work he admires, such as Heaney and Mahon, for the whole of the country, not just a portion of it. This is an attitude from which few Northern poets would wish to dissociate themselves, yet we're left with a feeling that Kinsella has carried things altogether too far in the effort not to weaken his assertion by suggesting a concentration of talent in a single area (i.e. the

North). We look in vain, in his book, for anything by John Hewitt, an important poet whose unostentatious manner has rendered him liable to disregard. Paul Muldoon is absent – it's true that he is ten years younger than the youngest of Kinsella's contributors, but John Montague got him into the Faber anthology. Simmons, Paulin, Carson, Ormsby, McGuckian ... the list goes on. Perhaps the most singular omission, though, is that of Michael Longley, whose *Poems 1963–83*, issued last year by the Salamander Press, shows a poet of incomparable fluency and discernment. When it comes to the Heaney selection (five poems), Kinsella has been rather unenterprising: nothing at all from *Station Island*, not even the masterly title sequence, only "The Gutteral Muse" from *Field Work*, and everything geared to display the popular, rather than the formidable element in Heaney's work. Mahon's "Disused Shed", with its starting-point in the grounds of J.G. Farrell's burnt-out hotel in his novel *Troubles*: this is in, and it's a choice with which no one can possibly quarrel. But where are "The Spring Vacation" and "Courtyards in Delft" (for example)? And why, among the Montague collections available for scrutiny, has *The Rough Field* been passed over?

Disputable absences and inclusions, which no editor can avoid, are more justly to be dwelt on in the case of an anthology like Kinsella's, which claims to be representative, than one like Muldoon's, which makes its impact, and asserts its purpose, by being very choosy indeed. Contemporary Irish poets, in Muldoon's book, can be counted on the fingers of two hands, and here they are: Kavanagh, MacNeice, Kinsella, Montague, Heaney, Longley, Mahon, Durcan, Paulin, McGuckian. No Muldoon, we notice straight away, which is understandable, if regrettable. Muldoon is famous for his oblique approach to things, and we see this feeling for indirection at work in the prologue to *Contemporary Irish Poetry* – not a manifesto by Muldoon, not even a note on his selection principles, but part of a BBC exchange between F.R. Higgins and Louis MacNeice on tendencies in modern poetry, broadcast in 1939 and printed in a *Listener* of the same year. Higgins's attribution of a special kind of purity to poetry in Ireland has less appeal for Muldoon, we can be sure, than the "common-sense" attitude adopted by MacNeice. "I think that the poet is a sensitive instrument designed to record anything which interests his mind or affects his emotions", MacNeice declared. "If a gasometer, for instance, affects his emotions, or if the Marxian dialectic, let us say, interests his mind, then let them come into his poetry. He will be fulfilling his function as a poet if he records these things with integrity and with as much music as he can compass or as is appropriate to the subject." Muldoon's 10 poets are all robust along the lines set out by MacNeice, and not in the least burdened with a sense of Irish spirituality, as Higgins would have it: "The sort of belief I see in Ireland is a belief emanating from life, from nature, from revealed religion, and from the nation." This notion of Irish spirituality, indeed, was very much a figment of the time, and it even came to be cited, once war had broken out, as a factor in Ireland's exemption from joining in. England, or so one argument went, had had it coming to her on account of her enthrallment with materialism. Dillon Johnston, at the start of his book, mentions the inevitable psychological result of neutrality in Ireland, in association with continuing censorship: undue introspectiveness. He notes a requirement of reactionary Irish readers: that "poetic truths" should be expressed in ways not inconsistent with certain political and moral assumptions. It didn't make for vigour or flexibility in Irish writing.

There were writers, however, who resisted the lure of chauvinistic restrictions, who bore in mind the limitless possibilities indicated by Joyce, and the immense achievement of Yeats, and activated their own literary impulses accordingly. Flann O'Brien comes to mind, along with the *Bell* magazine's editorial staff and contributors: the O'Faoláin dissentients. In 1951, Dillon Johnston reminds us, came the Dolmen Press, under whose imprint first collections by Thomas Kinsella,

Richard Murphy and John Montague were issued in due course. Dillon Johnston has a good deal to say about these poets and others, much of it enlightening; he is, however, a literary historian and critic, and not a social historian, and as a consequence the atmosphere prevailing in Ireland at various moments is not made altogether palpable in his book. Verse-patterns, tone and focus are the things that interest him, not the patterns formed by an interaction between historical circumstances and poetic practices, though he doesn't underestimate the importance of the latter. *Irish Poetry After Joyce* consists of six chapters, in four of which a present-day poet is juxtaposed with a slightly earlier one, to illuminating effect. Kinsella/Clarke, Montague/Devlin, Heaney/Kavanagh, Mahon/MacNeice: these are the arrangements, designed to show how each of the younger poets revises or extends or sidesteps the tradition embodied in the predecessor he's placed alongside. Johnston's opening chapter considers "the Irish poet and his society", though without placing too much emphasis on the extra-literary ingredients of that society; and in Chapter Six the author briefly adverts to the work of certain poets not appraised elsewhere, like Murphy and Muldoon. Whom does he omit? Most noticeably, Paul Durcan and Tom Paulin: the Southern jauntiness of one, and the Northern astringency of the other, seem to call for recognition in a study like this. Paulin's appropriation of the "Lagan Jacobins", the Presbyterian and free-thinking republicans of the 1790s, forms an attractive addition to those historical motifs which explain or enhance, for contemporary poets, some aspect of the present and its predicaments. Poems like Paulin's "Desertmartin" (included in the Faber anthology) look backwards and forwards at the same time: back in response to the "local stir", the consciousness of being in a special position, and forward to a recovery of something sorely missed, like the democratic spirit that went out with the eighteenth century.

In his preface, Thomas Kinsella explains his somewhat skimpy selection of recent poems by remarking that "the adequate presentation of contemporary careers would require another book". Muldoon, who includes no fewer than thirteen poems by any of his contributors (MacNeice has more than thirty), has surely provided it. He starts with Patrick Kavanagh and ends with Medbh McGuckian, and between these two – the exponent of the out-of-doors and the domestic prestidigitator – presents a range of poems shaped by criteria so exacting, and so felicitously composed, in almost every instance, that complaint on any ground seems out of place.

London Review of Books, 1986

AILING AND AISLINGS

Ann Saddlemyer (ed.), *The Collected Letters*
of John Millington Synge: Vol I 1871–1907

The language of Synge's plays is peculiar to himself; he
had no predecessors and no imitators. He forged his
dramatic manner from a handful of songs, folk tales and
some colourful Gaelic figures of speech. He travelled
to out-of-the-way places and emerged bearing a good
supply of incidents and ideas. Wicklow, Kerry and the
Aran Islands yielded up a store of decorative material.
Peasant flamboyance, as in the matter of lamenting the
dead or recalling past acts of violence, held a strong
appeal for him. His plays go in for rich and fanciful
imagery as well as embodying a form of Celtic fluency
unchecked by any dryness or awkwardness. The effect of
this fluency is hypnotic, whether the mood is poignant,
bold or wailful. Such a distinctive style, however, carries
a built-in element of self-parody. Synge's, moreover, is
entirely factitious; his intention was not to reproduce

the patterns of rural speech, either in Irish or English, but to superimpose stylistic flourishes in one language on the idioms of the other. It's not, as some critics have asserted, a matter of literal translation; Synge worked hard to get the utmost picturesque savour out of each expression he adapted. The Irish-language sources for a number of his lines make it plain that the original versions carried nothing like so high a charge of quaintness.

He was born in 1871, in time to catch the tail-end of the Celtic antiquarianism initiated by Sir Samuel Ferguson and others, and given a popular touch by Standish O'Grady. Its legacy for Synge's generation was the "fantastic, unmodern, ideal, breezy, springdayish, Cuchulanoid" outlook which so exasperated the playwright in the well-known letter he sent in 1904 to the friend from his Paris days, Stephen McKenna. Having had enough, for the time being, of Angus, Maeve and Fand, and all the rest of the "pale windy people" who flitted in and out of contemporary literature, Synge sought about for something stronger and lustier to put in their place, and hit upon the following revitalising course:

> We'll stretch in Red Dan Sally's ditch,
> And drink in Tubber fair,
> Or poach with Red Dan Philly's bitch
> The badger and the hare.

Here, Synge is advocating a return to the plainness and robustness of certain Gaelic folk-songs, some of which had recently been rediscovered in Connacht by Douglas Hyde. Synge's guidelines for a realistic approach, however, went awry in his own hands: his poetry is one thing, his plays another. The wayward antics of Synge's characters, in conjunction with the lush lines he put in their mouths, produced in certain members of his earliest audiences an outraged impression that Irish sensibility and Irish verbosity were being held up to ridicule. What they took for mockery was, in fact, admiration; all the same, native doubts about the Ascendancy playwright's attitude weren't altogether as fatuous as it might appear. Anyone might be excused for reading a humorous intent into lines like these about unmanageable sheep: "They were that wilful they were running off into one man's bit of oats, and another man's bit of hay, and tumbling into the red bogs till it's more like a pack of old goats than sheep they were … Mountain ewes is a queer breed, Nora Burke, and I'm not used to them at all …".

The charge of travestying the national character was the first that poor Synge had to contend with. A worse transgression, though, as far as his Catholic audience was concerned, was the aspersion he appeared to cast on Irish purity by conjuring up an image of women in their underwear. "It's Pegeen I'm seeking only, and what'd I care if you brought me a drift of chosen females, standing in their shifts itself, maybe, from this place to the Eastern world?" The subsequent ado, as the feelings of the audience got the better of them, went down to posterity as the Playboy riots; perhaps this was the only occasion when Irish belligerence erupted over an issue concerning bodice and soul. Gaelic League members who took part in the protest did so, presumably, in ignorance of the fact that the national language had produced a literature in which references to this particular item of underclothing weren't unknown. As an example we have the folk-song, *"Eadar Caiseal agus Úr Choill"* ("Between Cashel and the Green Wood") in which a girl rejected by one man declares that there are plenty of others who'd be happy to take her in her shift *(léine)*, if that was all she had. Synge, understandably annoyed by the business ("Did you hear that we had to have 57 peelers in to keep the stage from being rushed, and that for four nights not a word could be heard for booing?") got off to Stephen McKenna an entertaining account of Lady Gregory's first action in the crisis. She went backstage to consult the Abbey Theatre charwoman about whether or not a breach of decorum had been committed. The verdict was that "chemise" was the only acceptable word for the garment.

The outcry provoked by Synge's plays was modulated gradually until it had turned into an ovation. By

1910 the Gaelic League, or one of its representatives, had proclaimed a reversal of opinion in a magazine article which included the work of Synge, along with the *Táin Bó Cúailnge (Cattle Raid of Cooley)* and the anonymous ballad *"Slán Chum Pádraic Sáirséal"* ("Farewell to Patrick Sarsfield"), among the glories of the Gaelic tradition. The recantation came too late to gratify the playwright, who had been dead for a year. It's also, to be truthful, an assessment scarcely more judicious than the earlier nationalist denunciations. There are those who have argued that Synge's literary impulse was satiric, reading into his creation of Christy Mahon, for example, an intention to deflate the heroic Cuchulain figure of Irish romance. This is a plausible and illuminating speculation. What's certain, though, is that Synge's own writings provide for the satirist or parodist a target even more conspicuous than anything contained in the Irish sagas. Here is Flann O'Brien: "I have personally met in the streets of Ireland persons who are clearly out of Synge's plays. They talk and dress like that, and damn the drink they'll swally but the mug of porter in the long nights after Samhain."

Synge's verbal confections lend themselves to parody, but the author of the plays appears to have experienced no compulsion to send himself up in his other writings, either to indicate a degree of knowingness about the mode he invented, or to parade a nervous disinclination to take himself and his works too seriously. Only in a sentence of a letter to his fiancée Molly Allgood does he come at all close to joking about his stylistic eccentricities: "Remember in three little weeks there'll be another new moon, and then with the help of God, we'll have great walking and talking at the fall of night", he promises her. This mild burlesque is followed abruptly by a return to his brisker epistolary manner: "Do write me some decent letters before Tuesday's post."

The qualities that go to make the most captivating correspondences – discursiveness, a talent for gossip, the ability to turn personal mishaps into the stuff of comedy, and so forth – are largely absent in Synge. His descriptive gift is exhibited very sparingly in this volume. A view of some carageen-moss-pickers in Kerry – "Dozens of men and women … out in the sea up to their waists – in old clothes, poling about for it under the water" – is virtually the only extract to mirror the playwright's concern with pungent effects.

At their least engaging, Synge's letters are coloured by jealousy, whining, petulance, skittishness or dejection. And it is Molly Allgood who bears the brunt of his low moods. Worse, she is made to feel responsible for causing them ("I cannot understand why you treat me so badly"). He is constantly, he would have her know, trudging out in the rain to post letters to her, to the detriment of his health, and becoming fearfully aggrieved at her failure to do the same: "I don't know why you will not write to me, it is very strange."

Molly Allgood ("Maire O'Neill") was the Abbey Theatre actress who took the part of Pegeen Mike in the earliest production of Synge's *Playboy*. The author quickly fell under the spell of this capricious 19-year-old from a lower-middle-class Dublin family, and began addressing her as "Changeling". However, the playwright's beguilement was never sufficient to discourage him from assuming a pedagogic role in his fiancée's life. In his letters he proposes to take her education in hand, reminds her constantly how young and foolish she is, despises her taste in hats, complains about the shortness and infrequency of the notes she sends him, criticises her handwriting, and flies into a paddy over her insignificant betrayals of his trust. Molly proves less tractable than he might have wished, but the alliance endures none the less. Whenever the squabbling stops, the two go off on long romantic outings in the Wicklow hills ("Do not come of course if it is a wet day"); and Synge finally summons up the courage to mention Molly to his mother. Virtually everything about the relationship seems discordant, though: Molly's gaiety and Synge's intensity; her flirtatiousness and his fastidiousness; her vitality and his ill-health. In fact Molly in the end developed one or two ailments of her own, perhaps in retaliation for the pathetic reports she received in nearly every post: "I have a sharp headache, and the sweat is running down my face with the exertion of writing these few lines" (Synge said pathetically). The beginning of 1907 saw a brief exchange of letters between a miserable pair, one with a sore eye and the other with a sore toe.

The querulousness of the invalid, and the discontent of the incapacitated and suspicious lover – these feelings conspire to exclude from Synge's letters to Molly the possibility of grace, frivolity or anything at all in the way of aphoristic comment. A letter for him is not in any case a medium for effective or enduring self-expression. The bulk of the correspondence collected in this volume is flat, plain and businesslike in tone ("I very much regret delay in sending you the conditions we spoke of"; "Russell and I will draw up an agenda paper of the matters that are to go before the meeting"; and so on). The vicissitudes of the Abbey Theatre, the internal dissensions which racked it in its earliest years and the criticism it drew from the extreme nationalist faction, occasionally obliged Synge (co-opted on to the board of directors in 1905, and forming, along with Yeats and Lady Gregory, the third in the formidable Abbey triumvirate) to set out in writing his views regarding theatrical policy and the handling of troublemakers. However, a concern with particulars, natural in the circumstances but ultimately making for tiresomeness ("He thought she was not going to sign ... I heard barely that Miss W. had signed ..."), as well as an excess of caution and tact, leaves Synge's letters to his co-directors scarcely more absorbing than those to his publishers. Ann Saddlemyer, an indefatigable editor, collector of information and annotator, has included every extant communication of her subject's for the years covered, down to the note to Joyce (1903) which reads in its entirety: "You will say so as it is all the same to me." Make of that what you will. There is much in the letters, indeed, that's no longer open to elucidation, like this message for Molly Allgood: "I had no opportunity to speak to Fay about your teeth." The scope of speculation, however, is unrestricted. Did she bite him, or did she just need a new set?

Synge could be playful, as in the poem "Queens", in which the eighteenth-century practice of naming mythological women in order to point out the worthlessness of these in comparison with some present-day beauty (or personification of Ireland), finds a down-to-earth outlet. By exuberantly mocking this feature of *aisling* (vision) verse, Synge aligns himself with the last of the great Gaelic poets, Brian Merriman, whose splendid work, *"Cúirt a' Mheadhon Oidhche"* ("The Midnight Court"), was conceived as a burlesque of this particular genre. In his poetry, as in his book about the Aran Islands, Synge keeps well away from the high colour of his dramas and the colourlessness of his correspondence, and shows how his dramatic art might have flourished in an atmosphere more temperate than the one in which he chose to locate it. He is a writer, though, whose work gains in interest as a consequence of the confusions and paradoxes surrounding both it and him. By celebrating the energy he found within a dying tradition, he aroused hostility in those most strongly committed to preserving that tradition. (He never lost the disapproval, either, of critics suspicious of fakery or feyness.) You can make a piquant story out of the fact that Synge's uncle, a Protestant missionary, anticipated the playwright's journey to the Aran Islands by a number of years – where the uncle went to instruct, though, the nephew went to learn, and no doubt the islanders were able to appreciate the difference. Synge was not responsible for the actions and attitudes of his relations, which was probably just as well. One of the family estates in Co Wicklow was the scene of an eviction carried out in person by Synge's brother as late as 1887, a fact of no importance whatever in literary terms, but one guaranteed to stir nationalist agitators of the early twentieth century. They might have considered it instructive to set against the heady goings-on of Synge's peasants, this real-life episode of peasant suffering. The place where the brutal act occurred was Glanmore, and its literary associations come right up to date with Seamus Heaney's recent sequence of "Glanmore Sonnets", which is, felicitously, dedicated to the scholarly and enthusiastic editor of Synge's letters, Ann Saddlemyer.

Times Literary Supplement, 1983

THE ROARING
BORSTAL BOY

E.H. Mikhail (ed.), *Brendan Behan:*
Interviews and Recollections (Two Volumes)
Brendan Behan, *After the Wake*
(edited by Peter Fallon)

During his lifetime, Brendan Behan's exploits tended
to obscure his achievements; since his death, there
have been many attempts to redress the balance, to
find a place for him in the field of Irish letters on the
strength of an interesting autobiography and a couple
of exuberant plays. How far is the effort justified? It
is well known that drink and gregariousness eroded
Behan's capacity for concentration. His literary output
dwindled after *The Hostage*, and then stopped altogether.
Promises and obligations were not fulfilled. Playing the
unruly Irishman suited Behan all too well. His sense of
performance was stronger than his ambition to write
effectively.

Behan effortlessly converted incidents from his past into a series of pungent stories. Here you see him at six weeks, outside Kilmainham Gaol, held up in his mother's arms for the benefit of his father whose cell window overlooked the spot. Ireland is in the throes of a civil war, and Stephen Behan is serving a sentence for political activities. Next, you have the hardy eight-year-old supping porter with his grandmother in a Dublin slum. At 16, he is sent to a Borstal in Suffolk after being caught in Liverpool with a parcel of bombing equipment. *The Irish Times* of 9 February 1940 contained a report of Brendan Behan's trial. "He made a statement to the effect that he was a member of an organisation, and that he would blow up places if he got the chance." This, in fact, if it's reported accurately, amounts to nothing more than a piece of bragadoccio. The IRA of that time considered Behan something of a security risk, and packed him off to England as a way of keeping him out of mischief at home.

As far as Brendan Behan was concerned, Irish republicanism and socialism went hand-in-hand. He called himself a proletarian author and claimed to get on best with "ordinary blokes, taxi-drivers, house-painters, bookies runners", and so on. House-painting, as it happened, was the trade followed by his father and by himself, before literature and self-dramatisation gave him a way out of it. At one point – according to a celebrated anecdote – Behan was employed on a decorating job outside *The Irish Times* building, and on a writing job inside it. If his copy was late, the editor would throw open the window and roar at the workman standing on the scaffolding, "Behan, come up here and write your story. We're close on to deadline."

This incident, as related by Walter Hackett, appeared in *The Washington Post* in March 1964, two days after Brendan Behan's death. Hackett's piece is reprinted, along with many others, in E.H. Mikhail's two-volume collection of Behan material. Newspaper reports, extracts from memoirs, transcripts of interviews and snippets of Behan's own prose are assiduously assembled; you are left with a feeling that the views of everyone who knew the author, however slightly, were solicited at one time or another by every newspaper editor in the business. The resulting comments are not always marked by shrewdness or percipience. Going back to Behan's Borstal days, you have the impressions of C.A. Joyce, Governor of that institution, diligently recorded for *The Sunday Press*: "Brendan was a good boy at heart and he loved his religion."

Ingenuous though it seems, this was not an isolated opinion. Following his release from Borstal in November 1941, Behan began a 14-year sentence after being convicted of attempted murder by the Special Court in Dublin. (He spent four years in Mountjoy Gaol before being freed in a general amnesty for political offenders.) Like C.A. Joyce, Behan's new prison Governor was struck by the mildness of the would-be assassin's manners. "Basically", he assures us, the young Republican "was a very gentle person who in his senses would not hurt a fly." In Mountjoy Prison Behan brushed up his Irish and placed an article, "I Become a Borstal Boy", with Seán O'Faoláin's periodical *The Bell*. During this time, he was gathering the ingredients of his plays and stories, as well as acquiring a background wholly in keeping with his instinct for theatricality. Talent is especially intriguing when its occurrence is unexpected, and Behan made the most of his unique standing as an ex-convict and ex-labourer with a literary bent.

He did this, at least in part, by poking fun at it. The most pronounced of his assets was a gift for amiable mockery, with himself and his pretensions included among its targets. Of the miscellaneous items contained in the Mikhail volumes, the most entertaining is one of the three pieces contributed by Behan himself (the other two are newspaper paragraphs of very little consequence). "The Woman on the Corner of the Next Block to Us" was written for *Vogue* (American edition) in 1956. Here Behan, in merry mood, puts himself in the company of those Irish workers who write about their trade as an alternative to practising it, keeping *The Bell* well supplied with exercises in a picturesque mode.

Largeness of appetite was a benefit at first, and then a burden. John Ryan (in "The Home and Colonial Boy") relates how Behan, on one occasion, suddenly crammed into his own mouth the steak supper he'd prepared for some cats he was minding for friends. "God forgive me ..." he gasped. Such helpless voracity has a comic effect, indeed, generating indulgence for the person in its grip. Incorrigible showmanship – another Behan trait – helps to rivet the attention of the public too. There are many witnesses to his spectacular liveliness, wit and charm – qualities which flourished in the pubs of Dublin before a destructive element entered in. Injudicious camaraderie, waywardness, anarchy and buffoonery were always temptations for a character so extravagantly constituted. Behan was subject to extremes of behaviour, and after the success of *The Quare Fellow*, had the means to gratify his intemperate inclinations.

Before fame overtook him, Behan looked to his friends for the daily provision of such necessities as writing paper, food, drink, encouragement, the "makings" of cigarettes and so on. Later friends supported him in different ways, discouraging him from excessive drinking and, when that failed, extracting him from the pub-crawls and pub-brawls he was apt to get into. Those concerned for his well-being were often led on a dismal trek from bar to bar, as the wanton playwright became skilled at evasion. Most have recorded their efforts on his behalf, however unproductive they turned out to be. In the appalling last years of his life, between the futile bouts of sobriety and the hospital interludes, Behan carried on like some lurid figment of temperance propaganda, smashing everything around him, inviting assault charges, abusing his companions and often literally winding up in the gutter. His escapades by now have lost their savour and turned discreditable. Truly, Behan's wife Beatrice had a lot to endure. By all accounts she remained loyal to the end and suffered stoically, when suffering was unavoidable. She is foremost among those who stood by Behan when his disorderly habits had run completely out of control.

Beatrice Behan's autobiography, *My Life with Brendan* (1974) – one of Professor Mikhail's sources – was conceived as an antidote to "the writings of persons who had denigrated him during his lifetime" and who had subsequently attempted "to smear his reputation". Among these she probably included Ulick O'Connor, who, in his biography (*Brendan Behan*, 1970) adverted to the topic of her husband's supposed homosexual leanings – an aspect of his character she wishes to repudiate. In fact, as far as this matter is concerned, we have no reason either to disregard O'Connor's allegations, or to disagree with the view expressed by Anthony Cronin, that Behan's homosexuality was largely a pose. Cronin's account of his friendship with Brendan Behan and their eventual estrangement (extracted from *Dead as Doornails*, his study of three prominent Dublin figures, Behan, Patrick Kavanagh and Flann O'Brien) is among the most valuable and illuminating memoirs we have. It neither inflates its subject nor claims a special acquaintanceship with the "real", unembellished Behan. The majority of Mikhail's contributers take up one or other of these positions.

The Quare Fellow was staged at the Pike Theatre, Dublin, in 1954, and then at Joan Littlewood's Theatre Workshop, Stratford, in 1956 — the year of Behan's famous drunken appearance on television, with Malcolm Muggeridge in the interviewer's chair. "Like all drunks", Muggeridge recalled later, "he was a fearful bore." (He bored Kenneth Allsop too, according to Max Caulfield; though Allsop's obituary notice, true to the requirements of the form, is kinder in tone.) *Borstal Boy*, Brendan Behan's most substantial work, came out in 1958; and the first English-language production of *The Hostage* followed a year later. In its subject matter, Behan's second play bears a very close resemblance to one of Frank O'Connor's stories, "Guests of the Nation", as a number of reviewers pointed out at the time — perhaps prompting Behan's remark on the subject of drama critics who, he said, "are like eunuchs in a harem: they see the tricks done every night, they know how it's done, but they can't do it themselves." O'Connor himself mentions this piece of plagiarism, without rancour, in the obituary he wrote for *The Sunday Independent*, adding that the playwright, on his home ground, made no bones about acknowledging the source of his inspiration: "Ah sure, of course I stole the fucking thing."

After the Wake includes another version of this particular story, "The Execution", as well as a selection of Behan's *Irish Press* articles (published in that newspaper between 1954 and 1956) and other rediscovered pieces of prose. In spite of the intermittent vividness and friskiness of the writing, the effect of this collection is to remind us that the ways of discipline and industry were as alien to Brendan Behan as the practice of thrift. His striking delinquencies gained him an audience – and he was lucky enough, before the final deterioration set in, to succeed in making a way of life out of his habit of making an impression.

Times Literary Supplement, 1983

ROUNDING UP
THE STRAYS

Patricia McFate (ed.),
Uncollected Prose of James Stephens (Two Volumes)

In June 1907 James Stephens was employed as a
clerk-typist in the Dublin office of T.T. Mecredy & Son,
Solicitors, and his published works were a story, five
articles and a poem. Of this meagre output, it was the
last item that caught the eye of the poet George Russell (AE), who tracked the author to his solicitors' den
and accosted him at his typewriter, thereby initiating
a lasting friendship. Under the aegis of AE, Stephens
was recruited to literary Dublin which was flourishing
at the time, even if adversity had afflicted a number
of its luminaries: Synge, for example, whose *Playboy of
the Western World* at the Abbey Theatre had lately been
disrupted by riots; and James Joyce, who had failed to
secure a Dublin publisher for *Dubliners*.

The literary excitement was partly a product of the newly aroused nationalist consciousness and the heady discoveries it had brought in its wake. Not only were the Fenian and Red Branch sagas suddenly available to a new audience, but a whole storehouse of Gaelic treasures – love songs, religious songs and so on – was uncovered in Connaught by Douglas Hyde, who swiftly provided excellent translations for the benefit of those not fluent in the original language. In 1892, Hyde was already calling for the de-anglicisation of Ireland and finding a good deal of support for his views; by the beginning of the twentieth century, the cultivation of a mock-English outlook was equated, in Irish literary circles, with foolishness and a lack of integrity. Stephens's first essay (uncollected until now), which appeared in Arthur Griffiths's periodical *Sinn Féin*, typically derides the *Seoinín* (Little John, i.e. a follower of John Bull) and his pretensions. The sentiment can be traced back to Swift, who advised his readers to burn everything English except their coal, or to those Gaelic poets of the eighteenth century who deplored the ascendancy of certain anglified upstarts, along with everything else new-fangled in an English way. Stephens, true to the principles of the Gaelic League, recommends the Irish language and Irish styles of dress to his readers, and suggests they accord a proper reverence to the mythological heroes. "I have heard of a yacht called

Oscar, of a horse called Finn, and of a dog called Oisin", he states severely, not yet having developed the mischievous, whimsical, animated manner which makes the bulk of his writings so distinctive.

Still, for Stephens himself, it was a moment of metamorphosis. "My life began when I started writing", he once assured his stepdaughter Iris Wise. His autobiography begins here too, in 1907 or thereabouts, since he did his best to obliterate every previous experience. The earliest of his letters to survive was written in 1907; and in that year too he emerged as a husband and father. About Stephens's childhood we can be sure of nothing, not even his date of birth; 2 February 1882 is the one he claimed, but there is evidence pointing to a slightly earlier date. However, we have no reason to doubt that he was the James Stephens enrolled in a Protestant orphanage, the Meath Industrial School for Boys, in 1886. This makes an odd breeding ground for an Irish nationalist, let alone a poet, humourist and eccentric.

Stephens soon learnt to captivate his readers with the calm and sedate delivery of an unexpected observation: "Bigotry is a life force. Tolerance is decadence and disease." It is part of his stock-in-trade to seem engagingly opinionated. The unthinking veneration of humour displeased him: "The witty mind is the most banal thing that exists." His journalism aside,

Stephens himself, of course, could hardly write a line of prose without infusing it with his own brand of wit or drollery. His most celebrated work, the 1912 novel *The Crock of Gold*, sets out, among other things, to mock the pedagogic impulse – and incidentally succeeds in embodying all the charm of the literary revival, and none of its intensities. Stephens's cherished gods appear in the book, in profusion: around this time, as he acknowledged later, he "sowed gods with both hands". Deities and fairies, indeed, nearly overwhelm the final section of *The Crock of Gold*; only a continuing note of asperity saves the whimsy from becoming unendurable.

Nothing Stephens does is unoriginal. In his poem "The Goat Paths" the object is to devise a verse equivalent of the winding goat-tracks; the lines themselves twist and meander in a comparable way. Another, about a mountain, is specially constructed to procure breathlessness in the speaker as he reaches the summit. A fake-childish outspokenness is one of Stephens's traits:

Now cry, go on, mew like a little cat,
And rub your eyes, and stamp, and tear your wig,
I see your ankles! Listen, they are fat,
And so's your head, you're angled like a twig,
Your back's all baggy and your clothes don't fit,
And your feet are big.

He understands that, for him, the best results come from tackling things "with the particularity of a grub working through an apple", though he goes on hankering after the "Mount of Transfiguration" method recommended by AE. By and large, in his own work, Stephens is wary of both the approaches guaranteed to produce bad verse in Ireland in the early years of the century: the high-flown and the homespun. He can be taxed with quaintness but not with artlessness, and there is a good deal of justification for the mild complaint he uttered in 1917: "I have not been well reviewed in the sense of true comprehension, and it has not been seen that under the apparent ease ... of the narrative there has been an infinite, patient, curious care to do the work well." He stands against philistinism, even to the point of repudiating the literary products of those who sang for Ireland: "A country is in a pretty serious condition when its poetry has to become national ...". For a present-day readership, though, there is something a bit limiting in his contention that poetry cannot accommodate a "subject" without turning into rhymed journalism; certainly it's an odd view for a professed follower of Browning. It took the events of 1916 to get a quasi-political poem from Stephens; but when he succumbed to nationalist feeling, he did it thoroughly: "Be they remembered of their land for aye, / Green be their graves and green their memory."

With his family, Stephens had moved to Paris in 1913, and there he stayed for about a year, writing *The Demi-Gods* (gods again!). In this novel we find the usual commingling of mortals and immortals, with the resulting picturesque group of travellers which contributed a new motif to Irish fiction. Eimar O'Duffy and "Richard Rowley" were among those who adapted it to their own purposes; and it turns up, during the 1930s, in the children's novels of Patricia Lynch. It's natural, of course, that Stephens's singularity should attract imitators; what's inimitable about his fiction, though, is its zest. At times his prose is as decorative as a Toby jug; at others it is plain and pithy. A talent for aphoristic comment is one of his assets.

As far as the merit of his contemporaries was concerned, Stephens was apt to make eccentric judgements. He admired AE and Seumas O'Sullivan; he had no time for Pound or Eliot, and none for Joyce before 1927, at which time he and Joyce struck up an equivocal friendship. Stephens has left a diverting account of the earliest meeting between the two which took place in Dawson Street, Dublin, in 1912. There they stood, one very tall and the other very short, each more-or-less politely disparaging the other's achievements. Joyce, who began by advising Stephens to "give up writing and take to a good job like shoe-shining", came round, belatedly, to a state of approval for his fellow-Dubliner.

More than anything else, it was the coincidences surrounding the two of them that prompted his change of heart: their common Christian name, common place and date of birth (as far as anyone could tell), the character "Stephen" and the surname Stephens, and so on. All this encouraged him to put to Stephens the proposal that he should take over the writing of *Finnegans Wake*, if Joyce for any reason became unable to complete the project. What especially appealed to him about the idea was the possibility of getting "JJ and S" (a contraction of John Jameson and Sons, the Irish Whiskey distillers) on to the title page. Stephens acceded to this peculiar proposition; however, after his initial enthusiasm had receded, nothing more was heard from Joyce on the subject.

By 1925, Stephens's ingrained Anglophobia had been modified sufficiently to enable him to take up residence in a London suburb, and there he stayed for the rest of his life, apart from a period during the war when he and his wife took refuge in a disused chapel in Gloucestershire. High-spirited as ever, he'd no sooner arrived in England than he began contributing articles to *The Evening News* about the difficulties he was experiencing in finding his way around: "Leaving Trafalgar Square, I reached the Strand in nine buses."

Patricia McFate has diligently rounded up all of Stephens's stray journalistic pieces, thrown in a few rediscovered stories and added the texts of a couple of plays. It's a worthwhile exercise, in the interests of completion – however, through it all, no more than a trace of the author's usual exuberance and inspired frivolity is discernible. Literary and national topics, on the whole, make Stephens dull. We miss his virtuosity and aptitude for mimicry – and, above all, the quality he himself attributed to Lord Dunsany: "a vividly out-of-the-world imagination".

Times Literary Supplement, 1983

THE STATE
OF THE COUNTRY

William Trevor, *The News from Ireland*

In his novel *Fools of Fortune* (1983), William Trevor
looks back to a past condition of Ireland as it affected
an Anglo-Irish family; the parts of the book not set
in the present are concerned with a Black-and-Tan
atrocity and its aftermath. It also alludes to the actions
of one compunctious Anglo-Irishwoman at an earlier
date – the 1840s, famine years, when she, the wife of a
landowner, "travelled the neighbourhood ... doing what
she could for the starving and the dying, her carriage so
heavy with grain and flour that once its axle broke in
half". Trevor, who demonstrated his flair for historical
evocation in this novel, does so again in the masterly
title story from his new collection. The year is 1847,
when the news from Ireland was no less disquieting
than it is at present – wretchedness and starvation in
the countryside, and inadequate relief measures such

as soup kitchens and the construction of roads going nowhere. Distress and futility everywhere.

In the Trevor story, the Pulvertafts of Ipswich, having inherited an Irish "big house" and choosing to live in it, are acclimatising themselves to the customs of the country. To practice benevolence without looking for gratitude is one such custom. The poor are succumbing to edginess, and worse. At one point, news of a so-called "miracle" in the locality, the birth of a stigmatised child, is brought to the well-placed family, who utter conventional expressions of outrage and disbelief.

The unexceptionable activities of the Pulvertafts are observed by two people attached to their household: a poor Protestant butler called Fogarty, and a young English governess, Anna Maria Heddoe. Fogarty, who would like to see the Pulvertafts pulverised, has nothing against them – only that they did not stay where they belonged. With their arrival, it seems to him, some obscure restorative process has been vitiated. Left to itself, the house would have gone back into the clay, attended unemotionally by him and his sister. As it is, he says, instead of the past, it's the future that's withering. Fogarty, spokesman for no one, neither the stricken without nor the sheltered within, inflicts his thoughts about the plight of all of them on poor, well-meaning Anna Maria, who hasn't any use for his intemperate claims. It's a typical Trevor confrontation: unstoppable truth-teller and unwilling confidant. The urge to de-hoodwink those gulled, or lulled, into a wrong opinion is strong in certain characters created by this author.

Earlier in the story, Fogarty has planned a similarly divulging role for Anna Maria: telling her about the mutilated child, he expects a proper horror to carry her to her employers. "She will stand in the drawing-room or the hall, smacking out the truth at them, putting in a nutshell all that must be said." Smacking out the truth at them, in one way or another – this is a climactic act in much of Trevor's fiction. But Anna Maria refuses the role, being like the liberal Pulvertafts in her wish to get a moderate perspective on Irish matters. The pressure she is under is insufficient to cause a disruptive outburst. Like the Pulvertafts', her faith is grounded in kindness and reason.

Trevor arranges things, in "The News from Ireland", so that the emphasis falls oddly but tellingly, allowing an ironic viewpoint to go hand-in-hand with the depiction of malaise. Elsewhere in this vibrant collection, we have the story "Virgins", in which a splendid young man, not destined to live long, upsets a friendship between two romantic girls. "Bodily Secrets" concerns a late marriage between two people, one a widow, and both harbouring imperfections they'd rather not reveal. In "The Wedding in the Garden", a girl in an inferior position in a hotel forms an alliance with the son of her employers, is ousted from her job, and retaliates – unusually for a Trevor story – by *not* blurting out the truth, at the young man's wedding. Keeping mum, while she goes about her humble business, will constitute a more subtle revenge. "Two More Gallants" – an exercise in deftness and brevity – has the *Dubliners* story behind it. We remember Corley, who took himself off to lay a Dublin skivvy, and to touch the willing girl for a sovereign, while his crony Lenehan wandered the streets, awaiting with anxiety the outcome of the transaction. Suppose the skivvy had a real-life model? And suppose – the time in question being 1950 or thereabouts – she is still around to remember confiding her troubles to Mr Joyce, never dreaming that he would put her in a book? These quite groundless suppositions are foisted on a Joycean scholar and professor of English by a wily, over-age student in the grip of a grievance, who has found, coached and paid an old housemaid to act the part (a pound note is the sum involved) as a means of getting his own back for a very small slight. In this intrepid story by the incomparable William Trevor, the vogue for fiction mirroring other fiction finds a singularly felicitous outlet.

Times Literary Supplement, 1986

THE POWER
OF THE UNSTATED

Elizabeth Bowen, *Collected Stories*

Elizabeth Bowen held decided views on the tone and construction of the short story. "Poetic tautness and clarity", in her words, were essential ingredients, along with a single theme or mood which is pitched in a fairly high key. The story, with its brief span, cannot accommodate those troughs of slackness which properly separate the moments of climax in a novel. It should not contain anything which might "weaken, detract from, or blur the central, single effect".

How far does her own work measure up? Reading this collection, which brings together 79 stories for the first time, you get a sense of steady progress, of increasing mastery of the form, which culminates in the astonishing *Demon Lover* stories (1945): the title story, "Ivy Gripped the Steps"; "Mysterious Kôr"; "The

Happy Autumn Fields". She shares with the novelist Henry Green (as Angus Wilson notes in his valuable Introduction) an ability to render with the utmost keenness the sights and sounds of wartime London.

Her earliest stories (*Encounters*, 1923, and *Ann Lee's*, 1926) are exercises in observation, rounded out by guesswork; she takes account of mannerisms and imagines their sources, or follows up their implications. Her characters are meek, pompous, put-upon, confused or contrite. She evokes gaiety only to undercut it with an ironic repudiation of its shallowness. Mockery, "the small smile of one who, herself, knows better", is never too far away. Bowen is hardest on the arch, the effusive, all those who would attribute to themselves a "fearful" sensitivity. She shows from the start an essential soundness of outlook, and this makes a basis for the experiments in intricacy she carried out later. Emotional indecorum always affronted her.

Her own terse verdict on *Encounters* and *Ann Lee's* – "a blend of precosity and naivete" – still holds good. In 1949, obliged to cast a cold eye over her early work (for the preface to a new edition), she found it frivolous, effervescent, full of pretty detail – the soft furred edges of a tea-gown dripping out of a wardrobe; the parasols; the wisps of smoke rising from a small wood fire – but always lively, and illuminating at times. She was 20 when she began to write prose, having failed to be a poet and being, she says, in the course of failing to be a painter. Her stories showed at once a striking accomplishment in evoking scenes and settings; as yet, however, character – in its solid and enduring aspect – interested her rather less than the characteristic pose.

Bravado, the quality above all others she noted in Anglo-Irish writing, is discernible in her own – but bravado with all sense of the flashy removed. She was born in one of Dublin's Georgian terraces in 1899 and inherited, along with an ancestral home – Bowen's Court in Co. Cork – a tradition in style which subscribed to the classic idea. The Irish Protestant Ascendancy, to which she belonged, valued nonchalance, show, sociability, and a kind of emotional hardihood, akin to courage. The "big house people", Elizabeth Bowen wrote, "admit only one class-distinction: they instinctively 'place' a person who makes a poor mouth."

No more than a handful of Bowen's stories and a couple of novels are set in Ireland (two further novels, *The Heat of the Day*, 1949, and *The House in Paris*, 1935, have Irish interludes). She left the country when she was seven, following her father's severe nervous breakdown. The Dublin winters and Bowen's Court summers of her early childhood were at an end. In 1907, her mother took her to live in Folkestone – a radical displacement. "From now on there was to be … a cleft between my heredity and my environment." (The slightly younger Louis MacNeice embodied a similar dichotomy: "Torn before birth from where my fathers dwelt,/Schooled from the age of ten to a foreign voice...", he wrote in an autobiographical poem.) The classical facades of the Ireland she knew were replaced by an abundance of architectural frivolities: the balconies, bow windows, stucco and plaster decorations of English seaside villas. It was, in fact, a heady experience for someone who was always exhilarated by the unfamiliar.

England made her a novelist, by firing her imagination; but Ireland had already marked out her way of seeing. Toughness, melancholy, wit, and a stubborn, oblique romanticism that feeds on loss, are among her characteristics. Her first Irish novel, *The Last September* (1928), grew out of a fear: that Republican revolutionaries would burn Bowen's Court. (In this phase of the Tan war, at the end of 1920, the homes of the Anglo-Irish, the landed gentry, were considered legitimate targets.) Danielstown, the house in the novel, goes up in flames in an extraordinary final evocation. (In fact Bowen's Court survived, but without the money to keep it going; it was sold and demolished more than ten years before Elizabeth Bowen's death in 1973.) The author, it is plain, is not susceptible to the romance of insurrectionary Ireland; the lost cause engages her sympathy not at all. She is, instead, a custodian of those values Yeats revered – "Traditional sanctity and loveliness" – though they take a wayward, unsettling shape in her books.

It's sometimes been claimed that the "big house" tradition in Anglo-Irish literature (a tradition stretching back to Maria Edgeworth's *Castle Rackrent* of 1800) came to an end in 1955 with Elizabeth Bowen's *A World of Love* – a novel full of "summer emptiness darkening along the edges" and hypnotic skies, with a family more gallant than grand insecurely in residence in the house called Montefort. In fact, the tradition has not died yet. The Northern Irish episodes in Caroline Blackwood's *Great Granny Webster* (1977) testify to a continuing preoccupation, on the part of "big house" people, with the symbols of their own degeneration. Blackwood's Dunmartin Hall is dramatically lacking in income to keep it intact. It has bats in the bedrooms, and pots and jam jars are placed at intervals along the corridors to catch the drips of rainwater from the disintegrating roof. Elizabeth Bowen, too, understands the symbolic significance of the Irish big house roof, and the inexhaustible struggles of the so-called rich to keep it in place.

In the best of Elizabeth Bowen's writing, you hardly find an incident or an image which fails to set off reverberations, or draw into its vicinity all kinds of complex feelings. Her earliest stories, delightful though they are, are bound to seem slight by comparison: they're constructed on one plane only. They abound in swift, vivid perceptions – "a person who came quickly and frothily to the boil, like milk"; "Elise wrote a terrible letter, full of horses and brothers" – but lack the sense of an undercurrent which distinguishes her later work. This begins to be apparent in "The Tommy Crans" (the first of the 1930s stories), with the feckless eponymous couple kept in the background, and a debilitating emotional delicacy (a recurring trait) informing its principal characters. Then, after a foretaste of Elizabeth Bowen's electrifying use of atmosphere in "Look at All Those Roses", and the striking mood of decay – "There was no wind, and the woods stood heavily tense; against their darkness, in the toneless November evenings, the oaks were still yellow and shed a frightening glare. Everything rotted slowly" – which permeates "The Disinherited", we reach the superb group of wartime stories.

These give shape and definition to "a particular psychic London", a London distorted by the physical and the psychological effects of war. At night, the eerie city resembles "the moon's capital – shallow, cratered, extinct". No wonder, then, that one of Bowen's protagonists begins to dwell on an imaginary refuge – Mysterious Kôr, from Rider Haggard's *She*. Psychic dislocation comes into the *Demon Lover* inscape too: in the enormously resonant story, "The Happy Autumn

Fields" (the title borrowed from Tennyson's "The Princess") a fragment of intense experience in the life of an unknown Victorian Irish girl blots out the present for the bomb-shocked heroine in her damaged house.

The childhood trauma described in "Ivy Gripped the Steps", on the other hand, is the hero's own – a devastating instance of betrayal, casually disclosed. Gavin Doddington, revisiting in his forties the seaside town he last saw at the age of ten, remembers his childish infatuation with his mother's fascinating friend Mrs Nicholson, whose guest he was, and the painful moment when he grasped to the full the element of mockery in the lady's affection for him. Gavin is among those characters, common in the work of Elizabeth Bowen, in whom some emotional faculty is significantly deadened.

The title story from the 1945 collection, "The Demon Lover", is a masterpiece of conciseness and consternation, as it builds up to its unnerving climax. Bowen's feeling for the supernatural – which, austerely, she kept out of her novels – finds an outlet in some of her shorter fiction, and is often treated as an invigorating force. And, when her aim is not to examine the power of suggestion (as in "The Cat Jumps"), or devise an arresting embodiment for the numinous, she has fun with her ghosts. In "The Cheery Soul", for example, a playful spirit (in life a drunken cook), leaves cryptic messages about fish-kettles, and rude injunctions to her one-time employers. Especially during the 1930s, Bowen had recourse to episodes straight out of the popular press: at her instigation, lurid accidents, outbreaks of murder, are zestfully recreated as ghost stories, comic-horror pieces ("One of Mrs Bentley's hands was found in the library ... But the fingers were in the drawing room"), or psychological dramas ("Himself they had all – always – deprecated").

She is, as well, a deadly observer of social ploys and foibles. She views infelicitous or unruly behaviour with coolness and amusement. The bumptious, insensitive Heccombs of Waikiki, Seale-on-Sea (in *The Death of the Heart*, 1938) have come to exemplify her faculty for satire. At Waikiki, the dining table is made from synthetic oak, and breakfast is eaten off crockery "whose pattern derived from the Chinese". You could say this author is averse to the factitious. In fact, in even the most perplexed or disturbing of her narratives, an oblique comic vision is often detected doing its work. Her own emotions are never caught up in anything mawkish, as even her revered Katherine Mansfield's sometimes were. When we find a "dear little table lamp, gaily painted with spots to make it look like a toadstool" (in the story "Mysterious Kôr"), we know this object is far from being "dear" to the author.

An element of sarcastic admiration (the only permissible way, we learn from "The Jungle", for a schoolgirl to express approval of a friend's achievement) gets into her treatment of children in general. Childhood, with its fickleness, its odd formalities, its devious attachments and antipathies, always engaged Bowen's deepest interests. Young people in her fiction are envisaged with a peculiar clarity, whether they're pert schemers like Maria in the story of that title, comically blundering like Theodora in *Friends and Relations* (1931), or harrowed by an unmentionable stress like Roger in "The Visitor", whose mother is dying. It is true, as she said, that in childhood nothing is banal; inexperience means a capacity to be perpetually stimulated. However, "it is not only our fate but our business to lose innocence": this curt declaration says much about Elizabeth Bowen's temperament. Loss of innocence, betrayal, "the wrecking of an illusion": these characteristics (as she has it) of Katherine Mansfield's stories, are also major themes in her own work, as they were in Henry James's – but always enlarged by paradox, irony and complication. She relished the incalculable too. She is adept at isolating moments of strung-up awkwardness or incommunicable dismay.

Angus Wilson, in his introduction to the *Collected Stories*, takes mild exception (rightly, I think) to the plethora of "ever so queers" and "did oughts" which produce a monotonous effect in the lower-class monologues ("Oh, Madam ...", "Love", etc) Elizabeth Bowen sometimes felt obliged to attempt. Only in her wartime novel *The Heat of the Day* does she raise vernacular speech patterns to a high level of stylisation. Louie and Connie, factory and ARP girls, engage in conversations like this:

> "... Often you say the advantage I should be at if I could speak grammar; but it's not only that. Look at the trouble there is when I have to only say what I can say, and so cannot ever say what it is really ..."

And so on. We're reminded, as with the London blitz scenes, of the very eccentric use of dialogue in Henry Green's novels ("We'll not possibly make anything out of you that's one item dead certain"). Both authors, indeed, show a striking gift for idiosyncratic documentation. "Idiosyncrasy" is the word, and sometimes to the point of alarming readers. Elizabeth Bowen's "swanky vocabulary" as a subject for amiable derision on the part of certain critics, is noted by her friend and one-time lover Seán O'Faoláin – and he can't resist having a go himself. Her most extravagant mode he designates charmingly "the Bowen 707 or Take-Off Style". However sardonically expressed, though, his admiration for her work (we shouldn't doubt) is genuine.

No one understood better than Bowen did the

creative possibilities of evasiveness, the power of the unstated, the fascination of the unaccountable. Take-Off style aside, her work is elegant, dispassionate, ironic and restrained. She was – to adapt her remark about Virginia Woolf – an extreme and final product of the Anglo-Irish liberal mind, but with her own originality of approach, her own toughness and delicacy of touch.

New York Review of Books, 1981

ANGLO-IRISH ATTITUDES

W.J. McCormack, *Ascendancy and Tradition in Anglo-Irish Literary History from 1789 to 1939*
Gerald Dawe and Edna Longley (eds),
Across a Roaring Hill
Seamus Deane, *Celtic Revivals:
Essays in Modern Irish Literature 1880–1980*
Hubert Butler, *Escape from the Anthill*

In a recent *Times* article, Philip Howard pounced on the word "valorisation" which seems to be edging its way into the English language. "To enhance the price, value or status of by organised ... action", is one of the meanings he quotes for it. Here is an example of one such usage: "the literary critics' valorisation of tradition". This phrase occurs towards the end of W.J. McCormack's dissection of Anglo-Irishness as a literary and historical concept, *Ascendancy and Tradition* – a book, for all its merit, unduly full of academic obfuscation. At one point we catch the author considering the way in which Joyce and Yeats "as a binary and mutually dependent cultural production confront the totality of history". There the two unfortunate literary figures stand, symbiosis thrust upon them. At another moment, the history of Ireland is called "bifurcated", which makes it sound like a pair of trousers. It is very provoking of W.J. McCormack to write in this benighted way. He is perfectly coherent, felicitous and illuminating whenever he chooses. But, it seems, the less he has to say, the more fussy and fustian his manner becomes. On the poem "Nineteen Hundred and Nineteen", for example, we get this:

> The title employs words, not numerals, but it employs one of several possible verbal for-mulations. It prevents us from particularising the year as One Thousand, Nine Hundred and Nineteen; it prevents us from slurring it to a loose Nineteen Nineteen. Thus, the element Nineteen is repeated but not emptily so, for we are directed to the middle term, indicating the completed nineteenth century and its nineteen year excess. The post scriptum date, on the other hand, is unpronounceable, or at best variously pronounceable.

So it goes on … McCormack's main contention, when you get down to it, seems to be that "ascendancy" and "tradition" alike are figments of the imagination of W.B. Yeats. It is well-known, indeed, that the Protestant Ascendancy of the eighteenth century (a term not current, in fact, as McCormack reminds us, before 1792) didn't actually embody all the qualities Yeats attributed to it – courtesy and decency, a high-minded approach to political matters and an aristocratic lineage. As far as the last is concerned – well, there's the hidden Ireland uncovered by Daniel Corkery in 1925 (his study of eighteenth-century Munster appeared under that title), inhabited by people who took a very poor view indeed of the new English-speaking aristocracy which had ousted the old Irish-speaking one. "Valentine Brown", as these purists saw it, was the kind of ludicrous name an arriviste landowner might call himself – someone who'd installed himself in a demesne of the great McCarthys, now dead or dispersed. In this world, the speaker of "cunning English" quickly got himself condemned for opportunism, everything English being associated with the kind of baseness Yeats decried. Still, it was quite another Ireland the poet had in mind when he singled out the eighteenth century, labelling it "the one Irish century that escaped from darkness and confusion". Swift, Berkeley, Burke, Goldsmith and Sheridan: all these stood for clarity of thought, while Dublin gaiety, Belfast liberalism, and the sense of national consequence acquired at Dungannon, all contributed something to the Yeatsian image of a mellow era. That this particular form of Irishness was conceived in opposition to an unsatisfactory present – "Man is in love, and loves what vanishes" – and (as Louis MacNeice has it) "in defiance of the Gaelic League" and all it stood for, doesn't in the least detract from its efficacy.

As for "tradition" and the literary critics' "valorisation" of it – McCormack advises us to bear in mind the original legal meaning of the word ("handing over"), and to ponder the distinction between "the handing over of an object or a property, and the handing over of ownership or rights to such an object or property". The author (who has written far more cogently on tradition elsewhere) goes on to specify the social and cultural dynamics of the process of handing down – whatever these are – as the crucial factor in the business, but he doesn't uncover them in any individual case, or tell how, once enumerated, they can enlarge our understanding of what isn't, after all, a concept especially difficult to grasp. Such assertions as we find in these pages can only arouse in the reader an urge to stick up for "tradition" and the way in which it's commonly interpreted.

However, the McCormack study has much to recommend it. Among other things, its consideration of Edmund Burke is exhaustive. Burke, one of those eighteenth-century figures whose apotheosis was ordained by Yeats, has lately been attracting the attention of academics like McCormack and Seamus Deane, both of whom have written about him in the periodical *The Crane Bag*. Burke's social observations are worth repeating: Irish cabins, he said, were "scarcely distinguishable from the Dunghill" and the furniture they contained "much fitter to be lamented than described". The food consumed in these places wasn't up to much: potatoes and sour milk, and even worse in times of scarcity, when many people were driven back on boiled weeds and blood stolen from cows. "Pain, destruction, downfall, sorrow and loss" – in the words of the poet Aoghán Ó Rathaille – doesn't seem too strong a term to apply to the condition of the penalised Irish. From Burke, opponent of anarchy and advocate of Catholic emancipation, came a formula for British liberalism in the nineteenth century, as Seamus Deane points out in an article on "Arnold, Burke and the Celts", reprinted in *Celtic Revivals*. McCormack, in a *Crane Bag* essay, has linked Burke's writings, and especially the *Reflections*, to the body of Anglo-Irish fiction which began with Maria Edgeworth. (In this essay, he sensibly remarks that, "though there are difficulties attaching to the term 'Anglo-Irish literature', it is too late to purge it from our critical vocabulary" – an attitude one wishes he'd displayed more often in the current book.) Burke's

Reflections, McCormack now asserts, uses the "big house" as a dominant metaphor, and moreover shows it getting into a familiar state of ruin. From Maria Edgeworth's "the wind through the broken windows ... and the rain coming through the roof" to Caroline Blackwood's Dunmartin Hall (in the novel *Great Granny Webster*), with puddles in the corridors and warped doors, the Anglo-Irish house has characteristically fallen a victim to disrepair. There are, of course, a good many symbolic points to be adduced from this.

W.J. McCormack goes to some lengths to show that Maria Edgeworth's "Castle Rackrent" was only "a house of the middle size", not great at all by the standard of English houses, and he jots down the probable cost (between £1000 and £1100), with the number of bedrooms, living-rooms and so on, that a typical squire's house might contain. However, as he says, Castle Rackrent shrinks or expands at the author's whim, just as the events of Sheridan Le Fanu's *Uncle Silas* are cast in a perpetual autumnal haze (as Elizabeth Bowen noted), in defiance of the usual arrangement of the seasons. Anglo-Irish disdain for the tedious requirements of naturalism? Certainly a moral pattern takes precedence over verisimilitude, in Irish fiction before the twentieth century, and it's usually to do with some form of reconciliation: typically the interdenominational marriage. You also find — as the effect of Burke's ideas worked its way further and further down the literary scale – a lot of aristocratic heroes who believe in a strong form of government tempered by kindness to the governed.

In his effort to let none of the latent meanings of a text escape him, McCormack sometimes pounces on a particle of import that isn't there, like a demented lepidopterist making an assault on a shaft of sunlight. Take the Joyce story "Eveline". The most satisfying account of this story that I'm aware of comes in Hugh Kenner's book *The Pound Era*, and is properly mindful of Joyce's Dublin knowingness. "Eveline" opens with a perfectly felicitous and unobtrusive metaphor: "She sat at the window watching the evening invade the avenue." McCormack gets his teeth into "invade" and won't let go of it until he's forced a connection between it and the "soldiers with brown baggages" alluded to in part two of the story. Next, we're told that "behind both nominal heroines" (the Countess Cathleen is hitched to Eveline here) "lies the personification of Ireland as 'Patient Woman', *an tsean bhean bhocht*". Leaving aside the fact that *an tsean bhean bhocht* can only be translated as "the poor old woman", not a tag applicable to either the Joyce or the Yeats figure – leaving that aside, isn't the grafting on to Joyce's story of another, nationalist story a bit gratuitous? When McCormack proceeds to wonder if Eveline – poor, romantic Eveline – opts for "some domestic form of Home Rule in North Richmond

Street", he is being either fatuous or facetious, I am not sure which.

Ascendancy and Tradition covers roughly the same ground as "The Protestant Strain" (playfully subtitled "A Short History of Anglo-Irish Literature from S.T. Coleridge to Thomas Mann"): McCormack's contribution to *Across a Roaring Hill*, a collection of essays on "the Protestant imagination in modern Ireland". In both these undertakings, the short and the long, McCormack displays a salutary impulse to acknowledge all the complexities, social, ideological or whatever, underlying the term "Anglo-Irishness" and affecting its outlets in literature. However – through a fear of what he calls "isolationist aesthetics", meaning, I think, an insular approach – he draws altogether too much into the vicinity of his subject: economics, Nazism, authoritarianism and so on.

It's McCormack who quotes Louis MacNeice on the benefits of being Irish, with the sense of belonging to "a world that never was" among them; but it is Seamus Deane who incisively enumerates the sources of the various transformations – heroic, chivalrous, folklorish and so on – to which the idea of Irishness was subjected. Deane quotes Joyce on Ireland's "one belief – a belief in the incurable ignobility of the forces that have overcome her" – and goes on to consider the ways in which the concomitant notion of Irish integrity was enshrined in literature. In 1903, when Joyce made this remark, it was customary to differentiate between the adulterated and the "real" Ireland, though perhaps not between the real and the chimerical. The West of Ireland was the place in which the country's strongest substance was thought to reside (as McCormack points out). It was through his contact with the West that Padraig Pearse devised his prescription for a nation (as he put it) "not only Gaelic, but free as well; not only free, but Gaelic as well". J.M. Synge, on the other hand, believed that the essence of the Gaelic West – bursting with colour and vitality – could be rendered in English, though an English not current in any locality before or since, if we leave aside the haunts of those play-actors observed by Myles na gCopaleen, who "talk and dress like that, and damn the drink they'll swally but the mug of porter in the long nights after Samhain". Synge's Irish-English, true enough, achieves its narcotic effects at the expense of both Irish dryness and English wryness of tone.

Seamus Deane includes in his collection a couple of good essays on Pearse and Synge; nothing is missing from the latter but a touch of mockery at the succulent Irishness portrayed by the author of *The Playboy*. On Pearse, Deane remarks that the "former apotheosis of the martyr has now given way to an equally extreme denunciation of the pathological elements involved" (you can see a comparable process, considerably speeded up, taking place in the literature of the First World War). Pearse's programme for national regeneration certainly contained elements not in keeping with the proprieties of the present. "His nationalism teetered on the brink of racism", Hubert Butler noted in 1968, in one of the pieces assembled in *Escape From the Anthill*. Deane doesn't go as far as this in his appraisal of the architect of 1916; but he does, astutely, connect Pearse's Gaelic revivalism with "what used to be called 'muscular Christianity'". Going into the fight "white", indeed, was a concept Pearse would have cherished.

Seamus Deane and Hubert Butler are both authoritative commentators on the depleted condition of Irish letters during the middle part of the twentieth century – "once the major excitements of the Revival were over", as Deane has it, and with a pair of gauche states, one north and one south, struggling to find their feet. The atmosphere prevailing in both parts of the country at this time would greatly have discomfited the fosterers of Irish spirituality. Butler, in a *Bell* article deploring the unruly literary views of Patrick Kavanagh, distinguished between the parochialism of 1901, which contained the potential for enlargement of outlook, and that of 1951, which didn't. He likens the mind of the Mucker poet, when it's not engaged with poetry or fiction, to "a monkey house at feeding time". It was in the same year, 1951, Deane tells us, that John Montague, also writing in *The Bell*, called for an end to the apathy which seemed the predominant feeling about cultural matters, and at the same time "demanded of his generation that it reflect Catholicism as a living force in Irish life". His implication, like Kavanagh's contention, was that the Anglo-Irish Protestant impulse in literature had run its course – as indeed, by 1951, it had. However, for some time before this, and in the wake of the major achievements of the Revival, writers like Seán O'Faoláin and Frank O'Connor had been reflecting Catholicism like billy-o, as a force to be repudiated or encouraged, or just in acknowledgement of its inescapability. Hadn't the time arrived to dispense with sectional assertion in any interests whatever? Or perhaps it couldn't be done, given the tendency of every social group to claim exclusive access to certain tracts of the national consciousness. Thus we have Patrick Kavanagh (as Butler says) light-heartedly arguing that "you cannot be Irish if you are not Catholic"; and Butler himself insisting that to be Irish and Catholic debars you from possessing any insight at all into the mentality of Anglo-Ireland.

Hubert Butler – born in 1900, and Anglo-Irish to the core – goes in for amiable castigation of the bumptious or unenlightened, and for discursiveness and frankness of manner. He also has a knack for a diverting comparison: "Her intellect, like a barrage balloon that has lost its moorings, hovers uncertainly between Fishguard and Rosslare." (On Elizabeth Bowen.) He has a thing or two to say about Catholic Ireland, especially in its more bizarre manifestations: for example, we have the case of a man who, in 1895, roasted his wife on the kitchen fire, in full view of relations and neighbours, having convinced himself and them – or so it appeared – that he was trouncing a changeling. Butler reminds us of the interest in fairy lore which was widespread at the time in scholarly circles. The colourful business at Ballyvadlea – fairy rath, herb doctor and all – shows the obduracy of superstition in the face of priestly admonitions. A more orthodox variety of mad Catholicism asserted itself in a Wexford village in the late 1950s. A Protestant mother, married to a Catholic, chose to enrol her six-year-old daughter at a local non-Catholic school. The outrage aroused by this act was such that a boycott was organised against every Protestant in the district. A bishop congratulated the people concerned on their "peaceful and moderate" protest. In the third of his articles considering the peculiarities of Catholic life as they get reported in newspapers, Butler recounts the tussle which occurred in 1955 between the writer Honor Tracy and *The Sunday Times*. A "graceful sketch of an Irish village", complete with ironical aspersions on its frantic fund-raising operations when a new house was wanted by the local canon, appeared in that newspaper. Its author was Honor Tracy. The paper's staff had taken the village to be imaginary. However, once the sketch was published, an angry canon from Doneraile in Co Cork promptly surfaced clamouring for restitution. The newspaper capitulated. Miss Tracy, who read into its apology to the canon a criticism of her conduct as a journalist, turned on the paper. A court case ensued. The author of the article was awarded costs and damages. At this juncture, the inhabitants of Doneraile, on whose behalf Miss Tracy had thought she was campaigning, took up the cudgels for the canon. A demonstration in support of him and his new house was organised, with the parish choir, the Gaelic League and the Children of Mary out in force. Such exhibitions of Catholic fervour aren't uncommon. We're reminded of an episode in Peadar O'Donnell's novel of 1934, *On the Edge of the Stream*, when a similar crowd assembles to repudiate in public the message of a socialist agitator. O'Donnell views this outbreak of Catholic piety with mock amazement: "grown-up men and women", he assures us, stood there singing in unison "I am a little Catholic". It's not unusual either to hear heated voices raised in Ireland against the avarice of clerics. However, Hubert Butler isn't writing to endorse any such emphatic view. He isn't on anyone's side in the

Doneraile dispute. Miss Tracy, not an Irishwoman, is taken to task for implying that she had got the measure of the natives. So are those who attribute the whole affair to Irish dottiness. The spectacle of Catholic solidarity, and its implications for moderation in Ireland, can hardly have pleased Hubert Butler any more than anyone else, and neither can he have relished public debate on the messy business of possible self-interest in priests. Yet, as he says, it is no very comfortable matter for an Irish Protestant to criticise any instance of priestly greed, even if it should be proved to exist, when the countryside has so many half-empty rectories, deaneries and episcopal palaces, "for whose maintenance Catholics and Nonconformists once paid tithes". There is scarcely one of them, he adds, into which the Doneraile canon's "little house would not fit several times over". It is this fair-minded attitude, along with his perceptiveness about the achievements and the charm of the Anglo-Irish, that makes Hubert Butler's essays so agreeable.

London Review of Books, 1985

ON TARGET

Hubert Butler, *The Appleman and the Poet*

In 1985, the newly formed Lilliput Press in Ireland became involved in a tremendous project. It was to sort, assemble and place before the public the distinguished writings of the Kilkenny humanist and essayist Hubert Butler, and the project got under way with *Escape from the Anthill*, for which the poet and architectural historian Maurice Craig was co-opted to write a forward. Sharing Butler's viewpoint (as he tells us), that of a protestant republican, Maurice Craig is well placed to applaud the nuances and assess the probable impact of the Butler oeuvre. "For all his elegance, Hubert Butler is no belletrist", he states. "For him an essay is a projectile, aimed at a particular target and freighted with what it needs to do its work: no more and no less."

Butler's targets include dotty and dangerous forms of superstition (e.g. "The Eggman and the Fairies", which considers the case of a man who took his wife for a changeling and burnt her to death in the kitchen fire); church interference in private matters, such as the authorised boycott of Protestant businesses in Fethard-on-Sea, following the decision by a Protestant woman married to a Catholic to enrol her daughter in a non-Catholic school (this occurred in the late 1950s); social and political abuses of every kind, whether in Ireland, Russia or Eastern Europe. His measured, astute and graceful appraisals of one striking situation or another immediately struck a chord with upholders of rational dissent in Ireland. Butler enthusiasts, a select band to begin with, soon began to proliferate. *Escape from the Anthill* was followed by three further volumes; and now comes the final collection in the series, *The Appleman and the Poet*, edited by Anthony Farrell who initiated this particular process of rediscovery back in 1985. The book includes a forward by Fintan O'Toole, who relishes Hubert Butler's "cool detachment and fearless curiosity" along with its corollary, the way in which every sentence "is guided to its target by an unabashed and irreducible human sympathy".

The Appleman and the Poet is full of human sympathy, but human displeasure gets a showing too, if always courteously expressed. Butler's "unnervingly civil tone", as Fintan O'Toole puts it, never falters even in the face of obduracy and benightedness (Paisleyism in the North,

Catholic ostentation and Protestant demoralisation in the South). It's a quality he shares with a fellow Irishman, Conor Cruise O'Brien, also a master of the mannerly reproof. A refusal to be ruffled suggests an effective detachment, a necessary objectivity. Butler doesn't need to raise his voice to get his point across; like the Northern poet John Hewitt, another writer secure in his Irish-nonconformist identity, he is geared to reach his audience, if he has to, "across a roaring hill".

The roaring hill might consist of nationalist or religious demagogues, and Butler's identity – that of "an English-Protestant Irishman" – which made him resistant to any kind of an ideological hullaballoo, also accounts for his unobtrusive assurance and occasionally provocative stance. He was born at Maidenhall, Bennettsbridge, Co Kilkenny in 1900, and died in the same ancestral house over 90 years later. He believed in continuity, conservation, tolerance, scholarship, independence of outlook and the kind of "sober and thoughtful nationalism" to which the Act of Union of 1800 had put paid. He is in a line of descent from Flood and Grattan, Berkeley and Burke: Anglo-Irishmen of a public-spirited, engaging, interrogative stamp. He has no time for the kind of post-Treaty Protestant patriot who goes around wearing a saffron kilt while reciting "The Shan Van Vocht". He disputes the idea that the rump of the Ascendancy is stranded in the new Ireland, with nothing at all to contribute to its advancement, like a beached whale, or like Oisin in the wake of the Fenians. There they sit – in the popular view – embroidering coats of arms on cushion covers, or poring over ancient family papers. No, says Butler: the country should be large enough to accommodate all its diverse inhabitants, from Catholic (or Protestant) apologists to "Urbane Unbelievers", and to require from all of them an input into its intellectual life. But he knows it's not as simple as that. The Ireland of the mid-twentieth century was not exactly hospitable to any such ecumenical initiative, and Butler himself came up against a fair amount of opposition to his prescriptions for enlightenment. Catholic Ireland at the time was in the throes of an anti-Communist furore; and when – for example – he spoke out against Church complicity in a wartime pogrom in Croatia, he was severely censured. It took a long time for the complaint against him to be retracted. He'd been dead for nine years when the Mayor of Kilkenny, in the year 2000, apologised in public for the long-ago hurt inflicted on Butler and his family, simply because he had "told the truth".

As a social commentator, he could do no less than tell the truth and damn the consequences; as an essayist of discernment and aplomb, he allowed full scope to his eye for an absurdity and pungent descriptive gift.

During the 1930s, Hubert Butler was employed as a teacher of English in Yugoslavia, and at the same time he travelled widely in Croatia, Serbia, Bosnia, Macedonia and Montenegro. His experiences abroad form a counterpart to his analyses of Irish society. In 1932 he visited the Soviet Union, and the opening essay in the new collection – "A Stroll Around Leningrad" – with its evocative and ironical observations ("It is impossible for the bourgeois visitor to avoid sentimentalising as he elbows his way along, however proletarian his sympathies ... Streets are up, workers' dwellings going up, and churches coming down, debris is everywhere..."), sets the scene for much of what follows. Back home in Kilkenny, for instance, he records with contained amusement the Resolution passed by the town corporation to remove from its precincts a bust of Gladstone, on the grounds that Gladstone stood for the English oppressor. "It had been presented by a former mayor", Butler writes, "a tribute to Gladstone's effort for Home Rule." So much for the corporation's familiarity with Irish affairs.

The title essay, "The Appleman and the Poet", testifies to the importance of local produce, a prescient Butler preoccupation. Locality, nationality and politics are key subjects through all five collections. Butler has at his fingertips every feature of the Anglo-Irish landscape. But you can't avoid the sense, with the current volume, that one or two inclusions are tending towards the scrappy. This is especially true of the autobiographical section. For example, the piece called "Charterhouse" begins by saying, "Fortunately there is little necessity to write about Charterhouse" as Robert Graves has already done it. End of story. Contemplation of his father's deafness (only a page and a quarter) brings on for Butler a recollection of a story his father told, about an obese Anglo-Irish lady on her way to a party in a carriage whose floor suddenly gave way, obliging her to grasp a bar below floor-level and run at top speed to keep up with the horses. This is very fine and amusing, but slightly diluted if we remember a different version of the same story making an appearance in James Lees-Milne's autobiography, *Another Self* (1970). In his case it involves the higgledy-piggledy arrival of himself and his mother at his prep school, following a similar mishap. Did both incidents actually take place? Perhaps it was a common hazard of travel by carriage. Or perhaps the account by one author had stayed in the mind of the other.

The position taken by Hubert Butler is always progressive and his arguments stimulating, but it seems the confined space of a sketch or an afterthought works less well for him than the extended essay, in which all the ingredients are marshalled with ease and everything falls into its place. But even his slightest musings are grounded in esprit and acuity. Butler is a connoisseur of estrangement and harmony alike, and everything that comes within his compass is illumined by the clear light of reason.

Times Literary Supplement, 2014

THE WORLD
AND ITS WICKEDNESS

Edna O'Brien, *Saints and Sinners*

There are many things to admire and cherish about Edna O'Brien's writing, and this new and compelling collection of stories puts us in touch with all of them. The author's customary coolness and confidence, her instinct for illumination, her prodigious descriptive gift, draw us in and keep us engrossed. O'Brien holds an assured place in a line of magnificent Irish short story writers which includes John McGahern and William Trevor; like theirs, her stories eschew qualities traditionally ascribed to "the Irish story". They don't ramble or coax the reader into acquiescence or rely for their impact on a shocking denouement. They are simply and deftly constructed, whether in the form of a monologue, a detached glimpse into a distinctive way of life, or an episode of deflected reminiscence.

Reminiscence is a strong theme here. If you begin in Ireland, Elizabeth Bowen said, "Ireland remains the norm". Edna O'Brien has often acknowledged her debt to her birthplace and the things that happened there. Rural County Clare in the mid-twentieth century was prolific in repressions and privations, but it was also a place of charm and pungency: the lower field with its briars and young ferns and stalks of ragwort, and its millions of wild flowers – "little drizzles of blue and white and violet" – hiding underneath; lonesome rushes on the edge of a bog, and a curlew crying like "the uileann pipe that Billy Tuohey played in the evening". Particulars such as these added a luminous touch to O'Brien's first novel *The Country Girls*: an exuberant, poignant and lucid work whose unprecedented youthful candour (back in 1960) alarmed Catholic Ireland to the extent of drawing down clerical imprecations on its author's innocent – soon to be less innocent – head. But the banning and even burning which swiftly followed, couldn't stifle the upraised voices – the timely and necessary voices – of O'Brien's valiant country girls. And, in circles more enlightened than those presided over by Archbishop McQuaid in Dublin, or the parish priest of Tuamgraney, Co Clare, it was perceived that, with *The Country Girls*, something of a breakthrough had occurred. Irish girls and women were on the move.

The first book spawned a couple of sequels in which the country girls, Caithleen (Kate) and Baba – respectively impressionable and irrepressible – extend the scope of their girlhood concerns. By the end of *The Lonely Girl* (1962) they are "exultantly" on the Liverpool boat like many a talented misfit before them – fleeing Ireland, repudiating its harshness and backwardness, but also carrying it with them imaginatively for ever, its images and attitudes already ingrained. It was, indeed, essential to get away. Women in Ireland, at the time when Edna O'Brien began writing, were still largely excluded from the bustle of public, "masculine" activity, and therefore more intensely caught up in the emotional side of things.

O'Brien is acclaimed for her lyrical approach to matters of feeling and fancy; but, from the start, an astringent and sardonic viewpoint ("The Love Object"; "Girls in Their Married Bliss") was an invaluable asset which gave an edge to all her utterances. Her characteristic literary manner is clear-sighted and disabused, and this is especially true of the early unblemished novels, and of all the stories from *The Love Object* (1968) onwards.

Although she began as a novelist, and has continued to write full-length fictions (16 to date), Edna O'Brien has found in the short story a unique and graceful means of affirming an engagement with all of life's vagaries and inconsistencies. Predominantly, of course – though not exclusively – it is Irish vagaries and inconsistencies that come to mind in connection with this author: these are what set her going as a writer, and keep her instincts and insights working at full pressure. We remember "Irish Revel" with its village street littered with debris after a cattle fair, its Commercial Hotel, its hill-bred heroine's small expectations coming to nothing; or in "Cords", the anxious Irish mother's unsatisfactory visit to her daughter in London. Disillusionment is a major theme, along with loss and longing, countrified miseries and brutalities, and sexual entanglements, both destructive and life-affirming. A wayward streak, a fair amount of bitterness, nostalgia, an increasing urbanity and a fastidious touch: all these are attributes of Edna O'Brien's fiction through all its varied patterns and scenarios.

An overt or an underlying Irishness makes an inescapable motif, but doesn't lead to uniformity or repetition. Indeed, the first thing to note about the current collection, *Saints and Sinners*, is the range of tones it encompasses, from the wryness suggested by the title – are these to be taken as opposites, or are they different aspects of the same individuals? – to the complex despondency of "Send My Roots Rain", in which a shy and gawky Dublin poet fails to honour an appointment at the Shelbourne Hotel with a young provincial admirer. (I would take Patrick Kavanagh to be the model for the poet.) Through all the different narrative moods, or modes, you're aware of a certain romantic bleakness, which partly resides in stirring detail, freezing country buses in winter, "poplars like ghosts along a hillside", afternoon fiddle music issuing insidiously from the kitchen area of an all but deserted London Irish pub.

The last appears in the trenchant opening story, "Shovel Kings", in which a one-time navvy discloses, bit by bit, some elements of his past as an Irish construction worker, a tenant of dank bed-sitting rooms among an exiled community awash in drink and bravado. Frugal existences, small familial resentments and estrangements, moments of high drama: these come charged with an inspiriting briskness, whose effect is sometimes funny, sometimes arresting. Ireland, in these pages, goes on parading its potential for pain and irony and upheaval (although the most seductive and buoyant story here, "Manhattan Medley", which deals with the glories and absurdities of erotic intoxication, takes place, as its title indicates, elsewhere).

The mood deepens and darkens with the powerful "Plunder", set in a timeless war zone: it could be the seventeenth century or the present, Ireland or Eastern Europe or even some future place of horror and devastation, but for allusions to cars and mobile phones and someone playing the Irish air "Boulevogue" on a wooden flute. ("The townspeople hid, not knowing which to fear most, the rampaging soldiers or their huge dogs that ran loose without muzzles.") The theme is the savagery of armies – rape and intimidation and a shattered world – and it echoes and underscores a different kind of impending murderousness, as evoked in the unnerving story "Black Flower". Meticulousness and reticence are the keynotes of this, as a deadly pattern of betrayal and reprisal is worked out off-stage, while the country hotel setting epitomises the everyday. ("Just enjoy the view and the rolling countryside", advises the affable owner.) Tact comes into it too, in the sense that no judgements are made about motives or ideological will'o'-the-wisps, or the destinations to which chosen paths may lead.

"Inner Cowboy" is a troubling, beautifully realised piece about a blameless and not too canny youth, for whom the world and its wickedness prove too much. "Two Mothers" and "Old Wounds" are subtle and economical accounts of fraught relationships, rich in atmosphere, at which the author takes her usual straight and tolerant look. "Sinners" returns us to an instance of small-town anxiety, social unease and outrage, as the elderly female owner of a bed-and-breakfast establishment suspects three of her guests of getting up to goodness knows what improprieties under her good Catholic roof. Passing themselves off as parents and daughter, but clearly (in her mind) nothing of the sort, the three sinners bring with them a blast of sulphur, a shocking transgressiveness. Another rueful story, "Green Georgette", is cast in the form of social comedy, with an out-of-town mother and daughter elated to be invited for an evening visit by the local bank manager's lah-di-dah wife ("she wore a brown boucle coat that came almost to her ankles and she wore it open so as to reveal a contrasting coloured dress in muted orange"). The story proceeds from anticipation to indignation, with the country duo – as ever – left a bit let down and mystified before the occasion is over. This author's way with provincial niceties remains unsurpassed.

The short story, to quote again the infinitely quotable Elizabeth Bowen, "should be as composed, in the plastic sense, and as visual as a picture." The stories assembled in *Saints and Sinners* meet all her requirements, down to the approximation – it need only be an approximation – to "aesthetic and moral truth". Edna O'Brien continues to jolt, in the positive sense, enthral, entertain and hearten her readers.

Times Literary Supplement, 2011

A RECORDED DELIVERY

Ciaran Carson, *The Star Factory*

Towards the end of his remarkable new prose work, *The Star Factory*, Ciaran Carson has a footnote in which he quotes the entry on *Dinnshenchas* in Robert Welch's *Oxford Companion to Irish Literature. Dinnshenchas*, we read, "reflects a mentality in which the land of Ireland is perceived as being completely translated into story: each place has a history which is continually retold."

Dinnshenchas, or, more correctly, *dinnsheanchas*, has to do with the lore of place-names and the allure of places. In *The Star Factory*, Carson entertainingly subjects his native Belfast – "the dark city of Belfast", as he has called it elsewhere – to an extended reinvention. It's not the first time he has engaged in such an enterprise. Belfast has always loomed large in his iconography, but his approach to its particulars – its streets and edifices and flotsam and miasmas – is becoming increasingly spellbinding and idiosyncratic. "I think at first I had a pattern in my head, though maybe I think now / it changed", he wrote with a certain prescience in a poem called "The Patchwork Quilt" in his 1978 pamphlet *The Lost Explorer*.

Indeed, a change in tone and manner has been apparent since 1986, when *The Irish for No* (Carson's second full-length poetry collection) turned its back with a swagger on the simple lyricism and deftness of his earliest work. Carson's lines grew longer, his style took an anecdotal turn and his themes gained in pungency, redolent above all of Belfast in the 1980s, gritty, beleaguered and unregenerate. You can check the movement forward by reading "The Patchwork Quilt" with its unassuming impersonation – "It took me twenty years to make that quilt" – alongside the later "Patchwork", which assembles its images with bravado and originality. The same line ("It took me twenty years …") also gets into the second poem, but embedded in a much more elaborate evocation of potent swatches of the past. The same kind of constructive unravelling, or obsessive deconstruction, is a distinctive feature of *The Star Factory*.

Among the patches of "Patchwork" and the segments of *The Star Factory* is a remembered, or archetypal, excursion up the Black Mountain on the outskirts of Belfast. When "nearly at the summit", the narrator's father pauses to light a cigarette, a Park Drive or Woodbine, before gesturing downwards to indicate the components of their own home ground far below: Gallaher's Tobacco Factory, Clonard Monastery, the rows and rows of red-brick terraces, church spires and mill chimneys, barracks, schools, "mill dams, reservoirs, ponds, sinks and sluices", all bearing names which are infinitely conducive to storytelling.

Take the Star Factory of the title. This was, it seems, a boys' clothing manufacturer located at 322 Donegall Road, Belfast. (I was born and lived for 20 years at 551 Donegall Road, and I have no recollection of it – however, a repository of flannel trousers wouldn't have held much interest for me, unlike the Carnegie Library farther down the road, to which I, like Ciaran Carson, was drawn incessantly.) Over this utilitarian building, Carson superimposes a fabricated structure until it turns into a hectic workplace like something out of Fritz Lang's "Metropolis". It becomes the habitation of ghostly seamstresses, or a transformation zone where "words were melted down and like tallow cast into new moulds".

What gives *The Star Factory* its unique flavour is the alternation of foot-off-the-ground narration – not to say a stellar perspective, with the disembodied author hovering over the city like a recording angel – and down-to-earth concern with specifics: the names of businesses in Cornmarket, the hearths of houses (long demolished) in the Lower Falls, the smell of plaster pervading the half-rural housing estates.

Like its predecessor *Last Night's Fun* (1996), ostensibly about Irish traditional music but ranging over a good many related topics, this book is hard to classify. Part scholarly hotch-potch, part inscrutable memoir, part intensive appraisal of a singular locality, it engages to the full in the kind of "rambling ambiguity" applauded by the author in the hands of a master storyteller such as his father (an authoritative presence in the book), and thereby ducks out of any straightforward category. The dust-jacket has it down as fiction, but this is a misnomer. It is, as much as anything, a book about storytelling, with a structure determined by the principle of association. One thing leads to another, as in the traditional ballad or tale.

Carson has bilingualism among his literary assets. As the title of his award-winning collection, *First Language*, discloses, Irish came first – unusually for 1950s Belfast – though English wasn't far behind. He is also an accomplished flute-player and singer (he was Head of Music and Traditional Arts at the Arts Council of Northern Ireland between 1976 and his retirement in 2001).

One thing leads to another: here he is peering at the bole of a tree in the Falls Park, c. 1958; the next minute he's in the Ulster Folk and Transport Museum, comparing a reconstructed worker's house from Sandy Row with its Falls Road equivalent. Furniture and ornaments are the same, he says, on both sides of the sectarian divide.

So are other things. At one point he quotes a passage from Robert Harbinson's *No Surrender* (1960), about a Protestant upbringing. Very gingerly, the hero and his friends approach enemy territory – in this instance, the upper part of the Donegall Road, beyond the Bog Meadows. As in a mirror image, they might have seen their Catholic counterparts, equally tentative, coming towards them from the opposite direction.

The Star Factory is a book without an ideological slant. It deals, for the most part, with the ingredients of everyday life, transfigured by the intensity and clairvoyance of the scrutiny brought to bear on them. You can't, however, grow up in a place nurturing clandestine affiliations, such as West Belfast, without absorbing something of their exudations into your system. Carson's postman father learnt not only Irish but, we're told, Esperanto into the bargain – the latter "to subvert the world dominance of English". Carson, too, acknowledges "a tremble of loyalty" to the almost invisible, relatively innocuous republicanism of the mid-century, whose adherents included one of his uncles.

This *Odd Man Out* incarnation of Belfast is one of the versions of the city which get a showing in *The Star Factory*. It adds its seedy cinematic glamour to the local street-lore of Cathal O'Byrne, the fictional anti-Home Rule antics of George A. Birmingham, the Reverend O'Hanlon's mid-Victorian hellhole of gin palaces and debauchery, the deprived-but-buoyant territory of Robert Harbinson — all cited at one point or another. Carson has a poem, "The Exiles' Club", in which a group of Irish-Australians meets every week to reconstruct, in imagination, the entire Falls Road area. *The Star Factory*, more ambitiously, plots not only the physical city, but also a good many of the myths, memorabilia, layers of social history and customs associated with it. The postman's son, as you might expect, is adept at delivering all kinds of strange messages, postcards from byways and enticing packages. The result is a book to reread and savour.

Independent, 1997

RED HANDS
AND DANCING FEET

Ciaran Carson, *The Twelfth of Never*
Ciaran Carson, *The Ballad of HMS Belfast*

Among the traditional modes to be found in eighteenth-century Irish poetry is the celebration of abundance: the over-brimming trout streams, over-laden apple trees, endless creamy milk, and so on, which arose in tantalising counterpoint to the poverty and deprivation prevailing over much of the country. Ciaran Carson's marvellous new collection, *The Twelfth of Never*, which takes account of many pungent traditions, is equally attuned to abundance. In this case, it's an abundance of emblem and imagery, with every rag-tag credo overturned and every slogan playfully recharged.

The title phrase lends itself to the world of the imagination, to riddling and subversion and paradox. And, because this is a collection by an Irish poet,

Ireland's myths and symbols are taken to pieces and exuberantly reassembled. At the same time, the book doesn't have an exclusively Irish orientation. Modern Japan, eighteenth-century France and Russia get a look-in, along with Keats and Coleridge, Red Riding Hood and the land of the Jabberwock. This is not in any sense an insular undertaking.

Running through it, though, you find certain recurring indigenous motifs, like "the hand cut off and thrown to the Ulster shore": the original Red Hand, the emblem of Ulster. As the legend has it, the earliest colonisers of the northern part of Ireland were approaching the coast at high speed, having settled it beforehand that the land should belong to whoever touched it first. As it came within reach, the most determined among them hacked off his hand and flung it at the shore.

There is, indeed, a straightforward link between the first heraldic hand, the terrorist's bloody hand (in an earlier Carson poem), and being caught red-handed – implicated in nationalist fantasies of one sort or another. But, in Carson's hands, this striking image is absorbed into the compelling interplay between myth and reality, between steadiness of vision and colourful derangement.

One thing, as Carson's poems amply demonstrate, leads on to another. So the red of Ulster's bloody hand modulates into the red shoes of the fairy tale, and into a vibrant poppy-red – another versatile symbol whether attached to peace, to Flanders Fields or to the Opium Wars. Every item in this sonnet sequence is deftly slotted into the whole complicated super-structure, which itself is balanced by Carson's ease of manner and parodic impulse:

> As down by the glenside I met an old colleen,
> She stung me with the gaze of her nettle-green
> > eyes,
> She urged me to go out and revolutionise
> Hibernia, and not to fear the guillotine.

The effect is riveting, even for readers unfamiliar with every local nuance, those unequipped to identify the old song behind the new sonnet – for example, "The Bold Fenian Men" (in the lines quoted above), or the eighteenth-century "Churchyard of Creggan", the Gaelic *aisling* written by Art McCooey, which crops up elsewhere. Allusiveness isn't everything. You don't have to know that Carson's "The Lily Rally", which begins, "The Papists stole me and tried to make me play / Their Fenian music", is a branching out from that most amiable of Orange ballads, "The Oul' Orange Flute", or that "1795" harks back to Florence M. Wilson's 1917 poem "The Man from God-Knows-Where", her tribute to the United Irishman Thomas Russell, who was hanged at Down-patrick Gaol in 1803. It isn't necessary to be familiar with all the background notes to appreciate the verve and idiosyncrasy of *The Twelfth of Never* (even the title assumes a nod to Ulster's famous "Twelfth", the Twelfth of July). The game of spot-the-allusion only amounts to a surface gloss on a collection which encompasses all kinds of resonances. The whole heady assembly (77 sonnets in all) displays to the full the author's expertise when it comes to creative adaptation, or appropriation.

Carson is a Belfast-born poet, and a good deal of his work has concerned itself with mythologies of the city's streets and landmarks. *The Ballad of HMS Belfast* brings together his Belfast poems, many of them engendered while his birthplace "tore itself apart and patched things up again". The city-as-palimpsest is one motif, but Carson's strongest subject is more diffuse. It has to do with the hallucinatory effect achieved when various kinds of murderousness and destructiveness are superimposed on top of everyday life. Carson, though, is at the same time a storyteller, a joker and an ironist, so that even the most unsettling poems here – "Night Patrol" or "Queen's Gambit", for example – carry an upbeat astringency. His Belfast is in one sense close to Eliot's "unreal city", but also only too appallingly real – a place of unleashed badness, psychic distinctiveness, and a kind of harrowing glamour.

Independent, 1998

BYROADS AND BYWORDS

Benedict Kiely,
A Letter to Peachtree and Nine Other Stories

The author Benedict Kiely goes in in a big way for traditional story-telling devices such as hyperbole, digression, the incorporation of vivid motifs, celebration of local prowess and so forth. His stories on the whole eschew a standard, more or less straightforward approach. Rapid shifts of emphasis, odd angles of vision, rag-bag impressions are equally a part of Kiely's distinctive method, his readiness to cram a good deal in. The mixture is often exhilarating, especially when the ingredients boil down to something new and unified; sometimes they remain a jumble of bits and pieces, stray notions and recollections jammed together like so much lumber. Sometimes the author is run away with by the train of thought he sets in motion. More often, though, both a high degree of control and high pressure are maintained throughout. Kiely goes at things full tilt, like the two sides in the annual re-enactment of the Battle of the Boyne at Scarva in County Down, which he describes in the story "Mock Battle".

This story, in his new collection *A Letter to Peachtree*, has a good many typical Kiely components: a journey, a local event, an edgy relationship, some characters with strong traits, a lot of borrowed phrases and catch-phrases to contribute richness, an incident or two remembered from the past. A newspaper reporter, based in Dublin, and accompanied by his wife, has come north on the train, to be met by a photographer and driven to the scene of the celebratory skirmish. The reporter's wife keeps needling him about his friend-ship with a tennis-player named Alison, a bouncing girl. Other bouncing girls are scattered throughout the book, some with peculiar names like Maruna, and one, in the title story, identified only by the way she's dressed: Jodhpurs. Some, like the red-haired Gobnait in an evocative piece called "Your Left Foot is Crazy", are glorious girls from the distant past – 40, 50 years or more ago.

The backward look is a strongly developed feature of Kiely's writing. His "Letter to Peachtree", addressed by a research student over from America to study the works of Brinsley MacNamara, to a woman back in Atlanta, Georgia, recounts an Irish escapade – train journey, parochial hall, quaint Catholicism, late-night conviviality and all. It looks as though the author is under some compulsion here to present the whole thing as an elegy for old, mad Ireland, but his sardonic streak keeps him from going quite so far.

An elegiac tone, however, completely unadulterated, gets into one or two of the *Peachtree* stories, "A Walk in the Wheat", for example, concerning the return to his childhood locality of an old man with a grievance; and the vibrant story "The Jeweller's Boy", about the making of a journalist. Kiely, as ever, exercises his feeling for oddity and inflation; and his central theme is approached by some rocky byroad. Byroads and bywords alike appeal to him. Extravagant doings in out-of-the-way places: he's for ever latching on to these, and making something mock-heroic of them. The misbehaviour of a bullock on a fair day is enough to rivet his imagination. His temperament contains nostalgia, mockery and rumbustiousness in about equal measures.

He can surprise us, though, with a story ("Through the Fields in Gloves") about a molester whose trick is to spray paint at girls in their good clothes. "Secondary Top", too, has a teacher whose behaviour towards young girls in his charge isn't absolutely impeccable: letters of complaint signed "Worried mother" begin to reach the school. Two flippant detectives, posing as fishermen, arrive to sort things out. Kiely's resolutions are sometimes as haphazard as the contretemps that precede them.

A lot of singing and recitation goes on in these pages, to fill the odd moments when the talking voice isn't finding an outlet. "Now let me tell you something", says the narrator of "A Letter to Peachtree", as if that isn't what he, and all the rest of them, have been doing all along. Kiely's characters are a garrulous, memory-ridden, live-wire bunch; and this collection makes the most of their ebullient observations and outbreaks of reminiscence.

Times Literary Supplement, 1987

SEARCHING HIGH
AND LOW FOR A SONG

Ríonach Uí Ógáin (ed.), *Going to the Well
for Water: The Seamus Ennis Field Diary 1942–46*

On 2 July 1942, a young man named Seamus Ennis leapt
on his bicycle in North County Dublin and cycled west-
wards at high speed, never stopping until he reached
Kilbeggan and a break for tea, and then continuing on
to Ballinasloe and a good night's rest. The following day
he arrived at Oranmore, near Galway, and immediately
set about fulfilling his employers' requirements.

"I spoke to an old man", he wrote. "He sang '*Sí
Nóirín mo Mhain*' for me." Seamus Ennis was 23 at the
time, and abundantly endowed with energy and ideal-
ism, qualities essential for the successful completion of
his work. He was one of a team of dedicated music and
song collectors dispatched to remote Gaeltacht areas
by the Irish Folklore Commission, founded in 1935.

Their mission was to seek out, transcribe, record and preserve every aspect of an indigenous folk culture, before this endangered resource went the way of the woods of Kilcash, or the last wolf in Ireland. It still amounted to a living tradition, but only just; and, as yet, its importance to the country's psychic well-being wasn't widely acknowledged. (In fact, the context for Ireland's song-collecting was as much international as national. A similar preservationist drive in relation to folksong and dance was affecting other places, including England, parts of Europe and America.)

Among the assets Seamus Ennis brought to the job was his own expertise as a singer, flute player and uilleann piper. His musical gifts, along with his proficiency in Irish, helped him to gain the confidence of local "tradition bearers", who weren't always inclined to be forthcoming about the riches of song and story entrusted to them by earlier generations. People coming in from outside to observe, to marvel and to appropriate local idiosyncrasies, had been a Gealtacht hazard for a good many years. And the work of the Folklore Commission, though undoubtedly good in itself, was in some instances faintly tarred with the same provoking brush.

Was there a point, tradition carriers might have worried, when dissemination equalled devaluation? Was a fiercely guarded culture in danger of having its lifeblood diluted? For example, one old man, a fiddle player from Dungloe, Co Donegal, was willing to pass on a particularly cherished air *("Sliabh Sneachta")* to Seamus Ennis as a fellow musician, but wouldn't have it going anywhere near the Commission or any other "official" body. He was adamant about that.

A fear of handing out something precious to all and sundry was one thing, but you also had simple exasperation brought on by a stream of pestering folklorists. "… I am tired of teaching you songs. Someone comes to bother me nearly every day", complained one old Donegal woman, whose proximity to the Irish College at Gaoth Dobhair made her a target for earnest *Gaeilgeoirí* arriving in droves. Other performers, confronted by Seamus Ennis and his Ediphone Recording Machine, simply "will not play for me" – or required considerable coaxing to come up with the goods. But these were the exceptions. Most people were disarmed by the young man's evident appreciation and knowledge of the subject, and collaborated with his project willingly. Perseverance pays off, he found, tracking down elusive singers who constantly seemed to be away from home whenever he called on them. Sometimes the dogged collector ended up sitting in the middle of a field of potatoes with a whistling farmer whose whereabouts he had finally located after many digressions, or taking down material from a man cutting turf in a bog.

It's all part of his pursuit of authenticity – he wasn't interested in songs learned from books, or those already widely familiar. Anything rare, distinctive or enduring is what set his collector's nose twitching. The pages and pages of song titles included at the end of his *Field Diary* testify to his achievement as a champion song collector and conservationist.

In the 1940s, the whole Gaeltacht civilisation was on a cusp between continuity and modernity, though the most extreme forms of modernisation wouldn't occur for another 30-odd years. The imposition of a bungaloid, garden-pond makeover on the West of Ireland was still a long way in the future. The mid-twentieth century was still a time of innocence and a kind of rugged glamour, when turf smoke ascended from every chimney, and the men of the place were adept at planting, seafaring, gathering scallops, road-making, building walls and interior decorating, making querns for grinding and much else besides. And nearly every family included one or more tradition carrier, those in whose keeping are the pure true notes of a vibrant singing culture.

The brilliant *sean-nós* singers and fiddle players and dancers were a focus of interest for strangers – outsiders – and the thing that drew them in to applaud, to learn what they could and to record for posterity. Seamus Ennis, himself among "the greatest pipers of modern times" (as Ciaran Carson has it in his book on Irish traditional music), was valued as a guest in the Gaeltacht for his powers of playing music, and also for the ease with which he accommodated himself to local life. In every Gaeltacht area from Carna in Connemara to Tory Island, he rolled up his sleeves and went out on the bog to cut turf, take part in potato-digging or hay-making, or spend a morning helping to launch a curach beached on dry land. All of which requires prodigious stamina as well as a spirit of cooperation. A measure of hardihood in the face of constantly atrocious weather was needed as well: "The storm and rain were very strong ... I had to take shelter from hailstones ... It poured in the evening and turned to heavy snow ... As Colm said [Colm Ó Caodháin, one of Ennis's dearest friends in Connemara], I had paid dearly for the songs I had written from him this evening."

While Ireland kept out of the war that was raging elsewhere, "the Emergency" meant an absence of non-essential cars on the roads, and frustrating shortages and delays (two weeks for a bottle of ink to arrive from Dublin). It meant the cut-off communities of the west were even more acutely driven in on themselves, with consequent enhancement of age-old attributes and activities. "We had spent the afternoon in the old world, among people such as our ancestors", Ennis observes after a visit to an old Donegal woman, Nora

Gallagher, whom he pictures sitting on a stool by the fire with her back to the bed in the chimney corner, "wearing the dark clothes of former times". It's true that, at the time, the settle bed and the chimney corner co-existed with broadcasts from Raidió Éireann and Ediphone recording machines, but the spirit of the Gaeltacht places was still geared to an immemorial pungency and self-reliance.

It was also awash in Catholicism, with processions and confessions, gatherings of friends and neighbours after Sunday Mass an important social ritual, and St Brigid's crosses made of rushes hanging buoyantly above every half-door. As a way of life it had much to commend it – especially if you didn't have to live it, hardship, poor sanitation, terrible weather and all – but it wasn't equipped to survive in the modern world. It hasn't survived, but something of its essence has: the songs and music gathered from the old custodians of *ceol dúchasach*. And this survival is due to the efforts of visionaries, scholars and collectors such as Seamus Ennis.

Going to the Well for Water, meticulously edited and translated into English by Ríonach Uí Ógáin, is a stupendous production, full of insight, gusto and intrepidity on the part of the author – and it comes complete with its editor's valuable end-notes, and with evocative images (mostly old photographs) on nearly every page.

Some of these images are in colour, and – sadly – show desolate landscapes and roofless houses where feats of piping, singing and conviviality once took place. But to set against the depredations of the present, including the loss of a building heritage, we have Seamus Ennis's enthusiasm and discernment, his ability to put us in touch, time and again, with a bygone exhilaration, "a great night's fun and a full hall".

The Irish Times, 2009

HIBERBOLE

Gifford Lewis, *Somerville and Ross:*
The World of the Irish R.M.

The first collaboration between Edith Oenone Somerville and her cousin Violet Martin ("Martin Ross")
resulted in a Buddh dictionary – "Buddh" being the
family word for members of the family, and the dictionary consisting of words peculiar to it. "Blaut", for
instance, in Buddh circles, meant "violently to express
immoderate fury". The insufficiency of ordinary English,
when it came to strong feelings, engendered a lot of
linguistic contrivance among the Somervilles and their
family connections. A feeling for the comically expressive phrase, we learn from Gifford Lewis's affectionate
study, asserted itself early in the literary cousins. They
couldn't have been better placed to gratify it, what with
family loquacity, and with Irish servants and tradespeo-
ple expostulating idiomatically all around them. "Sure

the hair's droppin' out o' me head, and the skin rollin' off the soles o' me feet with the heart scald I get with her!" That sort of thing. Readers of the R.M. stories gain a strong impression of lower-class Irish hyperbole. Edith Somerville carried around with her a notebook in which she jotted down any local extravagance of speech she overheard. (She also carried a sketchbook in which she drew, very efficiently, Irish huntsmen in pursuit of their prey.)

Edith Somerville, the oldest in a family of eight, was born in 1858 and grew up at Drishane House, Castletownshend, in County Cork. Her mother and Martin's mother were first cousins; Martin, of Ross House, County Galway, was the younger of the two by four years. Somerville and Ross, in fact, didn't meet until 1886, when Martin was 24. She, Gifford Lewis makes plain, was the weaker and more conventional of the two: it took the boisterous Somervilles to bring her out of herself. Edith initiated the process by dressing in witch's clothing, for a prank, and frightening the life out of Martin and her party, who had come to Castletownshend on a visit. Ill-fed – diet being a matter of no consequence at Ross House – short-sighted and apt to pass out, Martin was peculiarly subject to mishaps. "There are many distressing descriptions", Mrs Lewis tells us, in a chapter describing the hazards of getting about in Victorian Ireland, "of her slight body being pitched from cabs and traps." When she wasn't falling out of conveyances or falling off horses (it's thought that a bad fall in 1898 led eventually to her death in 1915), Martin was tumbling down the crooked back stairs at Ross House and putting herself out of action for weeks on end. None of this deterred her from fox-hunting: vague but resolute, she would launch herself, and her mount, at any obstacle looming in the rough Irish countryside, hoping for the best. The side-saddle posture didn't help. Mrs Lewis enumerates the effects of sitting strained and twisted to one side for up to eight hours at a stretch. Conventional riding costume, moreover, included a skirt which was apt to prove lethal by getting entangled with the saddle. No matter: hunting provided an outlet for high spirits and hoydenism. Call it "pest control" and it became a social benefit too. No wonder the cousins were among those addicted to the wild sports of the west. Pity the poor fox that came within their orbit.

The really adept horsewoman was Edith Somerville, who schooled her own hunters and even obtained a part of her income from horse-dealing, which brought in more money than writing. Money was needed for the upkeep of both Drishane and Ross. The Anglo-Irish were hard hit by Gladstone and his Land Acts: one passed in 1881, for example, was geared among other things to do away with unfair rents. Landlords who hadn't exploited their tenants – in which category Gifford Lewis firmly places the Somervilles and Martins – suffered along with the rest. New-fangled acts of defiance sometimes caused them to suffer too. The Martin family, especially, was distressed by the attitude of its headstrong social inferiors who rejected Conservative Unionism in favour of Nationalism in the election held in 1872. Mrs Lewis attributes the death of Martin's father to this "betrayal" – and there's a poignant image of Ross House after it, temporarily uninhabited, and with rabbits scampering over the great steps before the main entrance.

Elizabeth Bowen, another Anglo-Irishwoman, applauds the sangfroid and ingenuity of "big house people" who refused to relinquish the reputation that dogged them, that of being "the heartless rich", while struggling to stay solvent and keep a watertight roof. (Their domestic disasters, like everything else about them, tended to occur on a grand scale. A female relative of Edith Somerville's, we learn from Gifford Lewis, once accidentally demolished the family mansion.) At Castletownshend and its outskirts, indeed, theatrical performances in the shrubberies, outings, dances and other merry activities continued unabated in the face of dwindling financial resources. Edith Somerville wrote indignantly in her diary in 1882 about the non-payment of rents to her uncle Joscelyn Coghill, adding that the threat of eviction would surely force the brutes to pay up. The rights and wrongs of land agitation didn't engage her attention greatly at the time. She had other matters to contend with – among them, we're given to understand, a love affair which came to nothing. The man in question wasn't rich enough to commend himself to Edith's father. Not too much information is available about this episode, which Mrs Lewis cites as a factor in Edith's opting for celibacy and a career. By 1886, when Martin came on the scene, go-ahead Edith had managed to get an art training in Dusseldorf and Paris, and was doing rather well as an illustrator.

The two thoroughly talented young women (Martin's talents included the ability to buck up a dull party by imitating a terrier with its tail trapped in the door) got their heads together over the Buddh dictionary, turned professional with *An Irish Cousin* (1889), and went on to write *The Real Charlotte* (published in 1894), which many people consider their finest work. It contains a lot of disagreeable characters all trying to better themselves at the expense of someone else. Charlotte Mullen is a strong-minded woman of 40, plain in appearance and absurdly infatuated with a neighbour who thinks very well of himself – too well to do anything to Charlotte other than borrow money from her. Francie Fitzpatrick, Charlotte's poor relation and the heroine of the novel, is a silly girl. The local grandees are an insane old autocrat in a bath chair and his unengaging wife. Class, chicanery and social transgressions are treated seriously in this book, but it was a jocular approach to these topics that gained for Somerville and Ross a vast popularity. *Some Experiences of an Irish R.M.*, in which an amiable Englishman comes face to face with Irish blether and buffoonery, first appeared in 1899. Major Yeates is the Resident Magistrate who soon discovers what an uproarious business life is in out-of-the-way Skebawn, and thereabouts.

Disraeli, who seems not to have thought highly of the Irish, once labelled the lot of them "wild, reckless, indolent, uncertain and superstitious", and it's as if Somerville and Ross latched on to this pronouncement and gave it a comic twist. The R.M. stories are very facetious and light-hearted, full of inoffensive belligerence and lovable improbity. The hunting contretemps is very much a feature of the R.M., with riders for ever "picking themselves in ignominy out of a briar patch", or entering a bedroom as a pack of hounds leaps off the bed. Consonants are thickened and vowels broadened all over the place – "throuble", "shneakin'", "dhread", "discoorse". A lot of readers found the antics and the idiom enormously diverting: but not, by and large, the Irish, to start with at any rate. In nationalist circles the figure of fun, however benignly presented, wasn't considered a suitable incarnation for an Irishman; and its prevalence throughout the nineteenth century was cause for affront. The jokey manner of Somerville and Ross ran counter to the spirit of organisations such as the Gaelic League (though Douglas Hyde, co-founder of that body, was on sufficiently friendly terms with Edith Somerville to translate for her an Irish ballad commemorating an exploit of her grandfather's).

"The plain people of Ireland", having had inferiority foisted on them, were fed up with it and its expressions in literature: hence the adverse reaction to the knockabout concoctions of Somerville and Ross, and even to the decorative peasant life enshrined by Synge in pungent language. These people resented, perhaps, the presumption of Ascendancy commentators who found in lives outside their own experience material for allegory or farce. Eventually, as circumstances changed, the R.M. stories gained an appreciative audience in Ireland, the thing to repudiate now being an inability to take a joke against yourself. Edith Somerville all along disowned any impulse towards satire (justly enough – the stories and novels aren't mordant enough for that), as well as rejecting the adjective "rollicking", which seemed to her to imply some want of authenticity. She had her notebooks filled with Irish expressions to testify to the correctness of the R.M.'s examples of rich native speech. It does, however, matter with the Somerville and Ross stories that the authors use dialect as the object rather than the instrument of ridicule (however good-humoured) – the clownish Irish act having palled.

Still, the energy and professionalism of the authors call for admiration; whatever they tackled, they did it with as much verve as they could muster. Their partnership lasted for nearly 30 years, being broken only by the death of Violet Martin – a break, indeed, that Edith Somerville refused to acknowledge. She had always been possessed of a degree of psychic power – we learn from Gifford Lewis that a small table once followed her across a room – and she insisted that her dead collaborator had a hand in the books that appeared (under both names) after 1915. Maurice Collis, who published a biography of Somerville and Ross in 1968, took the line that such closeness could only have come about as a result of a lesbian attachment between the cousins – a supposition very sensibly refuted by Gifford Lewis, who mentions the one authenticated sexual overture of this kind made to Edith, by Dame Ethel Smyth. Edith recommended that she exercise her passions elsewhere. "Hear from ES, her ears bad", she noted in her diary, when the composer wrote feelingly to her.

Edith Somerville, who was born in the year the Irish Republican Brotherhood was founded in America, went on living (and living in Ireland) until 1949,

by which time she had added 15 titles to the Somerville and Ross output – no more R.M. stories though,
as these required a jollier tone than she could manage – seen her brother murdered by Irish extremists,
developed a strong aversion to "immorality", practised
automatic writing, and witnessed the decline of her
own class in a reconstituted Ireland. Through it all,
she never lost the ability to make an impact: the girl
who'd danced a long-step mazurka down the steep hill
at Castletownshend in her nineteenth year, turned
up at her niece's wedding in 1944 wearing a stuffed
seagull on her head.

London Review of Books, 1986

THE POET UNDERTAKES A
REVIVING JOURNEY HOME

Thomas Lynch, *Booking Passage: We Irish and Americans*

Thomas Lynch is well aware of how his dual identity strikes others. At home in Michigan, he says, an
undertaker who writes poems has all the social cachet
of a dentist who does karaoke. In Ireland or England,
though, the eccentricity of these combined careers is
a cause of acclamation, given that the second is not
only followed against the odds, but followed brilliantly.

The poet-mortician is well to the fore in *Booking
Passage*. However, it's not so much professional as ethnic
duality that exercises Lynch's imagination here. He
brings a distinctive touch to his explorations of family
and kinship, broken and enduring continuity. The first
question he asks himself is this: what does it mean to
be more-or-less affluent American, while tracing your
origins to the bleak west coast of County Clare, an

area once famous for the intensity of its privations? In search of an answer, or partial answer, back in 1970, he travelled from Michigan to remote Moveen. Traditional Lynch territory then became, for him, a kind of home territory, where he gained some ties of affection and appeased ancestral promptings.

Thomas Lynch now owns the house in Moveen from which, in 1890, his great-grandfather, having had enough of poverty and disaffection, headed west to America. The house — two-roomed, thatched, two windows and a door to the front — remained in the family, who owned it outright after 1903, courtesy of the Land Purchase Act. It passed to the author, a hundred years after his ancestor left it, as an inheritance from his distant cousin Nora Lynch who, with her bachelor brother, had welcomed him to Ireland in 1970 — not as a returning Yank, but as a cherished relation.

Thanks to this pair, Lynch's visits to the West of Ireland began to seem less like episodes of time-travelling and more like a homecoming. *Booking Passage* is, as much as anything, a tribute to Nora Lynch, with her catchphrases, unpretentiousness and indomitability. One of her frequent sayings, "the same but different", betokens an instinctive attitude of tolerance for everything from idiosyncrasies of the outside world to local lapses of behaviour. We might do worse, the author implies, than to hold it in mind in our dealings with whatever conflicts with our sense of how things ought to be. Specifically, he's thinking of clashes of religion, race and nationality; but the proposition holds good in a general sense too.

Connections between people, between places, between times: this is a strong thread running through Thomas Lynch's book. It ties him into a celebration of friendship, with fellow-poets, with his brothers and sisters, with key figures in his life. If everything is connected, it makes for an enlarging outlook. If, for example, the house in Moveen links him to the life of his antecedents, it points forward too, with its up-to-date renovations. It's still the same, but different.

Something similar happened with the benign (in the author's view) Catholicism imported from rural Ireland into places like Michigan, where exorbitant forms of religious observation and prodigious procreative tendencies acquired an expansive American overlay. The family running to 18 or 19 children wasn't unusual. This Irish-American way of life has had to be modified, in recent years, not only by a potentially civilising secularism, but as a consequence of disclosures about priestly delinquency and the awfulness of Irish nun-run institutions like the notorious Magdalene Laundries. But, the author would contend, you can see beyond current derangements to an essential integrity in the Catholic church – though a more flexible integrity than it used to be. He's in a reflective mood here, but his book accommodates more than one mood.

By turns diverting, evocative and provocative, *Booking Passage* includes with its compass all the muddle and multiplicity of its author's lifelong concerns. It does so, to our enjoyment, in a spirit of discernment and delight.

Independent, 2005

QUIET VOICE OF A CREED
WITHOUT CLAWS

Frank Ormsby (ed.), *Collected Poems of John Hewitt*

For secular humanists and traditionalists like the poet and art gallery man John Hewitt (1907–87), there's an urge to see a pattern in the past in which morals, culture and politics all come together in the interests of some enlightened objective. In order to make sense of the community, one tries to take on board the whole of its ragbag of preconceptions, and at the same time, to emphasise what's invigorating about its singularity. Hewitt and Heaney, Tom Paulin notes in one of his poems, "trace us back to the Rhyming Weavers". Eighteenth- and nineteenth-century artisan poets of Antrim and Down, radicals, republicans, United Irishmen or Irish Luddites, these self-taught versifiers and social critics were egalitarians to a man, and as such attractive to left-wing authors of the mid-twentieth century on the look-out for literary precursors untainted by sectarianism. Hewitt's famous pronouncement to the effect that a writer needs to have ancestors – "not just of the blood, but of the emotions, of the quality and slant of mind" – sets the tone; and among his own adopted forebears were a lot of "assertors and protesters" (his term) – always in a just cause.

Hewitt devoted a good part of his life to a series of honourable explorations of what it meant to be Northern Irish (mostly in verse but occasionally in prose). The son of a Methodist schoolmaster, Hewitt was born in Belfast at a time when the future didn't look altogether bleak ("the century/scarce offered hint we'd not by now enjoy/a tolerant and just society"), and lived on to experience the disintegrations of the present, about which he wrote with bitterness and dismay. Frank Ormsby's splendid edition of the *Collected Poems* points up, among other things, the consistency of Hewitt's concerns. Even the early proletarian verses, which are frankly propagandist and not very sophisticated – "hungry men that dumbly suffer wrong,/And barefoot children in the smoky street", that sort of thing – show an author who is principled and compassionate, and searching for a style to express these qualities to the full. It didn't, in fact, take Hewitt long to discard the socialist simplicity, along with the artlessness of his earliest work; the grievances and tatters of the unemployed were subsumed under an altogether more thoughtful and complicated engagement with social issues, political abuses, and – a particular Hewitt topic – the claims to integrity of Irishmen of Planter descent.

Conscientious in his poetry as in his life, Hewitt took pains to make his position on all these matters abundantly clear – and sometimes it shows. The gems among his poems – "Conacre", "The Colony", "An Irishman in Coventry", "Once Alien Here", "The Scar", "Because I Placed my Thought", and so on – are those in which an intent craftsmanship is accompanied by inspiration, when the decent, pedestrian, discursive element in Hewitt's verse gives way to something rarer, richer, and more enticing. The point may be illustrated by quoting some well-known lines:

> I should have made it plain that I stake my future
> on birds flying in and out of the schoolroom
> > window,
> on the council of sunburnt comrades in the sun,
> and the picture carried with singing into
> > the temple.

and some less well known:

Awareness of time has always been
the chief quality of a certain type of mind;
gardeners have it, and cricketers and some
                              librarians ...

The first of these quotations is chock-full of resonance, while the second shows Hewitt getting down to
it in a dogged way, taking care not to let his thoughts
run away with him. However, reading the complete
oeuvre makes us grateful for the author's painstaking approach, since it clearly led him towards those
moments of illumination which crown his output:

The sullen Irish limping to the hills
bore with them the enchantments and the spells
that in the clans' free days hung gay and rich
on every twig of every thorny hedge,
and gave the rain-pocked stone a meaning past
the blurred engraving of the fibrous frost.

So I, because of all the buried men
in Ulster clay, because of rock and glen
and mist and cloud and quality of air
as native in my thought as any here ...

As native in my thought as any here. This is a key
assertion in Hewitt's poetry, from "The Colony" on,

with its flaring beacons, uprising of the dispossessed and acknowledgement of Planter guilt ("for we began the plunder"). The narrative voice, characteristically, is thoughtful, unintense, never wishing to shirk responsibility for wrongs committed, but none the less proclaiming a proper local attachment: "for we have rights drawn from the soil and sky". Such poems stick up for settlers – or those not activated by animosity towards the native Irish, at any rate – while advocating a due regard for whatever seems most alien in the different tradition. Tolerance: this is what it all boils down to – the quality that somehow got excised from the Northern Irish psyche, and which latitudinarians like Hewitt have been trying to reinstate ever since.

One of the ways to go about it is to engage continually in productive debate: argument for the sake of expanding one's viewpoint. But everything said in Ireland carries considerable risks; even Hewitt's instinctive aversion from Catholicism (a matter of temperament, not bigotry) was apt to get itself misconstrued. There were those who felt this aversion was atavistic, and betokened a political standpoint (equally atavistic). This is far from being true. When he writes lines like, "I fear their creed as we have always feared/ the lifted hand against unfettered thought", Hewitt isn't pronouncing himself an Orangeman, just allowing expression to a particular cast of mind (careful and spirited). He goes on: "I know their savage history of wrong/and would at moments lend an eager voice/if voice avail, to set that tally straight."

That assertion comes in the poem "The Glens", a poem which ushers in the topic of Hewitt as a nature poet – rain, bogs, stony hills, the bleat of sheep, a bare thorn hedge – and the fact that the boy from Cliftonpark Avenue, Belfast, couldn't quite make a countryman of himself (though he tried). "Even a lifetime among you should leave me strange." He is, however, a felicitous commentator on country ways and landscapes: "Ossian's Grave"; "The Ram's Horn"; "Footing Turf"; "Sunset over Glenaan". And his animal poems are respectful and delicate. He even got himself accepted as something of an honorary Glensman, on the strength of his affection for the place. But it is, above all, an idea of social justice, how it may be fostered and the fearful consequences of disregarding it, that pervades Hewitt's work and strengthens it. "The Coasters", for example (from *An Ulster Reckoning*, privately printed in 1971) is a bitter poem about the inadequacy of the liberal drift among the middle classes of Northern Ireland. "You coasted along",

Relations were improving. The annual processions began to look rather like folk festivals.

When that noisy preacher started
he seemed old-fashioned, a survival.
Later you remarked on his vehemence ...
But you said, admit it, you said in the club
"You know, there's something in what he says."

Not one of Hewitt's more meticulously crafted poems – but one that really struck home, with its acerbic observations and economy of tone, to anyone even in the smallest degree culpable among its readers. The central image of an infection left to deteriorate until it becomes a raging fever, leaves us in no doubt about Hewitt's view of an administration dangerously empowered ("the old lies festered"). And it's the cherished community – the whole of it – that pays the price. There's another poem of Hewitt's – "Ulster Names", written in the 1950s – which needs to be read in conjunction with the "Postscript" of 1984 to get the sharpest flavour from its innocent enumeration of some treasured localities:

I take my stand by the Ulster names,
each clean hard name like a weathered stone;
Tyrella, Rostrevor are flickering flames:
the names I mean are the Moy, Malone,
Strabane, Slieve Gullion and Portglenone.

As Helen Waddell said of W.F. Marshall's, this is verse to keep the spirits raised. In the postscript, written in a blacker mood, the listed place-names have a different connotation and effect:

Now with compulsive resonance they toll;
Banbridge, Ballykelly, Darkley, Crossmaglen,
summoning pity, anger and despair,
by grief of kin, by hate of murderous men,
till the whole tarnished map is stained and torn,
not to be read as pastoral again.

Social outrage, the strong theme indicated but held in check: this is what saves John Hewitt's poetry from a Georgian primness, undue circumspection, or a leaning towards the merely decorative. It adds an edge to his work and provokes him to his most profound or lyrical utterance. There's a quatrain by Dr William Drennan (1754–1820) which Hewitt very nearly appropriated as a comment on the modesty of his own accomplishments:

Man of taste, more than talent
Not learned, though of letters,
His creed without claws,
And his faith without fetters.

But it doesn't do to take this too seriously. It was in Hewitt's nature to eschew self-aggrandisement, along with flamboyance: he never made a show of himself or his work. And it's wrong to underestimate his gifts or his achievement. As Frank Ormsby says in his incisive introduction to the *Collected Poems*, no other Irish poet has gone to greater lengths to define the culture ("a particular fractured culture") he found himself confronting. Ormsby also takes up John Hewitt's own point about the "quiet voices" that make themselves heard, even while others "posture and mouth in bigot pantomime". Hewitt's voice goes on reverberating, sounding its distinctive notes of sanity and decorum.

Times Literary Supplement, 1992

A PEACE IN VIEW

Frank Ormsby (ed.), *A Rage for Order:*
Poetry of the Northern Ireland Troubles

Good political poetry, like any other sort, arises out of
a steady contemplation of the issues in question, as well
as depending for its impact on an individual approach.
The trouble with the last "Troubles" anthology, *The
Wearing of the Black* (1974), edited by Padraic Fiacc,
was its genesis in an ill-advised immediacy which sanctioned a rush to the head of outrage and other emotions.
Ineptitude on the part of too many contributors didn't
help. What struck you, with that collection, was the
banality of the sentiments expressed – and then, the
sudden change of register when something splendid
appeared. Good poems were scattered throughout the
book like street-lights in a fog. The effect produced by
the Ormsby anthology is rather different. It embodies a more sophisticated sense of the complexities

surrounding the theme – and as a consequence, it's the odd inferior inclusion that hits you in the eye. A handful of poems, no more, fail to earn their place among the riches otherwise assembled.

We'll come back to one or two of the sub-standard pieces in a moment, but first it should be stressed that this is a marvellous gathering-together of all, or nearly all, the most cogent, and pungent, deliberations on the state of disaffection prevailing in the North of Ireland (not a recent state, as the choice of poems indicates, though the emphasis falls on events of the past 20-odd years). The contents are arranged illuminatingly in six categories, beginning with history: "the clash and blend of different traditions in the North, the endless interaction, for better or worse, of past and present." History: you can't get away from it. "My diehard countrymen like drayhorses/Drag their ruin behind them", as Louis MacNeice expressed it in a poem not included. But you can make the effort to understand it, to put it in its place or allow its pressures to work creatively. The last, indeed, is an important and enriching strategy in a good deal of recent Irish poetry. With one or two exceptions, Frank Ormsby's anthology excludes fanaticism or extreme partisanship – no nationalist verse of the "martyr's fate" type, and only Rudyard Kipling wearing his Orangeman's hat to put the case for the Ulster Unionist rebels of 1912. Kipling and

Joseph Campbell are the oldest contributors to the book, though the usually luminous Campbell is unfortunately represented by a rather weak outcry against the Planter community: it really isn't reasonable or thoughtful of him to inform the subject of his poem that his head's a block. (He is elsewhere equally rude about an Orangeman, but brisker and funnier: "His faith, 'Sixteen-Ninety', His love, none; his hope / That Hell may one day / Get the soul of the Pope".) Following these two, in the chronological line, comes Robinson Jeffers (1887–1962), a bit wordy and over-the-top as far as imagery is concerned; and then things start to look up with Louis MacNeice and John Hewitt, and the sharp drift towards the present with all its variety, inspiration and expertise.

It's true to say that the really outstanding Northern Irish poets tend to separate themselves from all the others by a fairly wide margin. But one effect of their example has been an increased concern with craftsmanship among lesser poets: it's rare to find a Northern Irish poem that isn't constructed with a measure of artistry. Frank Ormsby enables us to observe, at a glance, the range of talent fostered in the North, while allowing for a wider perspective by bringing in some percipient outsiders. There are striking poems here by Donald Davie, Tony Harrison, Fleur Adcock, Carol Rumens and others not native to the place; and

Southern Ireland gets a proper look-in too. (The whole anthology is presided over by the spirit of Yeats, who supplies two epigraphs, though Yeats himself is understandably absent.) One of the ways in which this collection succeeds is in keeping a balance between the bulk of the contributions, which are of recent composition, and the few significant earlier pieces, such as Section XVI from MacNeice's "Autumn Journal" (1938) and "The Colony" by John Hewitt (1950).

In the latter, which speaks out on behalf of Planter entitlements – "for we have rights drawn from the soil and sky" – while disguising Ulster as a Roman colony, you get in a rudimentary form the practice of obliqueness which has come to loom so large, and work so remarkably in the right hands (those of Paul Muldoon, for example, who is famous for indirectness, playfulness, and felicity of style, in that order). This is among the ways in which the province has dispensed with provincial overtones; there are no devices, tactics or influences unavailable to the Northern Irish writer, though the character of the place isn't thereby diminished. Its distinctiveness stays intact. And you have to take it all on board: atrocity, disintegration, impasse and all. I suppose one might say of *A Rage for Order* that it achieves a degree of order which hasn't the remotest chance of being matched in the political sphere. However, it assembles such a quantity of insight, intelligence and right thinking that it can only militate against excessive pessimism as far as politics is concerned. "Delight in art whose end is peace."

A quality of strangeness or unexpectedness illumines the most powerful poetry; there's a place for social or political comment, indeed, but only if it offers something over and above mere documentation. It needs to touch some subversive or atavistic nerve. There are poems in this anthology that take your breath away – among them (to list a few at random) "Gathering Mushrooms", "Hamlet", "A Severed Head", "The Butchers", "Courtyards in Delft", "Under Creon", "From the Irish", "Poem Beginning with a Line from Cavafy", "Wounds", "The Scar", "From the Canton of Expectation", "In the Lost Province", "Punishment", "The Field Hospital" – and many others to admire. A long way behind these come the few we could have done without. Ormsby has included a piece of exasperating nonsense by Rita Ann Higgins, for example, and the neurotic demotic mode of Padraic Fiacc gets far too substantial a showing. However. One thing is inescapable, that no alert reader of any anthology will fail to envisage amendments: a bit more of this or that, a bit less of the other. (I am sorry not to find Paul Durcan's deft and enigmatic poem about Belfast, "The Riding School", making an appearance in Section Six.) As far as quantity goes, Seamus Heaney comes out top with

28 poems (though the abrasive and inspiriting Tom Paulin runs him close). But the subject of the anthology should be borne in mind: it's poetry from, or about, the intractable state of Northern Ireland that is specified, and some poets have undeniably been more exercised by this concern than others. Frank Ormsby has tackled this important undertaking with flair and vigour, and gets a degree of drollness into his juxtapositions. Where else, for example, would you find Rudyard Kipling rubbing shoulders with W.R. Rodgers?

Times Literary Supplement, 1993

ANCESTRAL ANOMALIES

Glenn Patterson, *Once Upon a Hill*

1920 was an eventful year in the history of Ireland, of Northern Ireland, and of the town of Lisburn. In August of that year occurred the shooting, in Lisburn town centre, of District Inspector Oswald Ross Swanzy. Swanzy, for his own protection, had been transferred from Cork following his involvement in the murder of that city's republican mayor, Tomás MacCurtain, earlier in the year. He was thought to be out of harm's way in the North – but vengeance caught up with D.I. Swanzy as he emerged from a church service at Lisburn Cathedral. Republican marksmen had him in their sights. What next transpired points up the deadly cycle of "faction and reaction" in Ireland, as Lisburn fell victim to mob violence and hatred. In reprisal for the killing of Swanzy, Catholic homes and businesses were burnt and looted, nearly the whole of Bow Street was destroyed, and terrified Catholics fled, some making their way on foot across the Black Mountain towards the relative sanctuary of Belfast.

These events are at the centre of Glenn Patterson's doughty new book. Part memoir, part family history, part idiosyncratic commentary, *Once Upon a Hill* proceeds in its quirky way, intrepid and compelling. Basically, it tells the story of Patterson's Lisburn grandparents, who, in the aftermath of the Swanzy affair, found themselves in rival sectarian camps. We're invited to envisage Kate, or Catherine, Logue, with her widowed mother and five-year-old daughter, crouching, panic-stricken, perhaps in a neighbour's cellar, while Protestant/loyalist fury ran its course above her head. Patterson would like to believe that his grandfather Jack acted not ignobly in the circumstances – that rather than running with the mob, he kept the safety of his wife-to-be and his daughter paramount in his head. But he can't be sure of this.

As with all families, any ancestral lapses or shortcomings are apt to be kept under wraps. In 1920, Kate and Jack Patterson were not yet married, due to the opposition of Jack's formidable mother, whose ideas of social betterment precluded embracing as a daughter-in-law a mill-girl and a Catholic to boot. The couple had to wait for Eleanor's death in 1925 before tying the knot. In due course, their Protestant son, the oddly named Phares, became Glenn Patterson's father.

One of Patterson's aims, in this book, is to juggle with family myths and facts, finding striking connections in the plots of different lives. Connections, indeed, are not confined to the actual narrative. The wonderful, humane and illuminating *Once Upon a Hill* comes with copious footnotes, as the author's surplus exuberance spills over into intriguing asides ("Shoving vehicles down Bridge Street had a bit of a pedigree"; "Suffragettes, as it happens, were particularly active in Lisburn"; "Apologies, good burghers, I am setting you up here something rotten"). The book ends with Patterson and his infant daughters in Lisburn's Wallace Park, attempting to locate a famous "lost echo" – and thereby encapsulating the story's overriding theme.

Independent, 2008

HOLY AND UNHOLY

R. Dardis Clarke (ed.), *Collected Poems of Austin Clarke*

Many critics have commented on the relative obscurity of Austin Clarke outside his native Ireland – "relative", because he has always attracted a discerning band of admirers, even while being bypassed by other readers on account of his Joycean boyhood (already done to death), his incorrigible indigenousness or his (to some) bewildering switch from the pure lyrical note of "The Lost Heifer" (say), to the clotted cogency of "More Extracts from a Diary of Dreams". Born in 1896, Clarke began by composing verse along the lines laid down by some romantic exemplars: Standish James O'Grady, Douglas Hyde, George Sigerson, Samuel Ferguson, and above all the early Yeats, the Yeats of "The Shadowy Waters" and "The Wanderings of Oisin". "The Vengeance of Fionn", Clarke's remarkably accomplished first long poem, was published in 1917 – and the new *Collected*

Poems ends with the shorter and blunter "The Wooing of Becfola", which brings things nicely full circle, in a sense, even if something of a gulf separates the tone of the two retellings.

Subscribing to the literary cult of ancient Ireland did not preclude the deepest awareness of twentieth-century Ireland, in all its gloom and severity. Clarke became a strong social critic almost *malgre lui*, as the most repressive phase of Irish Catholicism got under way. A consciously "protestant" element animated his literary imagination, and among the things he was driven to protest against were clerical authoritarianism and a concomitant clamping-down on the sensual side of life. He knew what he was talking about, when he spoke out against priestly coercion. And he'd had Joyce before him to exemplify an independent stance in this and other matters. Born into a middle-class family in Dublin, Clarke attended Joyce's old school, Belvedere College, and in due course found an essential similarity between his predecessor's view of the education dispensed by the college, and his own. He also, in common with Joyce, possessed a sensibility attuned to the modern age despite the allure of antiquity, and a growing streak of dissent from the strictures of the time and place in which he found himself. A satirical attitude to Church and State was evolving in Austin Clarke, reinforced, no doubt, by the years he spent away from Ireland between 1922 and 1937, when he worked as an editor and reviewer in London.

Back in 1919 Clarke had suffered a nervous breakdown, which led to his incarceration in St Patrick's Hospital in Dublin. "Mnemosyne Lay in Dust", his fictionalised account of this episode, was published many years later, in 1966, and remains among the most accessible and widely relished of Clarke's later poems. It imposes a slightly hallucinatory outline over its Dublin particulars:

> The spike-ends of the Blue Coat school,
> Georgian houses, ribald gloom
> Rag-shadowed by gaslight, quiet pavements
> Moon-waiting in Blackhall Place.

Breakdown and recovery: the poems of his, and the century's, 1920s and 30s, hold on to a peculiarly Gaelic poise and gracefulness, with their classic emblems of Irishness – the holy well, horse dealers at Ballinasloe, the rushy glen, the fair day, balladmen and beggarmen. But at the same time they allow an access for the public house, the ugly box (the confessional), shopkeepers, cartwheels and corduroy trousers in all their dusty authenticity. If you think of these poems as being, for the most part, rainy, remote and ritualised, you have to take note, as well, of a new and defiantly non-poetic element which is entering in. "Martha Blake", perhaps, sets the scene:

> In the shadow of the nave
> Her well-taught knees are humble,
> She does not see through any saint
> That stands in the sun
> With veins of lead, with painful crown ...

That poem was published in 1938 in the collection *Night and Morning.* And then came the famous 17-year silence, before *Ancient Lights* in 1955 took up with renewed causticity the themes of hell and heaven and mediaeval Ireland, along with pungent autobiographical detail. An eloquent opacity marks Austin Clarke's later work, in conjunction with its counterpart, "verse ... simple as join-hands, yet ambiguous", as he puts it himself in the striking "Forget Me Not" of 1962, with its vivid topography, resonant childhood recollections and extraordinary horse imagery: Dublin cab horses, horses for slaughter, horses of myth and legend, horse meat in restaurants, the Gray of Macha laying her mane on the dying Cuchulain's breast.

Once he'd got the bit between his teeth again, it seemed that nothing could stop Clarke – racing all over Ireland ("Delightful to be in Tipperary ... Storm out of the South-West/From Banagher, Clonfert, across the flats …"), supplying new words for old harp-songs ("Mabel Kelly", 'Peggy Browne"), and, further afield, making an old-fashioned pilgrimage to the small, white, one-storeyed cottage of Edgar Allan Poe.

> The House of Ussher, mouldering,
> the woodland scent
> Of leaf-decay, poor wet-their-drawers,
> not one robust:
> The poet was frenzied by them
> in his thoughts, the bust
> Of Pallas in the shadow …

After Poe Park, contemplated with a raised eyebrow, the Whitman Launderette. Clarke's "Old-Fashioned Pilgrimage" is a wonderfully discursive and inclusive poem, sardonic, buoyant and resourceful. Add to these qualities the jocularity of "A Jocular Retort" to a critic in "the Literary Supplement/Of the London Times" who described Mr Clarke as "a garrulous rambling old Irishman", and the bawdy exuberance of a poem like "The Healing of Mis" (1970), and we're back with a kind of Yeatsian irrepressibility ("Why should not old men be mad … ?").

Yeats himself continues to loom large, as a subject for contemplation or evocation, long forgiven (one feels) for his inexplicable exclusion of Austin Clarke from his *Oxford Book of Modern Verse* in 1936; and other preoccupations of his early days – holy and unholy Ireland, life histories, erotic affirmation – continue to exercise Clarke's imagination right to the end of his life (he died in 1974). As Christopher Ricks remarks in the opening sentence of his idiosyncratic and invigorating introduction to the new *Collected Poems*, Austin Clarke loved returning to things; and each return brought a deeper, wittier or more wayward appraisal. Among major Irish poets of the twentieth century, he is to be cherished both for his singing lines, and for his singular insights.

Times Literary Supplement, 2009

MA LANGUAGE
IS DISGRACEFUL

Chris Agee *et al* (eds.), *The Other Tongues:*
An Introduction to Writing in Irish, Scots
Gaelic and Scots in Ulster and Scotland

It is sometimes hard to remember that standard English is not the only language in which powerful literature has been produced in various parts of Britain and Ireland; but moves are afoot to amend that situation. This anthology, for example – well named *The Other Tongues* – assembles rich material, past and present, in Scots and Ulster Scots, Irish and Scottish Gaelic (or Gallic), all testifying to the indomitability of these languages. Endlessly threatened by political or social forces working against them, they have seemed at times in abeyance, at others assertive, but have always kept going, whatever the obstacles. Near-obliteration is followed by revival, contempt by approval. During the three centuries covered in this book, the tongues in question (some a bit closer to standard English than others) have shown themselves to be resilient, flexible and compelling. As a medium of expression, they are second to none.

Two distinct linguistic groups are represented here. There is no connection between Scots/Ulster Scots and Gaelic/Gallic, beyond the odd borrowing, translation or transliteration. But one of the points made by the editors of *The Other Tongues* concerns the co-existence of these minority languages, through the centuries, with the orthodox English from which they – or their speakers – were alienated to varying degrees. The mother tongue, the hamely tongue, Gaelic *mhilis* (sweet Irish), and so on: these terms denote affection and esteem. No less than the Irish, poets and prose writers working in Scots/Ulster Scots – with Robert Burns the great exemplar – treat the native language as a resource, not a limitation. It is, after all, the mode of speech "my neighbours use, / Wha think shoon purtier far than shoes", as Hugh Porter of Moneyslan in Co. Down put it, writing in 1818. He went on to define his cherished idiom as "nor Scotch or English either, / But part o' baith mix'd up thegither", which is straightforward indeed, though perhaps with an undertone of mild defiance. Polite society might turn up its nose at vernacular speech and its outlets in verse, but those to whom the mode came naturally were not apologetic about it, ever. Move forward a century and a half, and you find Glasgow-born Tom Leonard sticking to his own articulation, despite discouragement: "Right inuff/ ma language is disgraceful" (or so he has been told).

Hugh Porter is not included among the contributors to *The Other Tongues*, but two of his contemporaries, Samuel Thompson and James Orr, get a showing in the anthology, along with the slightly later Thomas Given (1850–1917). All three wrote verse in vibrant Ulster Scots, with only an occasional lapse into English. Thompson, for example, confronted with a local jollification ("The Roughfort Fair" of 1793), finds the best way to convey its bucolic excesses is by means of a sparkling parody of Gray's "Elegy":

> The stiff-neck formalist, with bigot breast,
> That vain new-light men ever keen controuls;
> The subtle deist, held Religion's pest,
> Here fall together, all as drunk as owls.

English is appropriate here (though it rules the poem out for this anthology). Elsewhere among country poets the rural idiom predominates, with its hedgehog ("Thou grimmest far o' gruesome tykes") its "auld stane brig", its chirple of a cricket "snug behin' the wa' ". The details are important, proceeding as they do out of a bygone country life, and out of a faculty, with most of these poets, for sardonic observation. The worlds of the ploughman, hedge schoolmaster, linen-weaver, come into focus with all their privations and consolations.

These poets, or many of them, also count among their subjects the nightmares of history, the Penal Laws, the Highland Clearances, the suppression of cottage industries, the failed rebellions. James Orr, whom the editors describe as "the greatest poet to come from the rhyming-weaver tradition", was active on the side of the rebels during the 1798 uprising in Antrim, and went on to enshrine in strong verse a few of the less than heroic scenes he witnessed at the time. His poem "Donegore Hill" (the opening section is included here) has a comic/humane element, with its untrained farmer-soldiers losing their heads and succumbing to cowardice and confusion; but its overriding tone is ferocious and veracious – anti-romantic, in other words:

> The camp's brak up. Ower braes, an' bogs
> The patriots seek their sections,
> Arms, ammunition, bread-bags, brogues,
> Lye skail'd in a' directions:
> Ane half, alas! wad fear'd to face
> Auld Fogies, faps, or women;
> Tho' strong, untried, they swore in pride
> "Moilie wad dunch the yeomen",
> Some wiss'd-for day.

In contrast, a melancholy romantic note continued to be sounded elsewhere in Northern Irish writing. The eighteenth century was the heyday of the *aisling*, or vision, genre in Irish, and it is represented in *The Other Tongues* by part of Art Mac Cumhaigh's *"Úir-Chill a' Chreagáin"* ("Creggan Churchyard"), a poignant and idiosyncratic exercise in wishful thinking. (In other parts of Ireland, the anticipated redemption of the country was attached to the Stuart dynasty, while in the North it was still the great O'Neills, or their descendants, who were cast as agents of emancipation.) An obsession with some kind of redress for wrongs inflicted, or a bitter acceptance, prevailed. From Gaelic Scotland, too, came searing accounts of devastation, death and emigration, by authors such as Tormod MacLeoid and Elizabeth Jane Ross, with the quirky traditional dirge, "Hè na Filibhig", conspicuous among them.

Interspersed with the poems here are fine passages of prose. One of these, featuring Ulster bumpkins looking for a place of Presbyterian worship in Dublin, c. 1730, has been tentatively ascribed to Jonathan Swift – an interesting speculation, if nothing more. James Hogg is here, with a lively extract from his *Confessions of a Justified Sinner*; also Aodh Mac Domhnaill, with a cache of herbal notes to rival Culpepper's (in Irish), and Mící Mac Gabhann from Gortahork, Co Donegal, as a seasonal labourer tramping the roads of Scotland. The social history of Scotland and the North of Ireland is compressed, in *The Other Tongues*, into an array of telling moments.

Continuity is also important to the undertaking. From Robert Burns's "Mouse" to W.N. Herbert's "Mousse", a line of indigenous inventiveness holds. "Into Modernity", the third and longest section of the anthology, comes right up to the present with (among other things) Michael Longley's exuberant recasting of a piece of the Odyssey in an Ulster dialect ("I gulder to me da: 'Dinnae gut him wi' yer gully, / He's only a harmless craytur'"); the austere and incomparable Sorley MacLean, with one of his "Poems to Eimhir"; and Liz Lochhead in rueful mood, learning to "speak posh" on her first day at school, when "pu'ed oan" becomes "pulled on", "gie'd ma", "gave me", and so forth. (A grimmer instance of the same kind of cultural force-feeding makes an appearance in John Montague's long poem "The Rough Field", when the Gaeltacht child heard speaking Irish at school has a notch added to a tally stick kept for the purpose of gauging an appropriate punishment for the transgression. Or, we might think of Tony Harrison's poem about Cornish tin-workers and their adversaries, "Those gentlemen who scuppered the men's oath, / And killed the language that they swore it in.") From the mid-twentieth century, and from Rannafast in Co

Donegal, comes a fragment of Seosamh Mac Grianna's unconventional autobiography *Mo Bhealach Féin (My Own Way)*; a title that might sum up the modus operandi of all the writers included here. As evaders of linguistic conformity, they can count a measure of subversiveness among their assets, along with an impulse to uphold diversity and authenticity.

Alongside the well-known names – Hugh MacDiarmid, Iain Crichton Smith, Edwin Morgan, Kathleen Jamie, Robert Crawford, Cathal Ó Searcaigh – are many less familiar but equally rewarding: Anna Frater, Rody Gorman, James Fenton (not to be confused with the English poet of the same name), Pól Ó Muirí, for example. The editors of this superb book (all 12 of them) have made some inspired and illuminating choices, and their common felicitous touch extends to the images, many in colour, which accompany each extract. The voices of *The Other Tongues*, away from the mainstream, sound distinctively, bewitchingly, and clear.

Times Literary Supplement, 2014

TWO ENDS OF
AN IRISH EGG

Claudia Kinmonth,
Irish Country Furniture 1700–1950
James Howley,
The Follies and Garden Buildings of Ireland

"Here and there up and down the country / There are
still houses where the fire / Hasn't gone out in a century." Paul Muldoon's poem, "Lull", cites the kind of
two-roomed country dwelling in which the furniture
described by Claudia Kinmonth might be assembled:
the creepie stool, the sugan or ladder-backed chairs,
the two-tone painted dresser, the settle bed. The last in
particular was quite a dominant object in many country kitchens, and has assumed a certain prominence
in social histories and reminiscences. Claudia Kinmonth quotes the Heaney poem of that title ("Trunk-
hapsed, cart-heavy, painted an ignorant brown. / And

pew-straight, bin-deep, standing four-square as an ark"), along with a paragraph from Seán O'Faoláin's *Vive Moi!*, which recalls a County Limerick farmhouse before the First World War: "Once I stayed for a couple of nights … sleeping by the undying turf fire … in the excitingly novel settle bed – by day a plain long box of wood, at nights its seat and sides folding down flat on the floor." First mentioned in 1640 in a County Waterford inventory (and apparently peculiar to Ireland), this item of furniture was associated with poverty and space-saving. A survey of 1836 refers to "an abominable thing called a settle bed", often found in the poorest dwellings of County Limerick, and just one step up from the custom of sleeping "in stradogue" – that is, the whole family lying naked on the floor, under a covering of blankets and in front of the fire. You need only add the cattle at the other end of the house to get an image of peasant Ireland at its most pungent.

Other commentators have praised "the economy of space and function characteristic of Irish kitchen fittings" (E. Estyn Evans), with comparable dual-purpose furnishings including the dreadfully cumbersome settle table and over-elaborate press bed – both interesting only as curiosities. The settle bed, on the other hand, along with particular dressers, dowry chests, primitive chairs and so forth, has a robust beauty and evocative presence, as well as an obvious historical significance.

Kinmonth's champion study of Irish vernacular furniture is strong on social history and literary allusion, over and above its engagement with craftsmanship and aesthetics. It is also something of a pioneering undertaking, since this branch of indigenous culture has been more or less overlooked, with only the odd pamphlet such as Nicholas Loughnan's *Irish Country Furniture* (1984) to indicate the charm and importance of these traditional artefacts. The book, moreover, is copiously and wonderfully illustrated, with many photographs in black-and-white and colour of the furniture *in situ* – and never mind if the kitchens in which it turns up are sometimes grotty or dilapidated. The joy of discovering an eighteenth-century dresser – and one-time hen-coop – in a tumbledown lean-to, must be immense.

Kinmonth is at pains to place the furniture in an historical context, as well as going in for extensive field-work, and her book is full of riveting detail – for example, we learn that a certain street in Cork City, during the Famine years of the 1840s, was given over to coffin-making to the extent that it became known as Coffin Street. She has immersed herself in nineteenth-century literature with a single purpose in mind: to pick out references to domestic accoutrements, and thereby build up a store of information about their use and ubiquity. (The Clougher Valley novelist William Carleton is a good provider of data in this respect.)

It adds up to an extraordinarily rich and engaging account of the uses of bog oak, pine, straw, osiers and so on, in the furnishing of common Irish houses over a period of two and a half centuries.

To turn to James Howley's *The Follies and Garden Buildings of Ireland* is to move from one end of the social scale to the other. It requires wealth as well as inspiration to build the gazebos, temples, grottoes, rustic bridges, obelisks and so forth, which ornament the great gardens of Ireland. But two things unite the architectural frivolities enumerated by Howley, and the sturdy furnishings brought under the sympathetic scrutiny of Claudia Kinmonth. Nothing about either is at odds with the natural landscape of the countryside (whether this is a result of forethought or functionalism), and both produce in the beholder a strong sense of continuity and aesthetic well-being. John M. Mogey, writing in 1947 (in *Rural Life in Northern Ireland*), mentions the excavation of a house at Lough Gur, County Limerick, which was found to be of almost exactly the same dimensions as the typical nineteenth-century rural dwelling, "so that the Irish peasant house has an ancestry of at least 4,000 years". A number of Howley's follies, likewise, are derived from classical Greek and Roman models, which puts them in a line of monuments stretching back to antiquity. It's only the twentieth century that has undervalued such continuity and consequent build-up of potent associations. Kinmonth notes "the close relationship between traditional architecture and the furniture it houses", so that everything is fitted into place; while Howley cites as "a true example of *genius loci*" the graceful eighteenth-century Temple of the Winds at Mount Stewart, County Down, which epitomises an accord between "the natural and man-made worlds".

The Follies and Garden Buildings of Ireland, like *Irish Country Furniture*, is a work of sustained scholarship and relish for the subject. It's divided into chapters according to type of building ("Towers", "Mausoleums", "Bridges"), and part of the author's purpose is to put in a plea for the preservation of all such assets from the past. In England, the Landmark Trust specialises in restoring follies and similar architectural eccentricities, while in Ireland these intriguing monuments to past grandiosity or make-believe are frequently – and deplorably – left to moulder.

Some were devised solely in the interests of "Mirth and Jollity", some arose out of a private delusion on the part of the commissioner (one County Meath Master of Hounds, fearing – with reason – that he was going to be reincarnated as a fox, had a mausoleum constructed for himself in the form of a crude circular temple, known for ever after as "the Fox's Earth"), and some were initiated as Famine Relief projects, like the later roads-going-nowhere of the 1840s and endless demesne walls. Probably the most extraordinary of the lot is the "Wonderful Barn" of 1743 at Castletown, County Kildare, which rises up to a height of 70 feet and comes complete with outer spiral staircase, gargoyles and battlemented tower.

From Claudia Kinmonth we learn a good deal about the plain people of Ireland, what they ate (for example) and what they ate it on (or off). These are people so lacking in financial resources that an egg-cup was beyond their means – hence you find tables with holes cut in the top to accommodate a hard-boiled egg. The egg-as-finial turns up in James Howley, topping a folly built into the estate boundary wall at Tollymore, County Down – and between the two, you gain considerable insight into the customs and mentalities of Ireland and Anglo-Ireland.

Times Literary Supplement, 1993

DEAD BUT
WON'T LIE DOWN

Máirtín Ó Cadhain, *Graveyard Clay*. Translated
by Liam Mac Con Iomaire and Tim Robinson

Speaking at a symposium in Cardiff in 1969, Máirtín
Ó Cadhain voiced an opinion. The writer in Irish, he
said, "whether for good, bad or indifferent, is writing
for his own people and only for his own people". This
statement is quoted by Breandán Ó hEithir in an essay
he wrote in 1977 for inclusion in John Jordan's *The
Pleasures of Gaelic Literature*. Recalling his own over-
joyed reaction to *Cré na Cille (Graveyard Clay)* on its
first appearance in 1949, Ó hEithir commends the
book as an extraordinary departure in Irish writing,
and a bold riposte to the spate of homespun novels
enshrining "the little house in the corner of the glen,
the sexless Nabla and the gormless Tadgh". *Cré na Cille*,
indeed, cocks a snook at mid-twentieth-century Ireland

with its platitudes and pieties; but for all its indigenous orientation ("only for his own people"), the novel has a thing or two to say about small town, or townland, life in general, its bickering and belligerence, its feuds and clashes and energetic goings-on. That most of Ó Cadhain's characters are dead and buried in the graveyard of Cois Fharraige ("by the sea"), only adds a savour of the surreal. These are highly articulate, outspoken and opinionated corpses, whose loss of life has not in the least diminished their worldly concerns.

Máirtín Ó Cadhain was born in 1906, in an Irish-speaking area of the west coast of Ireland not far from Galway city. After training on a scholarship at St Patrick's College in Dublin he became a primary school teacher, but lost his job following some altercation with a parish priest. He was arrested and interned for Republican activity during the Second World War. Already the author of a collection of stories, *Idir Shúgradh agus Dáiríre (Between Merriment and Gravity)*, Ó Cadhain went on to publish a second collection, *An Braon Bróghach (The Cloudy Drop)* in 1948, as well as working on a project to standardise Irish spelling, and contributing to the preparation of Tomás De Bhaldraithe's *English-Irish Dictionary*. Eventually he was appointed Assistant Professor of Irish at Trinity College Dublin. By the time of his death in 1970, Máirtín Ó Cadhain was revered as an author by those whose Irish was equal to the task of getting through the whole of daunting *Cré na Cille*, and also by those who hadn't succeeded in grappling fully with its intricacies and idiosyncrasies. It had a limited readership, no doubt about it. Because of the seeming impossibility of rendering its stylistic flourishes, its word-play and exorbitance and sheer unstoppable vitality in another language, Ó Cadhain's difficult, enticing novel resisted complete translation for more than 60 years. But now, at last, we have not one but two superb English-language versions of *Cré na Cille*. Hard on the heels of Alan Titley's *The Dirty Dust* (2015) – and from the same publisher – comes Liam Mac Con Iomaire and Tim Robinson's *Graveyard Clay*. (With the latter, the publishers have done well to stick with the original cover and illustrations by Charles Lamb.)

In his introductory note to the latest version, Liam Mac Con Iomaire mentions Alan Titley's "markedly creative interpretation of the text's 'rich and savage' demotic base". Is he sounding here a faintly dry and dismissive note? It's true that expressions like "pissed off", "fuck them anyway", "he's a bollocks", "done the dirty", "that little wanker" do not entirely correspond to the speech patterns of Connemara Irish. The last, for example, is more like "waster" ("pipsqueak" is how Mac Con Iomaire and Robinson put it – "that little pipsqueak is for the clay soon"). In fact, in both recent versions, you find little tampering with the tone or spirit of Ó Cadhain's invigorating undertaking (I use that word deliberately), if one allows for inevitable variations in approach and choice of phrase. As Titley says, "there is no easy equivalence between languages", and so the translator is free to follow his or her instincts. He admits that he has taken some liberties with *The Dirty Dust* (not least the title, which has a suitably earthy connotation, but isn't close to the literal "graveyard" – or cemetery – clay). Many of the characters in the novel are known by a nickname – Siúán an tSiopa, Tomás Taobh Istigh. Titley opts for effective English equivalents – Huckster Joan, Fireside Tom – while the other translators make as little alteration as possible: Siúán the Shop, Tomás Inside ("Tomás Indoors" might be nearer the mark, for an old bachelor who seldom leaves the house but has his relatives running round in circles, and despising one another, in the drive to get their hands on his bit of land). But whatever their differences of tempo or phraseology, each of the current versions of Ó Cadhain's most famous book is gloriously attuned to the energy, copiousness, invective, ribaldry and so on, of the original *Cré na Cille*.

The people buried in Ó Cadhain's graveyard are all in the grip of assorted grievances. Foremost among them is Caitriona Pháidin, a 71-year-old widow who opens the proceedings by wondering if she's lying in the pound plot or the 15 shilling plot (unthinkable that her son should have dumped her in the half-guinea plot). Caitriona's motivating force in life, and death, is a heartfelt hatred of her sister Nell (who stole the man she had hoped to marry); and with the arrival of each new corpse in the cemetery, she's agog to hear bad news of the same sister. Underground, Catriona carries on an exchange of insults with her son's mother-in-law Nóra Sheáinín, whom she dubs Nóra Filthy-Feet, and others, while her sights are focused on getting a cross of Island limestone (in one version) or Connemara marble (in the other) raised above her grave. Each section ends with Caitriona threatening to "explode" or "burst" as news not to her liking filters down from above.

Máirtín Ó Cadhain was writing about a close-knit community in which everybody knows everybody else's business, and is abundantly endowed with the means to disparage it. This intimate knowledge makes for a great and rancorous hullaballoo. "If it was a stranger buried beside you, you'd be in a bad way not knowing what to throw in his face, since you wouldn't know his people for seven generations back." Knowing what to throw in people's faces is paramount here. As many commentators have pointed out, there are several threads running through the book, but very little in the way of narrative as such. *Caint na ndaoine* — the people's vernacular — drives the action, with little other than dialogue filling the pages. Stories evolve and stay in the mind by repetition and acerbic allusion. There's the story of the "Big Master", for instance (schoolmaster, school principal?), and his widow's prompt remarriage to "Billy the Post" (it isn't long before Billy joins his predecessor in the graveyard, the pair of them stretched out side by side, "like a couple of dogs with their tails tied together"). A whole range of minor characters, above and below ground, gets a look-in from time to time: Peadar the Pub, the Irish-language enthusiast, the priest's sister gadding about in a pair of trousers. A drowned French airman is buried along with others. Politics, Irish and international, come into the picture. The Second World War is in progress, and some of the *Cois Fharraige* corpses are rooting for Hitler, while others, more pragmatic, think of England as "a place where good money could be earned". Disputes ensue. Along with colourful catchphrases – "Bloody tear an' 'ounds" – and imprecations – "May the devil pierce him with his front teeth" – are parodies and highly garbled retellings of traditional folk tales, mixed-up recollections of political and sporting events, and even a bit of Synge-along: "Little moon, little moon of Scotland, it's lonesome you'll be this night, tomorrow night and long nights after, and you pacing the lonely sky beyond Glen Lee ...". It all adds up to an unprecedented exercise in Irish modernism, a compound of calumny and detraction and bracing humour, an account of schemes and grudges unfolding by way of rowdy repartee. Ó Cadhain's good luck – finally – is to have his "thorny masterpiece" come into the hands of inspired and dedicated translators (twice). It may have taken more than half a century, but it's been worth the wait.

Times Literary Supplement, 2016

SHRIEK!

Heather Ingman,
Irish Women's Fiction from Edgeworth to Enright

"It has been a quite unexpected pleasure", wrote the *Irish Times* reviewer of Rosamond Jacob's novel *Callaghan* in 1921, "after wading through so many ill-conceived, dull tales about things Irish, to come on a story so fresh ... and ... independent in its point of view." You may or may not agree with this assessment of *Callaghan*, but no one should be in any doubt about the proliferation, at the time, of ill-conceived, dull Irish tales — not all of them, by any means, the output of women writers. And you can sympathise with the author of *Irish Women's Fiction* on account of the sheer volume of these she has had to wade through. They include works by "George Egerton", Annie M.P. Smithson and a Kathleen Mannington Caffyn who wrote under the pen name "Iota" and created a fictional home in which an ex-Cambridge don and his wife spend all their time discussing and writing about mathematical problems. Disaster ensues.

From Heather Ingman's study we gain an inkling of what the would-be professional woman, in Ireland and elsewhere, was up against in the early part of the twentieth century. If it's not your husband deriding you as "a short-haired shriek [sic] with pince-nez and a beastly little notebook in [your] lean paws", it's the Catholic bourgeoisie of Limerick or Waterford restricting your options. Whether you consider yourself to be a New Woman or a Revolting Daughter, sometimes there is nothing for it – as the novelist and travel writer Beatrice Grimshaw found – but to take yourself off to a cannibalistic part of New Guinea and hope to steer clear of the cooking pot.

Between Maria Edgeworth and Anne Enright, there's a lot of Irish ground to be covered: home ground, sacred ground, shaky ground, moral high ground, very rough ground or very soggy ground. As Ingman notes, many of the novels under consideration here get off to an encouraging start as far as the feminist ethic is concerned, but then change direction to accommodate what she calls (and calls, and calls) "the romance plot" (specifically, "the heterosexual romance plot"), as commercial or psychological requirements kick in. Depressing developments in the social sphere didn't help to promote an avant-garde approach on the part of many writers. (I'm thinking of De Valera's Ireland and its backward trend.) After the New Woman came the age-old woman, married with two children and living in Dollymount. Some representations of this archetypal figure are designed to applaud it, and some to deplore the circumstances upholding it. And, as Irish women writers of every degree of skill and enlightenment got to grips with all the urgent issues of the day, from Suffragism to Sinn Fein activity and the Dissolution of the Big House, a gulf became discernible between the capable and the culpable (in literary terms). Ingman does not go out of her way to distinguish between the two. You find little, for example, to suggest a proper awareness of the difference between Maeve Brennan and Maeve Binchy.

Ingman is, however, a dab hand at summarising biographical information and providing plot outlines, and this gives *Irish Women's Writing* a high value as a reference work. It should come in handy if you need to know about the Dublin upbringing of Hannah Lynch (say), or discover the outcome of Kate Carmody's return to Co Cork after five years working in domestic service in the US (in Geraldine Cummins's novel of 1919, *The Land They Loved*). Ingman is familiar with current critical strategies, and does not wish in any way to dissociate herself from the views of others. A large part of her book consists of nods to her predecessors in the field: "as Vera Kreilcamp points out …"; "as Clair Wills has shown …"; "as Anne Owens Weekes has pointed out …"; "as Heidi Hansson has argued …". She is also unduly given to dispiriting turns of phrase: "the male-authored text of Northern nationalism"; "dysfunctional childhoods"; "gender issues"; "gender politics"; "gender roles"; "gender binaries". Moreover, once she's got hold of one of these expressions, she is reluctant to let go of it. The question of "identity", for example, is linked so many times to "fluidity" in these pages – "fluidity of identity"; fluid identity"; "her fluid identity" – that the whole undertaking seems in danger of becoming waterlogged.

Some of Ingman's authors can only with difficulty be claimed for Ireland. They include the very overwrought "Egerton" (born in Australia), "Sarah Grand" (daughter of a naval lieutenant stationed briefly in Donaghadee), and the splendid Olivia Manning, who spent some childhood holidays with her maternal grandparents in Bangor and attended a school there for a couple of terms at the age of six. Portsmouth was Manning's home town (and the place she was happy to see the back of). Iris Murdoch? Perhaps, through her Irish parents and the couple of novels she set in Dublin and the West – though Murdoch was never a resident of the country. Of those unquestionably Irish, the "native" and the "Anglo-" make two distinct groups (though Molly Keane's mother Nesta Higginson did her best to fuse the two with the verse she wrote in the persona of an Antrim Glenswoman called Moira O'Neill – verse abundant in "quare wee house, barefut childer" flourishes).

The poor Anglo-Irish, lumbered as they are with "a hyphenated identity", and seen here in a permanent "state of stasis", do not come in for any profound illumination: the topic has been done to death. Their culture is by and large a matter of horses and hunting, fraught relations with their social inferiors and chilly treatment of children: yes, we know that these are the tropes. It isn't helpful to have observations like the following quoted approvingly: "colonialism as a pervasive historical system ... appropriates the sexuality and lives of Anglo-Irish children". Appropriates how? And how does the author know? Such pronouncements are degraded by being based on assumptions, and over-familiar assumptions at that. Not that being less clichéd necessarily makes them any more cogent. Another person quoted by Ingman "suggests that [Dorothy] Macardle's preoccupation with the Gothic and the paranormal ... reflects her anxiety over the way the Irish state has developed ...". Many people experienced and expressed anxiety about developments overtaking Irish society in the mid-twentieth century – but relating the resulting state of mind to a rather bland ghost story such as Macardle's *The Uninvited* of 1942, set exclusively in the south of England, makes little sense.

Nor does Ingman's sober-sided appraisal of a novel like Anne Crone's *Bridie Steen* of 1948 (however praiseworthy the anti-sectarian impulse that got Crone going), which treats the miseries of a cross-bred orphan in Co Fermanagh and her end in a bog. And we might question Ingman's endorsement of Somerville and Ross in the area of "exactness in reproduction of Irish speech patterns" – think "throuble", "shneakin'", "dhread", "discoorse" and worse. She is right, though, to rate Pamela Hinkson's novel *The Ladies' Road* (1932) above her mother Katherine Tynan's rather dreadful Irish romances; and to acknowledge the out-of-date surface quality that has come to characterise the once popular works of Kate O'Brien.

If Anglo-Irishwomen had the Big House and fox-hunting, native Irishwomen had the Republican movement and the Catholic church to revere or repudiate; and every writer among them, with varying degrees of competence or inspiration, went about the business of airing their views in books. Mad Ireland hurt the lot of them into creativity. Ingman deals most effectively with those authors whose work is marked by flair, substance or originality, such as Elizabeth Bowen or Edna O'Brien (though O'Brien's self-aware heroines, as ever, duck out of any attempt to pin them down). She comes closest to an adept form of literary analysis when she reaches the latest, "postmodern" phase in Irish writing, setting out all the terrific new techniques and highly charged contemporary themes available to novelists such as Eilis Ni Dhuibhne, Anne Enright and Claire Kilroy. But Heather Ingman, on the whole, is not very intrepid as a commentator, or especially alive to the irony in any unfolding scenario. For example, she reports with a straight face the decision of Molly Keane to turn her back on literature following the dismal failure of her play *Dazzling Prospect*, and opt instead "for a life of domesticity in Ardmore".

Times Literary Supplement, 2013

WANDERING SCHOLARSHIP

D. Felicitas Corrigan, *Helen Waddell: a Biography*

Judging by the numbers of people who found her captivating, throughout her long life, Helen Waddell was clearly something of an enchantress. It was a gift to which she never attached much importance. Social success, for example, was a matter of indifference to her. However, it was thrust upon her, along with celebrity, in the period just before the Second World War. It came as a consequence of her novel *Peter Abelard* (reprinted 15 times in the year of its publication, 1933). Before this, and in spite of some early setbacks in her career, Helen Waddell had gained much credit as a scholar specialising in the Middle Ages. Enthusiasm, ease of manner and a vigorous approach were among the qualities she brought to her subject, the mediaeval Latin lyric and the men who composed it.

Born in 1889, Waddell grew up in Tokyo – her father was an Ulster Protestant missionary – and Belfast. After graduating from Queen's University in 1912, she was all set to move on to Oxford; but family commitments kept her at home. Her stepmother, whose character deteriorated as she got older and iller, was unable to live alone. Waddell took on herself the burden of looking after the invalid and incipient alcoholic. Over the next eight years, she endured without complaining a difficult home life, kept her capacity for merriment intact, published some Bible stories and a collection of lyrics from the Chinese, and gained a friend and mentor in Professor George Saintsbury of Edinburgh University.

Professor Saintsbury was not alone in his admiration for the cleverness, playfulness and underlying spiritual gifts he found in the young Belfast woman. The Revd. George Taylor, a missionary based in India, felt the lure of these traits too, to the extent of involving Waddell in a copious correspondence which was kept up until his death in 1920. (The long and detailed letters which passed between the two have proved an invaluable resource for Waddell's biographer.) Certain habits of mind were acquired by Helen Waddell during this period, among them – unfortunately – procrastination. For someone to whom ideas came easily, she was very selective in those she carried through.

Her stepmother died in 1920, leaving her free, at last, to take up the offer of a place at Oxford. From Oxford she went on to Paris, on a travelling scholarship, pledged to investigate "the literary importance of the Wandering Scholars", and there turned up the material that went into her book on that subject (*The Wandering Scholars*, 1927), on which her claim to be an innovator largely rests. She had a talent for communicating the pungency of the past – as well as being susceptible to this quality to a perhaps inadvisable degree. To get the flavour of her book absolutely right, she had immersed herself in mediaeval Europe – and a moment occurred, in 1924, when she seemed in danger of remaining there. She was in the Institut Pasteur, suffering from insomnia on top of a throat infection, when her modern, Presbyterian consciousness suddenly gave way to that of a twelfth-century abbess. Helen had turned into Heloise, "not as I had ever imagined her, but an old woman, abbess of the Paraclete, with Abelard twenty years dead; and I was sitting in my chair lecturing to my nuns on his *Introductio ad Theologiam*." So it continued throughout the night; by morning, however, Waddell was back in her own skin.

After such an experience, she could do nothing but get on with a book that had been in her mind for years: a retelling of the Heloise/Abelard story. It was unfortunate that George Moore had beaten her to it (his *Heloise and Abelard* having come out in 1921); but she hoped her version would be sufficiently distinctive to warrant publication. And so it proved. For one thing, *Peter Abelard* was a lot more accessible than the George Moore novel had been. You could say it was too accessible, in so far as this implies a want of astringency. It is not equal, in style or perceptiveness, to *The Wandering Scholars* or its companion volume, *Mediaeval Latin Lyrics*. Dame Felicitas Corrigan claims that sexual experience never came her subject's way; it is possible that this deprivation (if true) was not an advantage as far as her only novel is concerned. Peter Abelard contains plenty of evidence of scholarship, indeed, but a good deal of blandness and lushness informs it as well. There is more comedy, elan and inventiveness in Waddell's letters, of which Dame Felicitas has secured a good supply to include in her biography (it is not, however, an adequate tribute to these letters when she tells us, "They are so real, so human, so many-sided ...").

The strongest relationships in Waddell's life – if we leave aside her sister Meg and family, and her friend Maud Clarke – seem to have been formed platonically with men many years her senior. Another of these alliances, if a less platonic one, came into being in the late 1920s, when she met Otto Kyllmann (OK) of Constable (the firm that published her books). She became a reader with the firm, and, during the war, edited its review, *The Nineteenth Century and After.* And, inevitably – Dame Felicitas says – there came a day when she and OK fell into one another's arms. But he wasn't free to marry her, and, sex being out of the question on moral grounds, they had to suffer frustration for the rest of their lives. To make matters in this respect as bad as they could be, OK came to stay overnight with Waddell at her house in Primrose Hill, found the house to his liking, and stayed on for nearly thirty years. His behaviour does not meet with Dame Feliticas's approval (and common sense suggests it was worse than she surmises) – though she acknowledges his kindness to Helen Waddell towards the end of her life, when her mental powers were in disarray.

Dame Felicitas Corrigan, a nun attached to Stanbrook Abbey, and editor of Waddell's posthumous collection *More Latin Lyrics*, is a conscientious biographer, often energetic and spry in manner, and only occasionally flaccid ("The leaves, alas, were not the young green leaves of a Second Spring ..."). Undue stress, perhaps, is placed on Waddell's Christianity. and not enough on the contradictions in her nature – secular/celestial, scholarly/popularising, fertile/unproductive. The final chapter, which covers more than 20 years of Helen Waddell's life, is cut rather short; we learn very little about the onset of her illness (organic brain failure) or its distressing progress – just enough to show that

"Ulster's darling, the most distinguished woman of her generation" came to a very untoward end.

Times Literary Supplement, 1986

REDRESSING
THE BALANCE

Angela Burke *et al* (eds.),
The Field Day Anthology of Irish Writing:
Volumes IV and V: Irish Women's Writing and Traditions

When the original *Field Day Anthology of Irish Writing*
was published in 1991, in three hefty volumes, it provoked an outcry over its allegedly inadequate representation of Irish women writers. Its harassed general
editor, Seamus Deane, resolved to make amends by
inviting a team of women scholars and academics to
repair the deficiency by compiling two additional volumes themselves. These eight women then conscripted
more than 50 contributing editors to help with the
prodigious work of recovery and re-evaluation. Now,
11 years on, comes the new, monumental, female *Field
Day*, in all its grandeur and multiplicity.

At first glance, it is a breathtaking achievement: 3,200 pages testifying to women's contribution to Irish cultural affairs over 14 centuries. But it's not as straightforward as this suggests. We begin with a section entitled "Mediaeval to Modern, 600–1900", whose editor, Máirín Ní Dhonnchadha, is obliged to admit that "not one complete text ... can be attributed with absolute certainty to a historical woman until the early 17th century" – not even the famous, racy, "Lament of the Old Woman of Beare" ("I that had my day with kings,/And drank deep of mead and wine,/Drink whey-water with old hags,/Sitting in my rags, and pine.")

Never mind. There's an abundance of material affording insights into the representation, treatment and experiences of Irishwomen between these dates, the bulk of it fascinating. A problem for the editors is immediately identified, however. If you're going to allow in writing by women, about women, and even obliquely connected to women, then the scope of the undertaking will be too wide, and a certain unwieldiness become inevitable. A couple of sections, or sub-sections, seem a bit threadbare, while others are catch-alls for material that bulges out in all directions.

Take "Sexuality". This important topic had as much currency in Ireland as elsewhere, and even more need, at especially repressive periods, to present itself clandestinely. Sexual oppression, in both the feminist and the erotic sense, was added to political, social or economic oppression.

One of the aims of the new *Field Day* is to uncover and applaud sexual subversiveness, and this means enlisting not only lesbianism but a lot of male homosexuality to boot. The drive to be inclusive has made the editors occasionally self-contradictory (they've included passages by men describing encounters between men), dull ("Sexuality and the Polyvalence of Domination" is one sub-heading), or modishly outraged (indignation surfaces over "the cultural prejudice against lesbian writers in Ireland" – a prejudice here conspicuously redressed).

"Sexuality", indeed, is an elastic category, stretching from William Carleton's decorous account of his adoration of a girl he never got the nerve to address, to statistics of illegitimate births recorded at the Belfast Workhouse in 1903, and Margaret Cousins's shudder at the failure of nature to devise "some more artistic way of continuance of the race". The skimpy sub-section called "Explorations of Love and Desire in Writing for Children, 1791–1979", seems to have had the title forced on it to get it in under the general heading. It's as bad a fit as the shoe on Cinderella's sisters' feet.

The sprightly asexual Maria Edgeworth, the feverishly prudish L.T. Meade: what are they doing here?

And Kathleen Fitzpatrick, author of a single, glorious volume of stories about a family of children running wild in Co Down (*The Weans at Rowallan*, 1905): this spirited and mysterious writer, about whom nothing is known beyond her date of birth (1872), is a welcome presence in the anthology, but a more appropriate placement could have been found for her. On the other hand, some genuinely bawdy stuff, such as "The Story of Mis and Dubh Rois", is happily sited in the mediaeval section.

The excellent "Oral Traditions" grouping includes the lore and culture of Irish travellers, children's street songs and games, folk tales in Irish and English, along with traditional songs (also in both languages), and excerpts from the recollections of such distinctive Irishwomen as the Blasket autobiographer Peig Sayers. Politics, Irish society, hospitals, workhouses, convents and prisons are all covered copiously in Volume V. Here, we also – eventually – reach "Women and Writing, 1700–1960", only to find it unduly full of wild Irish girls and rowdy nights on Inisbofin.

Irish misery is extensively represented, as in this opening to a tale from a book called *Shamrock Leaves*: "One dark and dismal morning in the month of November 1846, a miserable group of human beings were assembled in the attic of an old crumbling house, situated in a filthy obscure lane in a large Irish city." The title of this exercise in abjection is "The Knitted Collar"; and knitting as a resource of women is also exemplified in Evangeline Paterson's more recent *Knitting Woman* (1994). The evangelical Mrs Phillpott with her extraordinary poem "The Knitting Needle" (1506 lines) doesn't get a showing, however – a pity, since the work has considerable sociological, if not literary interest. It was written to commemorate the establishment of a school of knitters in Co Antrim during the Famine year of 1846-47 ("You, who are blessed with means to give,/Remember, that they KNIT to LIVE!").

Others escaping the colossal round-up of significant Irishwomen, or commentators on Ireland, include the poets Florence M. Wilson ("The Man from God-Knows-Where") and Helen Lanyon; children's writers Rosamond Praeger, Eilis Dillon and Meta Mayne Reid; Gormfhlaith Ní Fhlionn, author of the very resonant "Lament of Nuala O'Neill" (in Irish); Marjorie Alyn, Maud Joynt, Julia O'Faolain, Evelyn Hardy and Jennifer Johnston (who is mentioned in passing). Some who are squeezed in deserve more space, such as Janet McNeill, Helen Waddell and Florence Mary McDowell.

Angela Bourke is one of the Field Day editors, and probably chose to omit herself for this reason. She is also, however, the author of one of those rare books that become an instantaneous classic, *The Burning of Bridget Cleary* (1999 – about a man who mistook his wife for a changeling and put her on the kitchen fire). An excerpt from this book would have afforded a frightening glimpse into primitive – late-Victorian – Ireland. Instead, we have coverage – why? – of paedophile priests and fornicating bishops.

No anthology can avoid irritating its readers for one reason or another. The new *Field Day*, because of its size, is more vulnerable in this respect than most. An undertaking in which so many people have had a hand is bound occasionally to get out of hand. (Some of its most egregious nonsense goes into the footnotes, in which we get – among other things – "Begob" glossed as "By God, an exclamation".) The last, vast section, "Contemporary Writing 1960–2001", doesn't exclude tedium, sentimentality, overstatement and the most staggering ineptitude. But this should not lessen our gratitude for the wealth of pleasure and illumination it also contains (indeed, this is true of the anthology as a whole). Ireland is still in the process of adjusting to the modern world, and if the final section of *Field Day* seems overgenerous in its inclusions, this may be because time has not yet sorted out the deft from the daft.

Independent Magazine, 2002

ROADS TOWARDS
THE RISING

Ruth Dudley Edwards, *The Seven: The Lives and
Legacies of the Founding Fathers of the Irish Republic*
Lucy McDiarmid, *At Home in the Revolution:
What Women Said and Did in 1916*
Ronan Fanning, *De Valera: A Will to Power*

Twenty years before the Easter Rising of 1916, the
seven signatories of the Proclamation of an Irish Republic were going about their pre-revolutionary activities.
The year was 1896, and Thomas Clarke, the oldest of
the Seven, was undergoing penal servitude at Portland
Prison off the Dorset coast. He was 39 years old, a
convicted Dynamitard, and two years away from release
on licence and highly motivated return to Dublin. In
the early summer of 1896, James Connolly, a married
man of 28 and a socialist agitator, decamped from

Edinburgh with his wife and daughters and installed the family in a Dublin tenement. Thomas MacDonagh, by all accounts the most agreeable of the Seven, was beginning an abortive training for the priesthood, while his future friend and colleague Padraig Pearse, then a Dublin schoolboy, was arranging weekly meetings with a few like-minded contemporaries interested in Irish literature. Eamonn Ceannt, later an accountancy clerk, was studying hard and imbibing the nationalist atmosphere of his Christian Brothers school. Sean Mac Diarmada, 13, was failing to master mathematics at his country school in Kiltyclogher, Co Leitrim. And Joseph Plunkett, not yet nine years old, was coping with an unorthodox home life dominated by his mother the Countess, complete with nursemaids and govern-esses, intermittent ill health and congenial siblings. The unlikely convergence of these dissimilar individuals, and its stupendous outcome, is the subject of a new, dispassionate and stimulating study by Ruth Dudley Edwards. She has set out, at the same time, to detach her eponymous "founding fathers" from the pantheon of Irish martyrdom, and to substitute complexity and diversity for the kind of monolithic heroism with which their names were once synonymous.

She goes about this purpose by bringing common sense and a measure of irony to bear on what she calls "the nationalist narrative". She is sceptical about

everything and loves to home in on anomalies. In the
century which has passed since Pearse stepped out of
the GPO in Dublin to read the Proclamation of Independence to a largely unenthralled audience, attitudes
in Ireland have been revised or modified in the light of
contemporary revelations and preoccupations. Some
may regret the erosion of nationalist certainties, but
few, I think, would wish to uphold the "blood sacrifice"
aspect of the Rising. "There's nothing but our own red
blood / Can make a right Rose Tree", as W.B. Yeats has
Pearse aver to Connolly. Only Pearse, indeed, actively
embraced the prospect of execution. Yeats again: Pearse
is "half-cracked and wanting to be hanged", he told Ezra
Pound. "He has Emmet delusions …". Connolly too
disliked Pearse's "red wine of the battlefields" rhetoric
and called him a blithering idiot. Pearse, in his turn, had
offended Eamonn Ceannt's "Irish-Ireland" sensibilities
by praising W.B. Yeats. And so it went on. However, as
Ruth Dudley Edwards remarks drily, relations between
the Seven, on the whole, "remained civil".

None of them, aside from Pearse, actually wanted
to die, though all accepted death as a likely outcome of
Easter Week. Dudley Edwards's succinct biographies
show the ways in which all of the Seven were attached
to their ordinary lives, before an overwhelming objective supervened. By a series of twists and eventualities it
came to be the same objective, even if the roads towards

it were very different. The Gaelic League, the Irish Republican Brotherhood, Sinn Féin, Irish Volunteers, Irish Citizen Army, the opposition of all these to the Irish Parliamentary Party, all contributed something to the impending insurrectionary undertaking. The old slogan about England's difficulty being Ireland's opportunity came into play as well: 1916 was a crucial year.

Ruth Dudley Edwards pays tribute to the dedication, courage and often inspirational leadership displayed by the Seven, while arguing the case for present-day detachment and judicious reappraisal of the entire revolutionary era. It's the legacy of 1916 in terms of violence and republican fanaticism that bothers her most. In 1966, she claims, 50th-anniversary "triumphalism" gave the go-ahead to physical force nationalism and ushered in the Provisional IRA. There's a lot to be said for this, but it leaves out the issue of Civil Rights and civil wrongs and the burning need for reform – reform which almost seemed to be on the cards, before everything ran out of control. Dudley Edwards is at the same time a level-headed commentator, and a stirrer-up of atavistic passions: the role of controversialist comes easily to her. (Elizabeth Bowen's comment on Lord Dunsany springs to mind: his memoir *My Ireland*, she said, was written "to please himself, and, please God, infuriate others".) With its sharp observations, though, its demystifying impulse and wry alertness to every nuance of 1916-symbolism, *The Seven* is an important book. It disentangles the strands of motivation and aspiration which previous generations had tended to lump together.

At one point, *The Seven* alludes to Padraig Pearse's notorious unease in the presence of women. Left alone in a room with a female visitor at his school St Enda's, he was soon observed scurrying away down the corridor at high speed, to the amusement of onlookers. However, in the run-up to the Rising, and while it was taking place, Pearse had no hesitation in employing women as dispatch riders, custodians of arms and ammunition, cooks, nurses and military auxiliaries. Not that he could have kept them away. Whatever needed to be done to foster strength of purpose or boost morale, women were there in the thick of it. Lucy McDiarmid's spirited study, *At Home in the Revolution*, gets to grips with every degree of female activism and commitment to the Irish cause. In the era of the suffrage movement, the Woman Question and radical First-World-War departures, revolutionary Ireland offered a complementary variety of feminist possibilities. It almost seemed, as McDiarmid has it, "that another revolution was expressing itself through the national struggle".

The role of women in 1916 has only been effectively assessed in the last few years, with the appearance of works like Senia Paseta's *Irish Nationalist Women* (2013) and R.F. Foster's 2014 study, *Vivid Faces* (many of which were female). *At Home in the Revolution* is in the same inspiriting mode. It presents an exhilarating overview of women's contribution to the Rising. This included gun-running, setting fire to key buildings and organising first-aid posts. Some women, most conspicuously Constance Markievicz, got into uniform and fought alongside the men. The events of the time produced some singular exigencies. One woman, Grace Gifford, hoped to get married before her bridegroom was executed (she made it, with only hours to spare). Lucy McDiarmid's scholarly book is enlivened by its recourse to contemporary accounts, letters, diaries and so forth, testimonies to the heightened atmosphere of the time. Guns stashed in the fireplace was not the half of it. Women's defiance of the hated regime took effect at different levels: wearing boys' clothes and bearing arms in the street, dancing a 16-hand reel in Kilmainham Jail. From some pre-1916 diaries, McDiarmid gained a sense of the Irish revolutionary enterprise as "jolly good fun" – rather in the manner of all those heroines of First-World-War children's stories who were simply longing to dash off to the Front. The reality (in both cases) proved rather different, indeed, and during Easter Week and in its aftermath, the buoyancy of the moment gave way to grief and implacability. And, in another parallel with post-war Britain (post- both world wars), the freedoms achieved by Irish nation-alist women soon went by the board. The Ireland of the mid-twentieth century was very far in spirit from the egalitarian future envisaged by the 1916 genera-tion – and indeed, from the drift of the Proclamation addressed specifically to "Irishmen and Irishwomen". From the Civil War on, a reactionary tendency was paramount in Irish life. Its principal architect and exponent was the ultra-Catholic, eventual president of Ireland, Eamon de Valera, a survivor of Easter Week who evaded execution by a series of flukes (including the fact that he was born in New York), and the only commandant at the time to keep women well away from his headquarters at Boland's Mill.

The extraordinary story of de Valera's emergence from a labourer's cottage in Co Limerick and ultimate arrival at the forefront of Irish political life, is well told in this sterling new biography by Ronan Fanning. *A Will to Power* – as the subtitle suggests – treats its subject as a public figure, paying scant attention to his private life. The great upholder of Irish Catholic domesticity, it seems, had few domestic instincts himself. He was rarely in the company of his wife and children. If he wasn't in prison, he was travelling through America seeking recognition for the embryo Irish Republic. Practising self-advancement came naturally to de Valera. He switched his allegiance from culture to military activity and then to politics, as circumstances dictated. He showed himself to be a master of the expedient course of action at nearly every juncture in Irish life. The exception occurred during the disastrous period of the Treaty negotiations and subsequent Civil War, when de Valera's customary sagacity appeared to have deserted him. But he came back, with renewed determination. The long years of what became known as "de Valera's Ireland" ensued. The phrase, Ronan Fanning admits, carries a decidedly critical connotation at present, with the Fianna Fáil leader held responsible for the blights and failures of mid-twentieth-century Ireland. Against these (his biographer says) should be set de Valera's achievements, most notably his achievement of an independent Irish state. You can't argue with this, or with the authority and conciseness of Ronan Fanning's account; but what seems to endorse the negative view is the shocking image (included among the illustrations) of de Valera on his knees kissing the ring of Archbishop John Charles McQuaid – an image that enshrines the two of them in a kind of apotheosis of obsequiousness and illiberality.

Times Literary Supplement, 2016

PIOUS GIRLS AND
SWEARING FATHERS

PIOUS GIRLS AND
SWEARING FATHERS

Kirsten Drotner,
English Children and Their Magazines 1751–1945
Mary Cadogan,
Frank Richards: The Chap Behind the Chums
Joyce Irene Whalley and Tessa Rose Chester,
A History of Children's Book Illustration
W.H. Shercliff, *Manchester Polytechnic Library
of Children's Books 1840–1939:
"From Morality to Adventure"*
Joseph Connolly, *Children's Modern First
Editions: Their Value to Collectors*

"An Adventure of Master Tommy Trusty; and his delivering Miss Biddy Johnson, from the Thieves who were going to murder her": this is the charming title of a story in the first-ever children's periodical, the *Lilliputian Magazine*, brought out by John Newbery in 1751;

and with its theme of character-moulding (a silly little girl is cured of vanity through suffering a fright) it set the tone for a good deal of juvenile magazine fiction for some time to come. Right up until the 1930s and '40s, characters in children's papers were still being amended, sometimes with equal suddenness, as defects such as snobbishness or spite were ironed out of them. But it was during the previous century that the reformist impulse in children's authors was at its strongest. Such papers as there were, were full of fearful warnings about the likely outcome of frivolity or disobedience. Give in to naughtiness, the message went, and you will pay dearly for it. After the misdoing (being boisterous on a Sunday, or coveting a pear), as likely as not, comes the deathbed scene. However, Kirsten Drotner tells us, pictures of dying children were sometimes juxtaposed with elephants and giraffes, presumably to keep readers' spirits from subsiding altogether. Not that all fictional children were depicted as wilful – on the contrary, the misbehavers had their counterparts in the horde of priggish young who set about eroding the turpitude of bad adults, as in the magazine story of 1827 entitled "The Pious Girl and her Swearing Father". Judging by her clinging attitude (she is illustrated with both arms clasped around his neck), he had plenty to swear about.

Kirsten Drotner has written a serious book about a subject more often approached in a spirit of snootiness or levity: children's ephemeral reading, its purposes and effects. She cautions us against judging the bulk of it unduly edifying to start with, or unduly obnoxious once the "penny dreadful" type of paper had caught on, which happened in the 1860s or thereabouts (when, we might gather, a barber had difficulty in distinguishing between his clients and his dinner). However tempting it is to view such material from the standpoint of the present – a practice geared to the arousal of merriment – Drotner believes it's wrong to extract it from the context of its own time. What she terms "the infelicity in separating cultural production from historical circumstances" is a failing her study doesn't sanction. She is, indeed, more interested in the context than the content of the periodicals under discussion, and while this cuts out the tedious recapitulation of plot, it also makes her book rather less diverting than it might have been. We find an abundance of social statistics, for example, in place of choice extracts from bygone stories: the numbers of children "born into artisan or servant families [who] died before reaching the age of five", but no examples of fortitude such as that displayed by the youth refusing laudanum on this deathbed: "I can bear pain ... but I cannot willingly enter the presence of my Creator in a state little short of intoxication." According to Drotner, nineteenth-century readers were perfectly capable of relishing the ins and outs of a story, while taking or leaving the moral message. This seems a sensible view, and it is, of course, salutary to bear in mind the ideologies of the day, before we succumb to outrage over the horrors once inflicted on inexperienced readers. During the 1860s, for example, the wholesale eating of the ungodly by cannibals or crocodiles, which occurred in papers like *Boys of England*, merely amounted to a forcible means of communicating a religious truism. Good adventurers never came to such bad ends – unless, of course, they were minor characters, and required to ram home the hideousness of heathen ways. Each age has its own ideas about the kinds of reality children can, or cannot, bear. The Victorians didn't shirk the reality of death, atrocity, gore, having an arm or a leg torn off, all in the interests of Christianity; while we believe quite young children ought to be conversant with all kinds of grown-up issues such as divorce and homosexuality, to inoculate them against intolerance. While the Georgians recoiled from fantasy and fairy tales, we disapprove of anything that upholds a preju-dice of the past (golliwog characters in picture books, or calling an underprivileged boy a "ragamuffin"), or which fails to foster intelligence in the reader. As far as the latter is concerned, it is surely impossible to estimate the retarding effect of low-grade literature. On the credit side, we have the testimony of Joseph

Connolly, antiquarian book-dealer and author of *Children's Modern First Editions*, who graduated from the *Beano* to *The Times*.

The *Beano* (first issued in 1938) is among the papers noted by Kirsten Drotner but not examined in detail, possibly because characters along the lines of Biffo the Bear don't afford much scope for sober scrutiny. Before we reach this period (and the heyday of the story papers) there's a lot of ground to cover, and one or two changes of direction. A certain lightening of tone becomes apparent with the *Boys' Own Paper* (1879) and its counterpart for girls. However, it wasn't until the early years of the twentieth century that entertainment, as we understand it, began to replace uplift in the children's weeklies. The person chiefly responsible for the new exuberance was Charles Hamilton, better known as Frank Richards, who made a Never Never Land of the English public school, but did it with such dash, amiability and authority that every subsequent generation, right up to the present, has contained its quota of Greyfriars enthusiasts. Greyfriars School came into being in 1908 along with Harmsworth's *Magnet*, its habitat until 1940 and the paper's closure; but it wasn't for another decade or so that Frank Richards really got into his stride as an outstanding school story writer. The very early *Magnets* have a touch of fustiness about them.

There's more than a touch of inappropriateness about Kirsten Drotner's appraisal of the *Magnet* and its companion paper the *Gem*. A kind of disorientation occurs when we're asked to view the boys of Greyfriars or St Jim's as a "pupil community"', or reminded of "tensions between norm and deviance [originating] within the school environment". Are these proper phrases to find attached to the most high-spirited of stories? ("'I say you fellows, it's a lark, isn't it?' chortled Billy Bunter.") Drotner doesn't seem to have studied her material with sufficient attention to grasp the characters of the boys – or, come to that, the names of all the girls, once she reaches the equivalent female papers, the *School Friend* and the rest of them. Horace Coker of the Greyfriars Fifth, for example, is heavy-handed but good-hearted, and not a bully as Drotner says. Indeed, we learn from Mary Cadogan's illuminating study of Charles Hamilton and his works that Coker was derived in part from Hamilton's elder brother Richard, whose Christian name supplied the famous pseudonym, and who, quite clearly, was anything but a lout in the eyes of the author. And there's a Cliff House character named Dolly whom Drotner persists in calling Jolly, as though to superimpose mood over nomenclature.

Drotner's book is written from a feminist angle, and the author remains alert to the presence of gender distinctions in the periodicals of the mid-twentieth century, even while the other great defining circumstance – social class – was decreasing in consequence. Referring to a staple theme of the 1920s, that of the scholarship pupil making good, in spite of taunts ("She can't really be a council schoolgirl. Why, her face is clean!"), Drotner explains how this is consistent with the "bourgeois belief that the individual [is] separate from, and above, social circumstances and economic impediments". After about the mid-1930s, children's papers turned rather more demotic in tone ("'Chase me round the gas works, it's Inspector Meadows', muttered Alf excitedly") – while girls, by and large, continued to get the better of boys only by means of some tongue-in-cheek method such as flattery, and boys were still being initiated into the belief that a good British punch on the jaw was worth any amount of foreign deviousness. Drotner touches on the psychological function of cherished periodicals – which, after all, were meant to be grown out of – noting how certain painful areas in children's lives (insecurity, low self-esteem, dangerous predicaments or whatever) are simultaneously tackled and converted into something altogether more momentous and intriguing. That she calls this process "conflict transformation" is a pity, since jargon forms an odd accompaniment to the slang of the stories ("'My hat!' gasped Jack"). However, her book is substantial and often quite briskly written, even if it never rises to funniness. Around the turn of the twentieth century, she tells us, girls started taking a more active part in adventures, though they never posed a threat to male supremacy, "perhaps because they were always too busy keeping their skirts below the ankles".

All the idiosyncrasies in Whalley and Chester's *History of Children's Book Illustration* are in the pictures; the accompanying text is informative, workmanlike and plain. "Children may not alter", say the authors, "but their expectations may do so", and, no doubt, by the early Victorian period, knowing young readers were looking askance at the nursery homilies tolerated by the previous generation, and demanding to be amused. At any rate, the first of the great amusers, Edward Lear, appeared on the scene in 1846 with his exhilarating nonsense ("There was an Old Man in a tree, / Who was horribly bored by a Bee") and matching lithographs. From this point on, there was no holding children's books or their illustrators. Cruikshank, Tenniel, Richard Doyle, Arthur Hughes and many others all contribute greatly to the decorativeness of Victorian England, as it's preserved for later generations. Technical advances soon acted as a spur to artists and publishers alike. Edmund Evans, after about 1870, perfected the technique of colour printing from wood blocks, and thereby opened the way for that celebrated trio of the late nineteenth century, Crane, Caldecott and Kate Greenaway:

vigorous, sportive and quaint respectively. Whalley and Chester note the influence of the Pre-Raphaelite and Aesthetic Movements on these and other styles of illustration, and show how Caldecott, in particular, affected later water-colourists like Beatrix Potter.

Their survey, in fact, covers pretty well the whole range of children's book design, from its seventeenth-century beginnings to Maurice Sendak – following on from F. J. Harvey Darton's *Children's Books in England* (1932, revised edition 1982) and Percy Muir's *English Children's Books 1600–1900* (1954). They distinguish between "hack" and acceptable woodcuts in the early chapbooks, showing samples of each; but otherwise, it is only the cream of the field that attracts their attention. (Even here we find omissions: the work of Harry Rountree, for example, is excluded altogether, and neither Charles Robinson's nor Harold Jones's gets a showing among the illustrations.) The authors allude to the "ubiquitous girls' school story", but tell us nothing about its illustrators – not even Mabel Lucie Attwell, who provided the colour plates for May Baldwin's *Dora: A High School Girl* of 1906 (and other pre-1920s Chambers titles), before popularity and vulgarity overtook her. (An Attwell drawing from *Mother Goose Nursery Rhymes*, published by Tuck, is included.) Reasonably enough, since this is a history of mainstream illustration, the type of periodical discussed by Kirsten Drotner is more or less absent from consideration, but an odd exception is made for the 1950s *Eagle*, whose first issue is reproduced in colour. What else? Prettifiers like Anne Anderson and Honor Appleton get in, but not the more distinctive Gladys Peto; Robert Lawson is here but not Lawson Wood, A.E. Bestall (briefly) but not Thomas Henry.

In compiling the book – which is, in fact very nearly comprehensive – the authors have drawn on the holdings of the Victoria and Albert Museum, in particular the Guy Little Collection in the National Art Library and the Renier Collection at Bethnal Green Museum of Childhood. Other, similar collections, on a smaller scale, have been amassed, or acquired, by various local authorities throughout the country, and by a handful of libraries (including Wandsworth and the Hertfordshire County Library). Manchester Poly-technic Library has now brought out a catalogue of its holdings covering a century of children's reading (1840–1939), arranged under 21 headings: "Nursery Rhymes and Alphabets", "Stories 1900–1939" and so on – splendidly produced, with colour and black-and-white illustrations, and giving a good indication of what's been available at various moments during this interesting period. We have only to glance at the catalogue to understand how the Edwardian idea of manliness was foisted on adolescent boys ("A Lad of

Grit", "By Sheer Pluck"), who might have felt unentitled to call themselves British if they didn't feel confident of playing up on a battlefield.

Children's fiction furnishes plentiful material for the social historian, as a good many recent studies (including Kirsten Drotner's) have demonstrated. For collectors, however, the sociological bearing of a children's book is probably incidental to its appeal as an object – though it's hard to define exactly what it is that drives specialists in the genre to pursue certain titles down to the last distinguishing mark on the cover. (If, for example, you own a first edition of Elinor Brent-Dyer's *The School at the Chalet* with a bit torn off the dust-jacket, you will likely be prepared to pay the earth – up to £100, according to Joseph Connolly – for an intact replacement.) Collectors are probably conservative by temperament, susceptible to evocativeness, and driven by some unfathomable pressure, like the frequenter of second-hand markets in Michael Longley's poem "The Rag Trade":

> Drifting between thrift and nostalgia,
> That ache to reach home before the dust's
> Final version of your school stories ...

Aficionados will spot immediately that not all the books in the Manchester Polytechnic Collection are first editions (though many are), and that few come complete with their dust-wrappers (though some enticing Arthur Ransomes and the first of Richmal Crompton's incomparable "William" series do). They may also wonder why a lot of dates aren't specified, including some clearly announced by the publishers — *The Rivals of the Chalet School*, for instance, is dated 1929 — and others not that hard to ascertain, whether of firsts or of reprints. Sometimes, as the most assiduous collectors know, a first edition is identifiable only by the colour of its end-papers, or by the presence of an asterisk on the title-page or verso.

Joseph Connolly, who caters for bibliomaniacs of all kinds, has produced a useful and ebullient guide to children's modern first editions. He's perhaps not so sound an assessor of girls' as he is of boys' writers, leaving out, for example, the lively (and collected) author Dorita Fairlie Bruce, exponent of the kind of schoolgirl honour that prompted a spirited repudiation from Stevie Smith:

> Girls! I will let down the side if I get a chance
> And I will sell the pass for a couple of pence.

Nor does Connolly, apparently, see any difference between a rare Elsie Oxenham title, like *Deb of Sea House*, and a separately published extract from a longer novel, such as *The Girls of Rocklands School*. Both of these he puts at up to £20. It's hard, though, to quarrel with his mention of £10 as the upper limit for a late Brent-Dyer — nasty in appearance and very peculiar in content, sometimes featuring thunderstorms, non-stop flooding and jars of green dye falling on people's heads — even though collectors have been known not to baulk at £37. Early Brent-Dyers, with delectable dust-jackets and illustrations by Nina K. Brisley, are another matter entirely.

There's a very funny story by J.I.M. Stewart in which an elderly connoisseur of boys' books gets himself suspected of a rather less innocuous addiction. Not that it makes much difference when the truth comes out; in most people's minds, an adult interest in the trappings of childhood counts as a quirk. Books like Connolly's, though, should go some way towards correcting the impression that everything to do with children's books is invariably infantile.

London Review of Books, 1989

LARKS

David Hughes, *But for Bunter*
Daniel Green, *Bunter Sahib*
Doris Lessing, *The Good Terrorist*
Alice Thomas Ellis, *Unexplained Laughter*
Fay Weldon, *Polaris and Other Stories*

"But for Bunter the result might have been serious",
says a character in the *Magnet* "India" series of 1926,
giving credit to the fat schoolboy blunderer whose
tomfoolery – quite by accident – has saved the day.
It's a custom of Bunter's to run headlong into things,
with preposterously beneficial results for all concerned.
David Hughes, in his latest novel, takes this trait and
turns it on its head: the outcome of Billy Bunter's
intervention in certain notable events of the twentieth
century is very serious indeed. In Hughes's book, Bunter
is personally responsible for the arrest of Crippen and
the sinking of the Titanic, not to mention the Somme

debacle and consequent prolonging of the First World War. The throne of England is rocked because of Bunter. A fiery act of Bunter's sparks off the General Strike. It's Bunter's tailor who runs up some subsequently notorious black shirts for Oswald Mosley and his followers. Churchill assumes power in 1940 at the behest of Bunter. Bunter is at the bottom of the Suez business. "The Waste Land" is a patch of ground at the back of the Bunter residence. David Hughes even devises a comic genesis, involving Bunter, for *Lady Chatterley's Lover*.

Billy Bunter? "Bunter", states Hughes's narrator firmly at the start of the novel, "was a character in a schoolboy paper called the *Magnet*. He came on the scene in 1908 when he was 14 and vanished from it, having added not a year to his age, when the paper ceased publication in 1940." (Actually, Bunter's age is fixed at 15.) A figment of popular culture, in other words, of no more substance than Desperate Dan. Ah, but Hughes imagines the future author of the Greyfriars stories, in or about 1907, doing the rounds of English public schools in search of characters to insert into his projected schoolboy series, and – having exhausted the possibilities of Eton, Harrow and so forth – pouncing jubilantly on an outsize figure found attending a rather less venerable establishment. Archibald Aitken. It's Aitken-Bunter who's imposed himself on the twentieth century, just as Bunter, a peripheral character to start with, imposed himself on the Companion Papers. "Billy Bunter's Own Paper" was the eventual subtitle of the *Magnet*. Bunter gained his hilarious prominence by displaying a lot of deplorable traits to the full. Greed, sloth, stupidity and bumptiousness are what chiefly distinguish him. (Leaving aside his celebrated bulk.) Sometimes these defects are modified to meet the requirements of the plot, but Bunter's behaviour remains largely incorrigible. He is comically deficient in manliness and knows no better. His sturdier schoolfellows make allowances for him. Aitken, in the Hughes novel, complains about the travesty Frank Richards made of his character: obese he may have been, obtuse never. There's the History Prize he won in 1910 to testify to his possession of actual brains in place of the low cunning ascribed to Bunter. It may also be meant to alert us to Aitken's later extraordinary impact on the history of his times. David Hughes has an eye for egregious ironies as avid as Frank Richards's own.

Having invented a striking prototype for an imaginary dumpling, Hughes goes on gleefully to appropriate some public figures for the rest of the Magnet cast. For instance, we are asked to suppose that Frank Richards (his real name was Charles Hamilton, but Hughes affects not to know this), scouring Eton with a literary purpose in mind, came face to face with a boy called Anthony Eden and put him down on paper as Harry Wharton. (In fact, this isn't too wide of the mark. Charles Hamilton has left a record of how he went about assembling his characters, picking up a podgy frame here, a pair of loud trousers there.) The author of *But for Bunter* has a lot of fun selecting later celebrities with whom to equate the jolly boys of Greyfriars, though this is something of a hit-or-miss procedure. It is just about possible, perhaps, to see in Johnny Bull an embryo J.B. Priestley, or to take Harold Skinner for the youthful Oswald Mosley. But there are no grounds at all for attributing a poetic sensibility to the brashest boy in the Fourth Remove, Richards's bony American Fisher T. Fish. Richards himself, on one occasion, envisaging his schoolboys 25 years on, referred to Fish as "the great American fish-paste king". Frank Richards knew what he was about. Neither would a future for Fish as someone like, say, Walt Disney, have seemed amiss. But Fish as T.S. Eliot we just can't swallow. The success of this particular game depends on the appropriateness of the linkages effected. For poor Mr Quelch – the formidable form master – Hughes crosses A.E. Housman with Jack the Ripper. It really isn't a suitable concoction. Mauleverer, though, seems a proper boyhood embodiment for the Prince of Wales – and Mrs Simpson is brought in satis-factorily to extend the role at Greyfriars reserved for

Marjorie Hazeldene, an especially ripping schoolgirl in everyone's view.

Where in all this, we might ask, is Herbert Vernon Smith, the Bounder of Greyfriars? Another strand in contemporary history might have been adumbrated by means of this figure: a delinquent one. Burgess or Blunt would have fitted the bill. But it's clear that Hughes has been chary of apportioning waywardness to anyone other than his hero, Aitken-Bunter. Some decided liberties are taken with the character of Bunter, not all of them justified by the assertion that Frank Richards got it wrong. That's fine for the purposes of Hughes's novel, but not when it's carried back to the *Magnet* Greyfriars stories. Bunter was never a mocker or a lord of misrule. He wasn't at "the head" of any clique. On the contrary, he epitomises the hanger-on. When Hughes alludes to Bunter's "magnificent frailty", we might ask how this attribute evolved out of such habits, peculiar to the Owl of Greyfriars, as tittering at others' mishaps and getting himself in a jammy state. It's a failing of *But for Bunter* that it resorts too often to hyperbole ("I think you're herding the facts into gas ovens. I think your cosy lunch was a cellar for torturing the life out of common sense"). But the theme of the novel is inspired and audacious. Even if he doesn't quite pull it off, David Hughes deserves credit for his attempt to furnish a merry commentary on the infatuation with the English public school and its ethics which persists in certain circles, and on the implications of this attitude for society at large. (You can, if you will, view the whole thing as a frivolous outlet for Hughes's continuing concern with "the evasions and fantasies" by which people live, noted by the *LRB* reviewer of his last novel, *The Pork Butcher*.) The mingling of the Greyfriars Remove and various historical moves makes a splendid ploy, but a slightly sharper touch would have been required to get the utmost entertainment out of it.

David Hughes's narrator is an overweight government employee named Patrick Weymouth, incompletely divorced from his wife and unsatisfactorily entangled with his secretary. Weymouth's present task, rather vaguely defined, is to draft a report on the state of culture in modern Britain, with emphasis on current children's reading. He prefers to recall with affection his wartime ingestion of *Magnet* back numbers under a Sussex hedge: like the old pork butcher in the novel of that title, "living off the fat of his memories" – or in this instance, his memories of a fatty. Weymouth is a Bunter addict. In the early days of his marriage, he and his friends behaved like members of an Old Boys' Book Club, "testing one another's memory of goings-on at Greyfriars". When, at the opening of the novel, his ex-wife Lesley remarks blandly that Billy Bunter is still alive, he thinks it's an allusion to his over-eating. However, Lesley is being literal. She means that the model for Bunter has become an 89-year-old *enfant terrible*, at present living in New Romney, Kent, in the charge of two peculiar employees named Smedley and Soames. (Frank Richards's Soames, we remember, was an ex-valet-turned-crook; and at one point in the saga we find a bogus schoolmaster passing himself off as a Mr Smedley. However, no special significance is attached by Hughes to these facts.) Weymouth, having been persuaded to confront this figment of schoolboy fiction in the flesh, finds himself inveigled by Aitken into an escapade: a day trip to France. What larks! In the course of a beanfeast in Boulogne, Aitken comes up with some exorbitant revisions to events of the recent past, as historians would have them: "he was now going on about Field Marshal Montgomery, and then Pandit Nehru received an inscrutable mention" – the inscrutability was no doubt terrific. Eventually we are brought up to the mid-1950s, with Sir Anthony Eden in a fit of pique brought on by Aitken. Suez ensues.

Daniel Green presents a blunter Bunter: not William George, but his supposed great-grandfather William Frederick Augustus. Enumerating the moral flaws which define Frank Richards's classic character, Patrick Weymouth (above) mentions greed, pride, sloth, envy and avarice (the last two unjustly), but leaves lust out of the list. Bunter Sahib isn't especially a prey to this drive either, but most of the laughs in Daniel Green's novel (odd to find a couple of reconstituted Bunters appearing simultaneously) arise from the fact that its plump young hero keeps coming up against concupiscence. It's his sexual allure that gets this particular Owl into a succession of scrapes ("If I'm an owl," he says defensively at one point, "it means that I am well suited to night work".) Nineteenth-century India is the setting for the lewd advances inflicted on Bunter Sahib, the innocent possessor of – as one importunate Begum puts it – "a pizzle a temple bull could envy". "Well, really!" Frank Richards might have exclaimed, seeing his schoolboy buffoon subjected to some unseemly transformations.

Authors sometimes go in for odd enterprises: with her last novel, for example, Doris Lessing turned her back on the expertise she'd been cultivating since 1950. The second part of her *Diary of Jane Somers* is a trite and tiresome piece of work. *The Good Terrorist*, on the other hand, shows a resurgence of the customary Lessing boldness and diligence, reminding us how purely readable this author can be whenever she chooses. The impulse towards irony is paramount again, along with a seriousness of purpose which "Jane Somers" lacked. The good terrorist of the title is Alice Mellings, a renegade from the middle classes, whose talent for housekeeping benefits a noisome squat. We follow with interest the processes – initiated by Alice – of getting lavatories unblocked, electricity restored, the refuse of ages dealt with. Alice has a special relationship with shiftless Jasper, close but sexless (he prefers men, she does without). These two, at the start of the novel, arrive at what looks like a radically impaired building. In it, however, some people indifferent to bodily comfort are already ensconced. They are all, or almost all, would-be revolutionaries, and a plan is afoot to seek affiliation with the IRA.

Nothing comes of this plan, as it happens. *The Good Terrorist* is far from being cast in the form of a thriller, though a fair amount of narrative suspense is generated in the final section. It is rather a matter-of-fact scrutiny of the ideas, activities and outbreaks of those for whom society's structures are inescapably equated with corruption. Lessing's central character is an over-age protester who likes to daub walls with slogans denouncing the bourgeoisie. Her unexceptionable family's claim to consideration she discounts entirely. She holds against her parents and their friends their inability to acknowledge Jasper's merits. Their refusal to subsidise his exploits she cannot forgive. She blots out of her mind the consequences of her behaviour towards them, and especially towards her mother, a prop for her and Jasper over a number of years. A selective helpfulness is practised by Alice. It is directed towards those oppressed by awful childhoods, nourishing spectacular grievances, or lumbered with distorted sensibilities. She finds kindred spirits among the socially enlightened (as it seems to her): campaigners for an improved future, humanitarians, non-workers, malcontents, freelance pickets. Alice, the good girl manqué, not without a spot of self-delusion, throws in her lot with some bad hats. A stubborn and deadly innocence is among her traits.

Not that we're invited, in these pages, to relish or marvel at anyone's depravity. Doris Lessing is too conscientious to be censorious, and her present purpose isn't satirical, or expository, or even very clearly aligned with any special political view. She merely takes two kinds of destructiveness, bureaucratic and anarchic, and examines the conditions produced by the pair of them. Her approach is thorough, factual, and oddly entertaining – the last an effect of her traditional narrative gift.

We are all, she seems to be saying, implicated in society's failure to manage things better. No one has any right to self-congratulation. People who require symbolic vignettes from their fiction need look no further than the opening pages of *The Good Terrorist*, with the top-floor rooms of a gracious, solid house (c. 1910) filled with buckets of shit. Such a house is the responsibility of all of us, we've allowed it to get into this state, and for all the effort that goes into its reclamation, it can't effectively be put in order.

The unexplained laughter of Alice Thomas Ellis's title has a celestial source; she's at the business of larking with the metaphysical again. Her light, worldly novels don't exclude a salutary touch of the ineffable. There is always, for this author, some unspoken observer of people's antics – and this makes things gloriously intriguing and rum. Her ability to shape flawless, droll, astringent sentences is a help as well. In this, her fifth novel, a not quite broken-hearted journalist visits a Welsh valley to recuperate after a cut-off love affair. The name of this engaging show-off is Lydia, she has a lot of curly hair in which a bow is sometimes placed, a sharp brain and a piquant manner. A plain and ordinary person accompanies her to her Welsh cottage – Betty, who, until she's disabused of the notion, entertains a worry that Lydia, left to herself, might do herself in. Betty is a good sort with no dash whatever. Lydia goes in for beguiling venom, envisaging disagreeable ends for her absconding lover – "She wished that Finn's caique might sink in waters infested with small sharks" – until it occurs to her, about half-way through the novel, that goodness might be a more chic attribute. This quality isn't easily attained.

In a nearby farmhouse lives a full-flavoured family: dour husband, downcast wife, young sister-in-law afflicted with an unspecified deformity. The last is Angharad, whose elemental view of things, inserted into the narrative in passages set in italic type, makes a counterbalance to the sportive malice of Lydia. When Lydia labels the home of these people "Farmhouse Grim", you feel it's to avoid uttering the phrase "cold comfort" – that byword since 1928 for queerness in the country. We find queerness in abundance here. But Alice Thomas Ellis, though she pokes fun with gusto, at the same time goes looking for the skull beneath the skin – an unsettling practice, and one altogether alien to the Starkadder spirit.

Fay Weldon's tone, in her new collection of stories, is as grimly chatty as ever: "Well now, friends, let's have a little light relief. Let me tell you the story of what happened to Esther and Alan in the twenty-fourth year of their marriage." So opens "Redundant! or, The Wife's Revenge". It's this author's agreeable custom to cast a sardonic eye on the accredited triumphs of woman-hood – marriage, child-bearing, an affluent way of life, etc. Her instructive little life-histories reckon up the cost of these attainments, in terms of psychological wear and tear. Hysterical paralysis in an apparently happy woman? You'll find a husband of unacknowledged frightfulness at the bottom of it. Uncontrollable list-making on the part of another? This must indicate some unseen lack. Weldon's warped wives – warped by men's mishandling, as it may be, or just by the thinness of the options available to them – are sometimes driven to take matters into their own hands, with a good deal of ado. The outrageous retaliation is a recurring motif; and behind it, Fay Weldon has a knack for discerning a crazy pattern in marital goings-on. Her characters are all unnaturally busy – busy storing up trouble for themselves, averting it or meeting it head-on. There are twelve stories in this new collection, composed in a range of moods from the vindictive to the amiable, and all of them marked by brevity and a certain showiness of style. Women's fates, in all their variety, continue to dominate Mrs Weldon's fiction.

London Review of Books, 1985

IT WAS SUDDEN
AND AWFUL

Barbara Comyns, *A Touch of Mistletoe*
(Introduction to *Virago Modern Classics* reissue)

Barbara Comyns is justly celebrated for her distinctive
manner, her feeling for the oddity and insecurity of
everyday life. She started with the quasi-autobiographical *Sisters by a River* (1947), which presents some vivid
scenes from an unkempt upbringing: the large old house
in Warwickshire, on the banks of the Avon, disasters
occurring both indoors and out of doors, the peculiarities of adults, domestic upsets and savagery. "Of
course everyone knew Daddy drank", says the ingenuous
narrator, "but they thought we were all queer and there
were many strange and untrue roumers [sic] floating
around." That tone, confiding and uncalculating, has
stayed with Barbara Comyns ever since (though the
childish spelling didn't persist beyond the first book).

The child's unclouded vision and candour – these are attributes of even her adult narrators. Her approach to fiction is gloriously unsystematic. "I know this will never be a real book that businessmen in trains will read ... All the same, I am going to write this book even if businessmen scorn it", announces Sophia Fairclough in *Our Spoons Came from Woolworths* (1950). It's a declaration of policy. "A foot-off-the-ground novel that came by the left hand": Stevie Smith's description of her own *Novel on Yellow Paper* applies equally well to everything Barbara Comyns has written.

A Touch of Mistletoe (her seventh novel) was first published in 1967, and it opens with two girls – sisters – on the steps of a run-down house in Warwickshire, c. 1925. Their grandfather has just died and been buried near "the terrible Mrs Willoweed" (from the 1954 novel *Who Was Changed and Who Was Dead*); their mother has embarked on a course of manic house-cleaning in the intervals of giving in to drink; and the lawyer is insisting that every household item not in use should be sold at once. It's a characteristic situation – dicey and picturesque. Comyns heroines do not come from settled or conventional backgrounds. They are accustomed to disarray and loss ("I had no relations with the exception of a sister and brother", states Sophia Fairclough in *Spoons*. "They had all died for one reason or another"), and singularly ill-versed in the ways of the world. In *Mr Fox* (1987), for example, the guileless heroine accepts employment as a nightclub hostess, without having grasped the obligations of the job. "The other girls were very clever at getting rid of men who didn't intend to spend much money, but the only way I could manage it was to leave them and hide in the ladies' convenience." Before anything untoward can happen to Caroline Seymore in this dodgy setting, she is struck down with lumbago and never acquires a first-hand knowledge of the hostess's role. Like most of her Comyns predecessors, she is undaunted by adverse circumstances and confronts things in a spirit of steadfastness, if not astuteness, which sees her through.

The heroine and narrator of *A Touch of Mistletoe* is called Victoria Green ("sounds like a station"), and the novel recounts the events of her life, from 18 on. She sets out sturdy and hopeful, having secured what promises to be an interesting job – and finds herself responsible for the care of defective bull terriers on the outskirts of Amsterdam. A bitten finger, which quickly turns septic, is only one of her troubles. It's a brief and dismal interlude, one of the trials that Comyns characters are obliged to undergo on the way to self-reliance. A fairy-tale element is strong in the work of this author – the edge of danger, deprivation and grotesqueness, the clarity and exactness of the writing, the heroines' composure in the face of emergencies, the pungency of the atmosphere. A Babes-in-the-Wood menace hangs over the child characters in these books, who frequently come to harm. They die by drowning and surface poignantly festooned with weeds; they tumble downstairs on their heads; or a fever gets them. A striking end is in store for young Alice Rowlands in the sedate and disquieting novel of 1959, *The Vet's Daughter*. And as well as deaths, deformities abound. *The Skin Chairs* (1962) contains a child born without a hand, and in *Mistletoe* a housemaid named Marcella Murphy has only one nostril to her nose. Alice Rowlands's friend is a deaf mute. If the central figures aren't alone in the world they tend to have awful relatives who say things like, "I'm just off to see a dear little baby with water on the brain ..." (*The Skin Chairs*). Sometimes in defiance of such relatives the girls go in for a mild bohemianism of the sort indicated in the title of *Spoons*, rejecting conventions dictated by mere stuffiness or dullness of mind.

They are happy with their bohemian lives, as long as these are leavened with affection and optimism about the future; it's then of no account if bailiffs are hovering and dead bugs emerge from the bathroom geyser. Comyns girls are always getting married to unknown artists with strong opinions about aesthetic matters, and an impatient attitude both to housekeeping itself, and the money to keep it going. Vicky Green duly embarks on this episode in her life, setting up house with a painter named Eugene Reeve. Some of the funniest moments in the novel concern the excruciating effect on Vicky's husband of certain ill-designed objects:

> Often he went out of his way to torture himself by looking at things that would upset him – furniture shops and windows filled with plaster little girls lifting up their skirts and gnomes and monks or demons twisted up in agony. These things were frightful but one could always look the other way. Gene would return home quivering with the horrors he had seen as if it had been cruelty to children or animals. I could tell by the way he walked upstairs if things were wrong. Sometimes I thought I must be insensitive that I did not worry enough about ugliness, unemployment and all the things that upset Gene; but life would have been frightful if we had both suffered so much.

This is funny, but it isn't long before an altogether more sombre note supervenes. These marriages always end for one reason or another, leaving the heroine with a child or two; Sophia, in *Spoons*, soon learns from experience that birth control entails rather more than having it firmly fixed in your head that you won't conceive. Vicky, likewise, is innocent and unassertive in a good many respects; but – like her creator – she is at the same time ferociously observant and endowed with a natural astringency and common sense.

Vicky's husband Gene has an image in his head of trees in France being stifled by mistletoe; even those which appear to be free of the growth are found to have a small bunch taking hold somewhere. Hence the title – "mistletoe" standing for universal miseries to which everyone is subject, though whether or not they swamp your life depends on the attitude brought to bear on them. Comyns heroines never go under, though a vicissitude motif marks their experiences to an extraordinary degree. They are accustomed to life going wrong, before their fortunes take an upward turn – and the cycle is repeated over and over. They inhabit a world in which childhood is strange and ramshackle, marriage eventful, and acute money troubles prevail ("if we left the rent unpaid an awful man in a bowler hat used to come"). "Sad" is a frequent adjective in the Comyns oeuvre, but it's an intriguing, never a dispiriting dejection that's evoked: "Right in the middle of spring cleaning Daddy died, it was sudden and awful"; "It was cold out there on the manure heap, and we became very sad." Barbara Comyns has a knack of getting to the heart of an atmosphere, or of conveying an emotion, neatly and without fuss. Vicky, on her evenings off from dog minding in Amsterdam, has nothing to do but wander through icy suburban streets in the darkness: "I ... bought a small bag of monkey nuts, and, lying down on a felled tree in a frozen field, slowly munched them as tears of misery and cold fell down my cheeks." Sophia in *Spoons*, though grateful for healthy employment in the country, confides at one point:

> I would have given anything to walk down a typical London street made of rather dirty yellow brick, the houses tall and semi-detached, with a flight of steps going up to the front door, and iron railings with rather straggly private [I think she means "privet"] hedges encaged behind, and every now and then a cat asleep on a window-sill.

Such grimy captivating streets, along with the Warwickshire village susceptible to flooding, encompass a good part of Barbara Comyns's fictional territory; and in *Mistletoe* the London of the 1920s and 30s takes shape before us in a highly decorative form. Vicky and her younger sister Blanche are trying to get by on very little money on the edge of Somers Town ("We used to buy grim little oranges for two a penny"), weeping into a towel on the back of a door when things become too much for them, and pawning some inherited rings to get money for evening dresses – you won't find a husband if you don't own an evening dress. Vicky has had a couple of terms as an art student, while a small legacy lasted; but then it's a matter of finding employment quickly and holding on to it, and never minding if a partner in the firm keeps obtruding himself on you. Comyns girls do not seem to be highly sexed, though they sometimes become the mistress of this one or that one; it's companionship they go in for, not lust. Vicky, when she reaches her third husband, has a habit of saying over to herself a five-line rhyme in bed: "and if I was fortunate I'd only have to repeat it all through twice". The child's view of the world persists, though by now we've been through the Second World War complete with Home Guard, evacuees and flying bombs.

Barbara Comyns has clearly drawn on her own experience for the substance of her novels – like Sophia she worked as a home help in the country after the war, like Mr Fox (in the book of that title) she got involved in property-dealing, and like Vicky she attended an art school in London (dog-breeding and antique-dealing come into the picture too) – but it is all transformed and heightened in the hands of the adept storyteller. Everything in the books is envisaged precisely, perhaps through a way of seeing derived from an art school training – sometimes her work recalls the illustrator

Harold Jones's, in its subtlety and charm, and sometimes it takes on a Rackham-like outlandishness – and the clearest possible outline is imposed on the narrative material. *A Touch of Mistletoe* is among the most purely engaging of Barbara Comyns's books, though it's not without its share of calamity and disagreeableness. It is especially abundant in comic detail – "a dog who looked like a mad rocking-horse", a hanger-on of an author, alluded to in passing, who suddenly makes a go of selling second-hand prams – as well as containing a characteristic Comyns heroine, gifted with a kind of unobtrusive panache, the idiosyncratic assurance that underlies all the novels of this invaluable author.

Introduction to *Virago Modern Classics* edition, 1989

THE WHITE AND THE RED

Barbara Comyns, *The Juniper Tree*

Barbara Comyns's new novel — her first since 1967 — is obliquely descended from the Grimm story with which it shares a title. (A variant title is "The Almond Tree".) Both story and novel open with the same enticing image: it is midwinter, and a beautiful, statuesque woman stands peeling an apple in the courtyard before her house. The knife slips, and blood falls on the snow. "'Ah', says the woman (according to Grimm), 'had I but a child as red as blood and as white as snow!'" In the novel, which is set in Richmond (south-west London) at the present time, the narrator Bella Winter simply observes the trivial accident which befalls a young woman who's about to become her friend. It is not a friendship of equals, since one of the two is rich and cosseted, while the other works hard for living, selling antiques in a shop across the River Thames at Twickenham.

The child as red as blood and as white as snow has already been conceived, and the friendship lasts just as long as Gertrude Forbes's pregnancy. She dies giving birth, of delight, as in the story; or, it may be, of "a haemorrhage amongst other things". Like the proto-type, Gertrude, in a whim of pregnancy, has eaten the fruit of the juniper tree which grows in her garden – a detail which may or may not be significant. The way is now open for Bella – also beautiful, though disfigured by a scar on her cheek – to take Gertrude's place and thereby bring into being an ill-fated little family like the one in the old tale: father, stepmother, daughter, stepson. The daughter is Bella's illegitimate black child Marline, or Marlinchen (more happily known as Tommy). Some years go by, and a mishap duly occurs involving an old oak chest, a storing place for apples. A broken neck is futilely bandaged, and a frantic interment carried out. Barbara Comyns at this point inserts into her modern story the emblematic objects distributed by the original dead-child-cum-bird – gold chain, red shoes and mill-stone – though she balks at the fairy-tale resurrection.

In some versions of the old story, the child's bones are boiled in a soup which the unknowing father sups with pleasure: "My mother killed me, / My father ate me", goes the refrain, merrily gruesome because, in the magic world, no real harm can befall the innocent. The blueprint calls for the restoration of any head chopped off through malice, and the proper dispatching of the evildoer. The modern approach is more equivocal. Barbara Comyns, for a start, turns the story on its head by making the stepmother her central character, and by declining to endow her with blackness of heart. Like other Comyns heroines, Bella recounts her singular experiences with a childlike directness and impassivity, which is very striking. "I told Helen my story and she went home and cried", goes the opening line of the 1950 novel *Our Spoons Came from Woolworths*. What is solicited is not so much pity for those ill-equipped to cope with peculiar troubles, like seeing your mother's ghost sitting in a rocking-chair (*Spoons*), or being obliged to make a show of yourself by levitating in front of an audience (*The Vet's Daughter*, 1959), but rather approval for the way the characters are not got down by atrocious circumstances. Comyns heroines, and her novels, are plaintive, strange and robust all at once.

The mood was established with her first novel, *Sisters By a River* (1947), which is really a string of childhood episodes recollected with ferocity ("Daddy was very fierse with us, we would suddenly hear an angry trumpeting noise and he would grab as many of us as he could and bang our heads together ..."), but tellingly underwritten. The childish spelling and unarranged state of the narrative produce a thoroughly ingenuous effect. The quirky viewpoint persists from book to book, but subsequent Comyns novels go in less for artlessness. *The Juniper Tree* is very cunningly contrived indeed.

The hump-backed lady bearing baskets of damaged china to the Twickenham shop, the shivering greyhound and the carved stone bear, the doll with a burnt arm recalled by Bella, Mr Crimony the coal merchant who seems to have strayed out of some Victorian card game: details such as these contribute to the homely but disquieting atmosphere in which the central characters are located. The old, outlandish tale makes an appropriate model for a novelist like Barbara Comyns, whose imagination is drawn to the odd, the macabre and the picturesque. As an exercise in reconstruction, containing the traditional ingredients but producing a fable for a different age, *The Juniper Tree* could hardly be more satisfactorily accomplished.

Times Literary Supplement, 1985

RIVETING DEVILMENT

Muriel Spark, *A Far Cry from Kensington*

Kensington is, in fact, the setting for Muriel Spark's new novel (her eighteenth): Kensington in the postwar years, recalled from a vantage point in the present. We're back in the territory of the May of Teck Club, of the enterprises observed with relish by Fleur Talbot in *Loitering With Intent*. It is indeed a far cry, the narrator thinks, from the life she is leading in the 1980s. Thinking of Kensington, too, in those days, she recalls a far cry which is at the centre of her story, the cry of someone on the brink of suicide. The book, as well, might be said to constitute a stand against those ills the author has always decried: bogusness, emptiness, malice, inexactitude and prolixity.

In *A Far Cry from Kensington* these disagreeable qualities are lumped together in a hack writer named Hector Bartlett, the narrator's bane. Mrs Hawkins, a war widow, 28 in 1954, is as fat as Jane Wright in *The Girls of Slender Means* and, also like Jane, insecurely employed in publishing. She is one of several occupants of a rooming house near South Kensington station, and works for a firm on the verge of bankruptcy. Waylaid one morning in Green Park by the red-haired hack, Mrs Hawkins comes out with an unforgettable epithet: *pisseur de copie*, she calls him. Pisser of prose, urinator of journalistic copy – it's a comment (borrowed, Mrs Hawkins tells us, from a French Symbolist of the late nineteenth century) on Hector Bartlett's literary manner, and on his manner in general. In the course of the novel it takes on the character of an imprecation, a three-word formula to undo the misuser of words. Nothing, neither entreaty from a famous woman novelist, nor the loss of two jobs, will induce Mrs Hawkins to retract the label. A pisser of prose is a pisser of prose.

The point about the insult is its aptness. "Any better phrase that you can honestly suggest might apply, I'll be willing to give it careful consideration", says Mrs Hawkins to Emma Loy, the famous novelist to whom Hector Bartlett has attached himself, and who is trying to promote his interests in order to be rid of the incubus. Mrs Hawkins is unshakeable in her whopping weight. To anyone not a pisser of prose she is always ready to extend a helping hand, weighing in with advice and reassurance; though, as events progress, she comes to feel increasingly lumbered with this bolstering role, for which, she thinks, her age unfits her. Having lost her job with a shady publishing firm and moved on to a more substantial one, she takes a look at her new colleagues and finds some peculiarity afflicting all of them: at this point she decides to do something about her bloated appearance. Mrs Hawkins's "buxom bulk", and its gradual reduction, have a bearing on the plot; the author, as ever, is at the business of imposing a vivid, capricious and wholly engaging pattern on the elements of her narrative.

The plot, which thickens as the narrator thins, concerns the inhabitants of the lodging house at 14 Church End Villas, Mrs Hawkins's publishing associates and the links between the two groups, with the central figure herself, in her phase of fatness, coping with some vicissitudes, her own and others', and some ill-doing. One of Mrs Hawkins's fellow tenants, for example, is a Pole acclimatised to suffering, a dressmaker bewilderingly undergoing persecution at the hands of an anonymous letter-writer. Wanda Polodek, like many another Spark weakling, has got herself into the clutches of someone unscrupulous. Many of this author's plots turn on blackmail, intrigue, the ferreting out and subsequent exploitation of secrets. (We remember Sir Quentin Oliver and his awful Autobiographical Association in *Loitering with Intent*, the wholesale skulduggery of *Territorial Rights*, the factitious letters in *The Public Image*.)

Muriel Spark isn't one to balk at full-blown wickedness. Her wayward approach, as a Catholic novelist, has been much commented on; what she has always maintained (a mite disingenuously) is that Catholicism endows her with a point of view, a position of moral soundness from which to contemplate all the riveting devilment her imagination devises. She started by applying her considerable comic gift to a literal working-out of certain theological truisms, such as the notion of a celestial author busy constructing the plots of people's lives, or an apocalyptic announcement coming through on the telephone. She has always been interested in symmetry and analogy – as in *The Bachelors*, for example, with its juxtaposing of epilepsy and mediumistic trances.

In literary terms, Catholicism offers a discipline as exacting as that of the fixed form (a form "such as a rondeau, triolet or villanelle") preferred by Fleur Talbot when it comes to the composition of poetry; and also a sense of the defectiveness of whatever ideology falls outside its scope. If it isn't spiritualism, it may be fascism, materialism, psychoanalysis, macrobiotics or some other kind of pseudo-science. In the current novel, a Box, a device pertaining to the cult of radionics, comes into the story, filling the fair-minded Anglo-Catholic heroine with revulsion, but also alerting her to an unnecessary bit of mumbo-jumbo in her own religious observance. She decides to stop reciting the Angelus every day at twelve noon. "My religion in fact went beyond those Hail Marys which had become merely a superstition to me." With religion, as with fiction, the aim is to cut out inessentials and attain grace, both procedures that come easily to this author. Everything written by Muriel Spark is both resonant and concise.

She has also felt free to pick and choose, to an extent, among the tenets of Catholicism, refusing, for example, to treat sex as a sin, or even to make a great to-do about it. Spark heroines aren't averse to adultery, which act they go about more or less merrily, according to temperament. Sex is on a level with child's play, thinks Barbara Vaughan in *The Mandelbaum Gate*, speaking for all of them; or if it isn't it's worthless. It is just a part of ordinary life, which may or may not be exalted by the attitude brought to bear on it, like anything else. (*Loitering with Intent*, in which the author takes as part of her subject matter her own practices as a novelist – the "light and heartless hand", and so on – is perhaps the Spark novel in which the commonplace, *pace* Sandy Stranger, is most thoroughly transfigured.) It is the custom of Muriel Spark to make the most of everything, while treating things coolly – "everything" including the spectacle of someone being deplorable to the fullest degree. A quality she admires, and shares, is aplomb. Miss Brodie, for example, has aplomb, and also a kind of innocence over and above her misguided goings-on, to which the knowingness of Sandy Stranger is opposed. (A lively element of paradox is a feature of Spark's work.) Certain peripheral characters, those who prompt approval, are endowed with aplomb: characters like the very old, very peculiar mother of Sir Quentin in *Loitering with Intent* – all pre-war draperies and "fluxive precipitations"; or Milly the Irish landlady in *A Far Cry from Kensington*, who reacts robustly to a lodger's bad end.

Unlike (say) *Territorial Rights*, which does without a protagonist, the new novel is centred firmly on Mrs Hawkins and her stout opinions, her captivating reliability; Mrs Hawkins with her eye for an abomination, whether pisseur or poseur. (Mrs Hawkins is eventually to be known as Nancy, once she has attained a normal shape.) It is slightly more discursive than usual, and full of the tang of an undiminished past – the past called up by Mrs Hawkins, in a state of cherished insomnia. We get the details – bomb damage staying unrepaired on the outskirts of London, the corduroy, in shades of brown or green, worn by those artistically in the know – and also the larger framework, the mood of those distinctive days. While the two previous novels by Muriel Spark drew on other works for the purpose of analogy and enrichment – the quasi-autobiographical *Loitering with Intent* has the autobiographies of Newman and Cellini behind it, while *The Only Problem* turns to the Old Testament and Job – and the current one doesn't, on the whole, stray outside its own terms of reference, all three are based on the essential Sparkian proposition (courtesy of Job) that we can't expect to receive good at the hand of God, and not evil. Starting from this point, Muriel Spark has shown herself, consistently, to be an endlessly resourceful, idiosyncratic and uncompromising author – not only funny and formidable at the same time, but also inspiriting, in the richest tradition of serio-comic fiction.

Times Literary Supplement, 1988

WHY IRIS MURDOCH
MATTERS

Anne Rowe, *Iris Murdoch*
Gary Browning, *Why Iris Murdoch Matters*

Since her death in 1998, Iris Murdoch has become something of an industry. Memoirs, critical studies, close examinations of her life and work abound. Most hold their subject in high regard; one or two are less than adulatory. All lay claim to an aspect of Iris, not least her husband John Bayley's accounts of her descent into dementia. It seems a long time since A.S. Byatt's *Degrees of Freedom* (1965) set the whole proliferating genre of Murdoch studies going. This book, indeed, was not undertaken as a critical survey, but rather as an attempt to elucidate the points Iris Murdoch's early novels were making. It remains, for the most part, cogent and convincing. But Byatt only had seven novels to deal with. Now the entire oeuvre is available for evaluation: fiction, philosophy, essays, letters and all. It has generated an unconscionable amount of comment and analysis.

And now that the centenary of Iris Murdoch's birth in 1919 is upon us, we can look forward to a further flurry of conferences, exhibitions, interviews and publications. Among the last are two short studies, both by respected Murdoch scholars. Anne Rowe is co-editor of Iris Murdoch's letters, *Living on Paper* (2015), and author of critical and biographical approaches to the novelist. Gary Browning, professor of politics at Oxford Brookes University, has, over the past few years, subjected Murdoch's writings to careful scrutiny, particularly with reference to their philosophical content. His new book, *Why Iris Murdoch Matters*, is part of Bloomsbury's "Why Philosophy Matters" series, and it begins (and continues) with an attempt to differentiate between Murdoch the philosopher and Murdoch the novelist – or at least, to estimate the extent to which the one has affected the other.

This question, as Anne Rowe says in *her* new book, "has both challenged and energised Murdoch scholarship for decades". Iris Murdoch's own response to the suggestion of a philosophical framework bolstering up her novels is well known: it filled her with "absolute horror". On the other hand, she conceded, philosophical discussions between characters in her books might legitimately occur, "because I happen to know about philosophy. If I knew about sailing ships, I would put in sailing ships". But it seems few critics are willing to let it go at that.

Why Iris Murdoch Matters is a thoroughgoing and stimulating engagement with Murdoch's ideas and practices. It does not offer a critical perspective on the novels, but rather places them within a context of general intellectual exploration and social shake-up. Following the upheaval of the Second World War, all kinds of new, or newish, projects and ideologies came into circulation, and Murdoch was no less susceptible to these than anyone else. Some affected her less enduringly than others. Her early socialism, for instance, was replaced in the late 1970s by a swing to the Right, a not untypical departure for many of her generation. She took against the trade union movement and Arthur Scargill in particular, and became an admirer of Margaret Thatcher. What did endure, though, was her preoccupation with the freedom of the individual and the ways in which it might be arrived at.

You learn a lot about Murdoch's influences and achievements from Gary Browning's book (the former, as we know, including Plato, Kant, Hegel and Simone Weil). But a fair amount of repetition gets into his expositions, especially where Murdoch's literary modus operandi is concerned. When he says on page 5 that her narrative strategy "allows for the reality of distinct characters that are not formulaic projections of an author's standpoint", and then goes on, a few pages later, to note her "imperative of finding a way for the novel to imagine real characters that can enhance our sense of the world outside ourselves", you have to wonder if the point isn't too obvious to require restatement. It's only when he gets to grips with Iris Murdoch's philosophical training and instincts, that Browning's academic critical procedures come into their own. Anne Rowe, in her short study in the Liverpool University Press's "Writers and their Work" series, has praise for her fellow critic's expertise, drawing our attention to his close reading of the political element in a couple of early Murdoch novels.

Anne Rowe is an exceptionally able and assured commentator, and her insights into Iris Murdoch's work, particularly the weirdly conceived and wildly orchestrated last novels, *The Green Knight* (1993) and *Jackson's Dilemma* (1995), are illuminating. (Of the latter she remarks that "Every chapter bears the mark of its creator and gives a unique glimpse of Murdoch's last, unguarded self-reflections".) Her book consists of five chapters and an Afterword, and considers the novelist as a product of her times, as a public intellectual, as an outstanding author, a woman of complex character, a seeker after truth and exponent of the long view. Her novels, Rowe contends, provide a link between august nineteenth-century realism and the freer, more experimental, anxiety-ridden modes of the twenty-first century. She created an inimitable fictional world, of great ingenuity and fascination. (She didn't have Elizabeth Bowen's effortless grace and density – say – or Muriel Spark's bite and aplomb, but she had something else: moral seriousness allied to elaborate plot-making.) It evolved over the years before falling to pieces right at the end, but some of its ingredients were already in place when *Under the Net* was published in 1954. They include an authoritative marshalling of characters, a sense of prevailing moral perplexities, a flair for strong definitive symbols and symbolic gestures. Sandcastles, sunken mediaeval bells, unicorns and all the rest, point up the novels' underlying forces and their essential concerns.

If Murdoch's profoundly alluring fourth novel *The Bell* (1958) represents one kind of moral comedy (anarchic and abundant), its immediate successor, *A Severed Head* (1961) embodies another. This one is coolly urbane and ironic, with its dizzying erotic realignments and its "London *cognoscente*" effects. It also contains one of those striking denouements, fundamental to Murdoch, in which someone in the throes of a crazy passion bursts into a bedroom where an episode of unlawful copulation is taking place. (Incidentally, it's surprising to find Anne Rowe confusing Georgie Hands in this novel with Jessica Bird in *The Nice and the Good* – similar roles, but totally different works.) Another of these scenes of monumental embarrassment, occurring in the novel *The Red and the Green* (1965), features a couple of overwrought nephews and their concupiscent aunt.

Towards the end of that novel there's a very funny set-piece – though the context is anything but funny – when one of the characters is thoroughly bewildered to find two of his relatives, a young British Army officer and an under-age, would-be freedom fighter, sitting side by side on the kitchen floor with their legs stuck out in front of them and their backs against the wall, one with bandages draped around his neck, and both apparently in a drugged or a comatose condition. How they got into this predicament has a crucial bearing on the plot. It is Easter week in Dublin in the year 1916, and momentous doings are afoot. *The Red and the Green* is Iris Murdoch's only historical novel, and one of only two "Irish" novels among her output. In fact, her emphasis in the book doesn't fall on the impending insurrection and the atmosphere surrounding it. Her attention is focused, characteristically, on family misunderstandings and entanglements, Irish and Anglo-Irish. She evokes the ambiance of dusty and dishevelled, but none the less elegant and imposing

Dublin streets (including her own birthplace, Blessington Street, "north of the Pillar"), but not the city's revolutionary stirrings. Late in life, Iris Murdoch said *The Red and the Green* was the one novel she wished she hadn't written, though I think this declaration had more to do with her changed perception of rebel fighters and the tradition they fostered, than with any shortcomings of style or structure.

The question of Iris Murdoch's "Irishness" is not straightforward. She was born in Dublin but taken to England before she was four months old. She never lived in the country again. Both her parents were Protestants; her father, indeed, came of Ulster Presbyterian stock, reinforcing her alienation from the Catholic population. Between them, the Murdochs endowed their only child with a heritage, and a standpoint, surprising to some among her later friends and acquaintances who took her for an IRA sympathiser – or at least, for someone sympathetically aware of nationalist grievances in the North. Not a bit of it. John Bayley recalls an occasion during the Troubles when Iris was invited to lecture at Maynooth, the Catholic seminary on the outskirts of Dublin. When her host and his fellow-priests expressed solidarity with "the men behind the wire" (i.e. republican prisoners), taking her concurrence for granted, she nearly burst, he says, with the effort to keep a smiling face. Bayley clearly approves of his wife's refusal to align herself with what he calls "the fashionably correct attitude [among London intellectuals] to Irish unity".

Nevertheless, Iris Murdoch called herself Irish and never lost an opportunity to visit the country of her birth. Anne Rowe, in the chapter in her book called "Writing the Landscape" considers Ireland and London as the two places most radically embedded in Murdoch's imagination. The descriptions of London life and districts and streets and architecture, from *Under the Net* on, are indeed sharply and superbly rendered. Ireland, or its wilder shores, is another matter. *The Unicorn* (1963), whose setting is never specified, though Bayley has identified it as the coast of Co Clare, relies for its Irish essence on mists and bogs. Otherwise, it could be any remote locality where disturbing forces are brewing up a storm of baleful eventualities. Sheridan Le Fanu is often cited in connection with this Murdoch novel, but it seems to me *The Unicorn* is more akin to a slightly different phenomenon of the 1860s, the "Cometh Up As A Flower" variety of "Sensation" fiction. *Cometh Up As A Flower, and Pusheth Her Husband Down a Well* – as some wit revised Rhoda Broughton's title – isn't without faint echoes here. By the end of *The Unicorn*, rather a lot of corpses are strewn about the place, and you can't avoid noting a certain diminution in Iris Murdoch's usual affectionately sardonic attitude towards her characters.

If flights and frights and fights continue to loom large in subsequent Murdoch novels, they are tempered, for the most part, by the author's ethical drive, and by the striking inventiveness she brings to her invigorating imbroglios. Her singular blend of artifice and authenticity has placed her in a category of her own. Themes and plot devices recur in a variety of configurations, some more intriguing than others. *The Nice and the Good* (1968), for instance, is one book that stays in the mind, with its *Midsummer Night's Dream* felicity of expression and its *All's Well That Ends Well* impetus. Elsewhere, absurd situations go hand-in-hand with serious social comment and abstract speculation – think of the half-naked girl concealed in a china cupboard in *The Flight From the Enchanter* (1956), or Bradley Pearson near the start of *The Black Prince* (1973) beset by wailing women. Murdoch can be read on different levels, and this is one reason why she matters. You can relate her trains of thought to her own time, and to the present time. She matters, too, because of her prodigious creativity, her intellectual gifts, and her standing as the author of engaging, engrossing works of fiction. Both Gary Browning's study and Anne Rowe's acknowledge this, in paying tribute to their subject's brilliance, distinction, and unique cast of mind.

Times Literary Supplement, 2018

OFF GAMES

Muriel Spark, *Curriculum Vitae*

Commenting on the spate of books about authors, biographies, critical studies, theses and the like, Elizabeth Bowen posed the wry question: "If anybody must write a book about Elizabeth Bowen, why should not Elizabeth Bowen?" The same thought has clearly occurred to Muriel Spark, another subject of "widely off the mark" assertions. "So many strange and erroneous accounts of parts of my life have been written", she tells us, "that I felt it was time to put the record straight."

Curriculum Vitae sets the record straight, but at a cost. "Straight" is the word. This most invigorating and idiosyncratic of novelists takes an unduly plain approach to the story of her life. Crinkles, contretemps and complications are all smoothed out. It's not that she is dull – dullness is as alien to her as inelegance – just that we might have looked for something a bit more pointed or playful.

As it is, we get the facts, or as many of them as she wishes to disclose: childhood in Edinburgh, relations and neighbours, schooldays. She was born Muriel Camberg in 1918 (for the first year of her life, you might do worse than turn to the wonderful story, "The First Year of My Life") and lived in a street in middle-class Morningside which retained its gas lighting, unlike the city-centre streets to which electricity had come. She wore knitted silk dresses and grew familiar with the ragman's cry as he did his rounds with a handcart. From a very early age she began to be fascinated by people's foibles. In due course, she attended a good Edinburgh school – though oddly, and seemingly by choice, didn't go on to university – and enjoyed tranquillity at home.

After school came a bit of teaching and office work. In fact, Muriel Spark's life seems to have been exceptionally free of alarms and discords until her twentieth year, when it took an untoward turn. At this point she left Edinburgh *en route* for Southern Rhodesia, to marry a man whom she'd met at a dance – not even alerted by his initials, S.O.S. (Sydney Oswald Spark). This decision puzzled and annoyed her father, and it puzzles us. "It was a disastrous choice", she admits, but virtually leaves it at that.

S.O.S., with his incipient "mental problems", doesn't even have a talking part in these reminiscences, though he gave her a name well suited to a novelist, and a son, Robin, born in 1938. He was working as a teacher in Southern Rhodesia when she went there to marry him, and it was there, she says, "that I learned ... to put in a peripheral place the personal sorrows, frights and horrors that came my way": a lesson stringently applied in this autobiography.

However, some at least of the frights and horrors have found their way into Muriel Spark's novels, suitably transfigured. Transfiguration, indeed, is prominent among her fictional strategies. A slightly unsettling achievement of *Curriculum Vitae* is to return us in some instances to the bare bones, divested of all imaginative embellishments. Take Miss Jean Brodie, for example. Yes, this redoubtable character did have a real-life counterpart – but one recalled with joy and admiration, and completely unbetrayable. Moreover, Miss Christina Kay, into whose hands Muriel Camberg fell at the age of 11 when she entered the James Gillespie High School for Girls, was far too devout to have slept with the music master, or anyone else. Then, the May of Teck Club appears here in a watered-down version, along with the Compound from *The Hothouse by the East River*. It almost amounts to a reversal of Fleur Talbot's amused amazement, in *Loitering with Intent*, as she goes about rejoicing at "seeing people as they were, and not only that, but more than ever as they were, and more, and more, and more". Still, the novelist's recourse to fun and games – Fleur Talbot's phrase – doesn't necessarily come within the autobiographer's brief.

Curriculum Vitae takes us up to 1957, when Muriel Spark was 39 and had been back in England for 13 years. In 1944, she secured employment with Sefton Delmer's Political Intelligence Department ("black" propaganda broadcasts to Germany), and worked for a time with German prisoners of war. Late in the 1940s she took over the editorship of *The Poetry Review*, and promptly encountered trouble on various fronts. She records a comment of John Heath-Stubbs: "You were too avant-garde for them." Someone else saw her at the time as "more of a Chinese cracker than a new broom".

There were squabbles over the question of whose name should or should not appear on the cover of the magazine. Dr Marie Stopes turns up siding against the new editor, and prompting the remark: "I think she was demented at this stage of her life. I used to think it a pity that her mother rather than she had not thought of birth-control." Brandishing of umbrellas, anonymous letters and general unpleasantness comes into the picture. Friction in abundance, indeed, to garnish the fiction: some of these incidents, we're told, get a later showing in *Loitering with Intent*.

In the 1950s came a measure of success (winning the *Observer* short-story competition, for example, and causing "quite a stir" in literary circles), though it was also a time of hardship – indeed, malnutrition – for Muriel Spark. It also saw the start of her literary association with Derek Stanford, whom she describes as amusing, hypochondriac, short, bald, eccentric, and living with his parents in Hounslow. He was also, it seems, very prone to get things wrong; and it's partly to correct the impression of her conveyed in his memoir, *Inside the Forties*, that Muriel Spark has written this book.

It is easy to understand anyone's annoyance at being subjected to garbled or inaccurate comment in someone else's reminiscence, but the Stanford section here amounts to only a very mild retaliation for any perceived affront. Much more devastating, for example, is Spark's treatment of the odious Hector Bartlett (the "pisseur de copie") in *A Far Cry from Kensington*; but *Curriculum Vitae* doesn't disclose the identity of this individual, though it offers several candidates for the part. The book, indeed, has more about friendships than enmities; its tone is more amiable than adversarial. Muriel Spark is among the most enticing and compelling novelists writing at present, and this first instalment of her autobiography is consistently engaging, even if it lacks a certain narrative spice.

New Statesman and Society, 1992

THERE WERE
ODD FOLK EVERYWHERE

Jane Gardam, *Crusoe's Daughter*

There is at present something of a vogue for novels reflecting other novels, ironically and obliquely (Peter Ackroyd's *The Great Fire of London* comes to mind, with *Little Dorrit* behind it; or even *Flaubert's Parrot* by Julian Barnes, though biography, fiction and all inform that eccentric piece of writing). These, at best, are neither extensions nor offshoots, but playful and original tributes to the work that has set them off. With Jane Gardam's latest novel, the background book and enriching ingredient is *Robinson Crusoe*. Mrs Gardam is not new to the practice. *The Summer After the Funeral* of 1973 has a heroine (aged 16 – it's ostensibly a children's book) who feels an affinity between herself and Emily Bronte, to the point of thinking deeply about reincarnation. *Wuthering Heights* has left its mark indirectly on this novel. *Crusoe's Daughter*, with its heroine Polly Flint metaphorically cast away, and not cast down by it, is rather more open about its literary appropriations.

Polly Flint, though, is a good deal more than Crusoe's parrot. Crusoe, for her, is both a solace and an exemplar, stuck there on his island – as she says late in the novel – "like women have to be almost always ... Imprisoned." Stranded, imprisoned, but calmly getting on with things, fashioning an umbrella for himself out of goat-skins ("Very useful in the great heats") and acquiring the skills of pottery and pastry-cooking. Among the children eventually fathered by Robinson Crusoe after his 28 years of sexual abstinence, Defoe mentions a daughter; but this daughter promptly disappears from the history of the central character, just as Shakespeare's sister (*pace* Virginia Woolf) disappeared from history. It's a masterstroke of Jane Gardam's to bag the role for a twentieth-century woman, daughter of a sea-captain drowned in 1904 on the coal run to Belfast. This is the year when the novel opens. Motherless Polly, soon to be fatherless at six years old, has washed up at a tall yellow house on a saltmarsh, somewhere on the Northumbrian coast. Nearby are a church, a nunnery, a folly, a Hall and an iron-works. All of these buildings, but especially the yellow house which faces the sea, are constantly at the mercy of strong winds blowing from the north-east.

At the yellow house live Polly's aunts, Mary and Frances, both of them too religious for their own good – a temperamental defect well understood by Jane Gardam. One is overtaken in the end by vagueness, the other by unaccountable flightiness, after a late marriage, on a voyage to India. Also their crabbed friend Mrs Woods, a knitter; and Charlotte, the faintly unsavoury servant who boils up her knickers on the kitchen fire. A double wrong has been done to Charlotte, and she's allowed her say in retaliation before exiting from the novel in a striking manner. Before this, she has instructed Polly (who is growing up) in the practicalities of menstruation – the aunts being too fastidious to do it – advising her, at these times, to avoid excessive washing. Polly's isn't exactly a jolly upbringing, what with Aunt Mary sleeping with the silver spoons to baffle burglars, Aunt Frances going ga-ga over awful Mr Pocock, the curate; and companions of her own age few and capricious. But neither is it especially bleak. Polly has a good many resources – conspicuous among them *Robinson Crusoe*. (They don't, though, at any stage, include the one adopted by her grandmother, a Victorian Archdeacon's wife, who boldly inscribed her name in her own copy of *Fanny Hill*.) Only one complaint is voiced by Polly, very tentatively, in a letter to her beloved Aunt Frances, when she mentions that, had she been a boy, "the money would have been found" to send her to school. We remember Defoe: "I have often thought of it as one of the most barbarous customs in the world ... that we deny the advantages of learning to women." And Moll Flanders asserting that courage was what women needed, and the power to "stand their ground". As Virginia Woolf noted. The author of *The Voyage Out* has quite a lot to do with *Crusoe's Daughter*, supplying an epigraph with her riposte to Dickens (he complained that *Robinson Crusoe* never made anyone laugh or cry), and even turning up on a lawn in Yorkshire at one point in the narrative, very thin and beautiful. The summer after the wedding of her Aunt Frances, Polly – aged 16 – is brought, via Darlington, York and Helperby, to visit a grand dame called Lady Celia, who keeps open house for artists and writers.

Polly takes the place for a madhouse, and not surprisingly. Lady Celia encourages artistic behaviour in her guests. A Mr Thwaite, mysteriously present at Aunt Frances's wedding, has whisked Polly off shortly after the ceremony. He is Lady Celia's brother, as it turns out, but seems more closely akin to Badger in *The Wind in the Willows*. A perfect English gentleman, "all gruffness, shyness and goodness". "Fearful weather", Mr Thwaite keeps grunting. "Really frightful weather." Polly is charmed. The next minute, matters are arranged so that she may experience one of the sudden infatuations

Jane Gardam specialises in, along with the equally sudden retraction which is sure to follow. An earlier novel – *A Long Way from Verona* of 1971 – contained a character who looked like Rupert Brooke; this one has someone who may *be* Rupert Brooke. "His profile is – oh Aunt Frances – most utterly perfect." Into the prevailing mood of steadiness, dictated by *Robinson Crusoe*, comes a romantic intrusion. It's around this time that "The Lady of Shalott" (misspelt "Shallott") is quoted – or rather, misquoted: it's three paces, not three steps, the lady takes in her agitated state when Tennyson's romantic attitude compels her to forsake the web and loom. All very picturesque and alluring, but it won't quite do for Polly, whose comment on the poem is this: "all of her so lovely and never even been for a walk." Quite soon, she is contemplating Paul Treece, the Rupert Brooke figure, and thinking: "I wanted to kick him." Whom one meets is a matter of luck, as Polly reflects at the end of the novel; and the men who come her way – it could be Robinson Crusoe who is speaking – are all "duds or shadows", not one of them, neither Paul Treece nor the more substantial Theo Zeit, a patch on Crusoe himself as far as vigour and tenacity are concerned.

A kind of fidelity, then, takes Polly back to the yellow house, where she and a competent young maid-servant, Alice, are soon dug in; and keeps her there for 70-odd years, while going on elsewhere, at various times, are two Great Wars (as the blurb has it) and a social revolution. "We are not free to choose by what we shall be enchanted", goes the epigraph – from W.H. Auden's *A Certain World* – to *The Summer After the Funeral*. "In the case of a false enchantment all we can do is take flight before the spell really takes hold." Can *Robinson Crusoe* be designated a false enchantment? It seems so only when Polly starts translating it into German and then, that done, subjects the book to analysis as "spiritual biography", all the time drinking a great deal of whisky, and remaining indifferent to the kind of hat she jams on her head. "All washed up and marooned and far away", is how Alice, the servant, sees her during this period. One or two of the lodgers – money is short – take fright at Polly's peculiarities; but another, a schoolmaster once given to lurking behind his wardrobe door when breakfast was brought in ("There were odd folk everywhere after 1918"), regains his confidence, and eventually provides Polly with a way to regain her equilibrium. Indeed, she really has no other option, with Crusoe's briskness and resilience constantly in front of her, to be taken either as a rebuke or an inspiration – not to mention the absence of fatuous longings among her hero's traits. Thus we find, on the day after the shipwreck, the following statement of policy by Crusoe: "It was in vain to sit still and wish for what was not to be had."

During the greater part of the novel Polly's age is less than 20; and so Jane Gardam is able to re-do certain set-pieces like the one in which a nervous but determined young girl confronts someone's grand, unlikeable and disconcerting mother. Adolescence offers plenty of scope for the kind of high comedy, elliptically presented, at which this author excels. But *Crusoe's Daughter* is not a novel of awkward adolescence, or a social comedy, or commentary, or a piece of pure historical evocation ("the dress was of pure silk muslin, golden-brown, with needlework bands and a high neck stitched with blue silk thread"), though it conforms to the rules of each of these categories in turn. It's not exactly an allegory either, more a sustained salting of one set of fictitious memoirs with another – a subtle undertaking. Jane Gardam, following her usual practice, creates dazzling effects out of bits and pieces: an Edwardian pony-and-trap bowling joyously along a beach, a train drawing away from the platform at Darlington Station, a telescope on a roof. Nothing is out of place in the details of setting or mood; as with other novels which assimilate some crucial text ("Crusoe, her King Charles's head"), and thereby gain the freedom to shift away from straightforward narration, certain kinds of verisimilitude seem not greatly to the point. Jane Gardam, for instance, makes no bones about endowing her under-age heroine with an unnatural cogency; and truly, it wouldn't have done to make Polly's literary judgements correspond with those we might expect to hear from an unschooled 16-year-old brought up long ago in a house full of women. "Form", she declares – at this formless age, and in a bygone age, not that it matters a jot – "is determined by hard secret work, in a notebook and in the subconscious and in the head." And *Crusoe's Daughter*, no less than *Crusoe*, could be said to bear out the effectiveness of the process.

London Review of Books, 1985

IT WAS FUN
IN THE FOURTH

Rosemary Auchmuty and Joy Wotton (eds.),
The Encyclopaedia of School Stories: Vol I,
The Encyclopaedia of Girls' School Stories, edited by
Sue Sims and Hilary Clare; *Vol II, The Encyclopaedia*
of Boys' School Stories, edited by Robert J. Kirkpatrick

In his collection *Our England is a Garden* (1979), J.I.M.
Stewart includes a story in which a distinguished
old gentleman is suspected, after his death, of having
indulged a taste for pornographic writings, a suspicion
fuelled by his communications with a specialist book-
dealer. However, the story's title – "Teddy Lester's
Schooldays" – would have alerted aficionados straight
away to the fact that the old gentleman's innocuous
addiction came into a different category altogether:
collecting boys' books. Not that it improved matters

greatly when the truth emerged, since one preoccupation seemed almost as much of a posthumous embarrassment as the other. The old gentleman's "intellectual eminence" remained at stake. Since the time of J.I.M. Stewart's urbane story, we've seen various attempts to upgrade the whole field of children's literature, indeed, and in particular, to separate the school story from the faint risibility which has always adhered to it. It has not been an easy purpose to bring about. You have only to name a title such as *Eric; or, Little by Little* or *The Jolliest Term on Record* – to take those examples – to provoke a derisive response (tempered by an amused indulgence, to a greater or lesser degree). And in fact, some aspects of the school story genre simply do not lend themselves to an unduly academic appraisal. No one endowed with a sense of the ridiculous can take a serious tone about incidents such as the theft of fireworks, cricket trophies, a cocker spaniel or a stuffed gorilla, plans to smuggle an owl out of the school, the recovery of missing title deeds from the bottom of a well, a spot of accidental arson, or the thrilling disclosure of the heroine's past abduction by an eagle.

However, the school story – girls' or boys' – does make as legitimate a focus for a scholarly enthusiasm as any other genre; and the current full-scale survey of the entire field (alphabetically assembled) should help to bolster its claim to respectability. This monumental undertaking comes in two volumes, male and female – and with the latter, a further area of defensiveness is immediately mooted. Throughout the greater part of the twentieth century, the term "school story" suggested to most readers the boys' school story; girls, sickly or silly, were relegated to the sidelines in their absurd gym tunics, clutching their inferior imitations of their brothers' jolly books. Feat and counterfeit, you might have dubbed the complementary genres. In fact, as the authors of Volume One are at pains to show, the girls' school story gathered considerable momentum from the 1880s on (when the term was first used), and quickly established its own distinctive procedures and flourishes. It has, indeed, received less critical attention than its counterpart, for a variety of reasons including its supposed disentitlement to sober scrutiny; however, the last 30-odd years have seen strenuous efforts to get *Six Sinners at St Swithin's, To the Fray, St Agatha's!, The Third's Thrilling Term* and equivalent titles out of the dog-house and into the critics' good books. Rosemary Auchmuty, for example, one of the overall editors of these Ashgate encyclopaedias, has contributed to the advancement of girls' school fiction with her study of 1992, *A World of Girls*.

Rosemary Auchmuty and Joy Wotton are the editors of these companion volumes, while individual entries are the work of, respectively, Sue Sims and Hilary Clare, and Robert J. Kirkpatrick (with a little help from experts in the field, such as Mary Cadogan and Brian Doyle, whose contributions are acknowledged). It adds up to a striking achievement. What do we learn? Well, to begin with, the school story proper could not come into being until a reversal of opinion had overtaken the idea of school itself. While schools were perceived as "unhappy, lonely, bleak places" in the Lowood or Dotheboys mould, it was no good trying to hitch them to high jinks. In fact, it took the new century to bring about a change in tone, as the irrepressible schoolgirls of Angela Brazil, and the merry boys of Greyfriars and St Jim's, burst upon the reading public – or at least, upon its juvenile component. It's true, as we are reminded, that Angela Brazil was not by any means the first or the most rewarding girls' school story writer (any more than *Tom Brown's Schooldays* inaugurated a new genre; at least 60 school stories had existed before Thomas Hughes was struck by his brainwave in 1856). But there were, and remain, certain key books and authors whose names are inextricable from the genre as a whole, and those of Angela Brazil and Charles Hamilton ("Frank Richards") are conspicuous among them.

The indefatigable compilers of these volumes provide a good deal of biographical information, astute assessments of plots ("*The Rivals of Maidenhurst* is an extraordinarily bad book"; "a fascinating index of change – social, educational and literary"; "well worth avoiding", etc), and lists of relevant titles. They are happily alive to instances of higher absurdity – "Nobody with a name like Cynthia", wails a character in one of the books, "could possibly want to have fun with a clay rat"; and, although they take a dim view of uninformed adult commentators who subscribe to the notion that all fictional schools are full of froth and frivolity, concede that one or two *are*. They have gone the whole hog into *Angel Pig* and *Top Dogs Versus the Duds*. They know what they are about. Dogged detective work has uncovered, among other things, a connection between the school story writer Evelyn Smith (*Val Forrest in the Fifth; Seven Sisters at Queen Anne's*, etc) and John Mortimer of *Rumpole* fame (she was his aunt) – though an opportunity is missed, in Volume Two, to mention that the son of the boys' writer Robert Leighton, killed in France in 1915, was Vera Brittain's fiancé.

The statistics alone – in 1923, for example, 43% of all new books for girls came under the school story heading – are enough to underscore the importance of these singular, once-flourishing, sub-genres of children's literature; but aside from that, the Ashgate volumes make fascinating reading, as well as furnishing all kinds of insights into memorable works of fiction, from *The Pranks of Doria* to *A Bit of a Bounder; or, The Surreptitious Cigarette.*

Times Literary Supplement, 2000

OPEN THAT WINDOW, MISS MENZIES

P.D. James, *A Taste for Death*
Barbara Vine, *A Dark-Adapted Eye*
Gladys Mitchell, *Dead Men's Morris*
Gladys Mitchell, *Laurels are Poison*
Joan Aiken, *Dido and Pa*

The epigraphs of P.D. James (now that she has taken to using them) are important. "There's this to say for blood and breath", runs the current one, from A.E. Housman, "They give a man a taste for death." Are we being directed to hold in mind those other lines of Housman's?

> Oh like enough 'tis blood, my dear,
> For when the knife has slit
> The throat across from ear to ear
> 'Twill bleed because of it.

Just such a shambles is evoked at the start of her new novel (her tenth), when the bodies of an ex-Cabinet minister and a tramp, each with its throat slit, are found in the vestry of a Paddington church. It's a splendid opening for a detective novel. Ruth Rendell likewise, under her new name of Barbara Vine, kicks off in striking style: "On the morning Vera died I woke up very early." Vera Hillyard, we learn within a line or two, is scheduled to be hanged at eight o'clock in the morning. It is Vera's niece Faith Longley, Vine's narrator, who discloses this information. What follows is an exhaustive look at the circumstances of the murder committed by Vera, and the life lived by her and her family before this event. We are soon in the past, in the 1930s and 40s, and engrossed in a story presented with all the expertise the thriller-writer can muster.

The Longley family is a heterogeneous one, accommodating various social classes. Class, social behaviour and sexual morality matter in 1939, in ways incomprehensible to those born into a freer society. The murder and the motive, the narrator emphasises, were "of their time, rooted in their time". Faith Longley, 30-odd years on, recreates her wartime sojourns with her father's sisters, Vera and Eden – the second still a schoolgirl in 1939, with her front hair rolled into a sausage shape – at their white-brick cottage in Great Sindon, Essex. Interspersed with Faith's recollections are pieces of research work by an author engaged in examining the Hillyard case.

The Sindon household to which Faith becomes attached is rather an odd one, what with querulous, prickly Vera, irresistibly blonde Eden, and provoking Francis, Vera's son, who spends his holidays from school devising torments for his mother. Within a year or two another child is added to the household, and it's a tussle over the custody of this child, Jamie, that brings about the pivotal outbreak in the drama. But in the meantime, Faith and her Sindon friend Anne Cambus rifle the life of Mary Queen of Scots for scenes to play-act in a derelict cottage, while the Battle of Britain rages overhead, and Eden, at her dressing-table, applies cosmetic preparations to her face. All this is set out with the surest feeling for the character of the era.

Ruth Rendell has written many detective novels of a fairly orthodox kind, alongside high-grade thrillers in which the course of events is determined by the maladjustment of someone among the leading players. With the second type of novel, it's the author's custom to lumber herself with outlandish or seemingly unmalleable ingredients, and then go on to surprise us by the skill with which she causes everything, in the end, to fall into its proper place. It is partly a matter of balance, as she handles two or more converging stories (within each plot) and keeps them from going off the rails. Only a slightly lurid aftertaste gets between these stories and our complete enjoyment of them: there's no element of parody or black comedy in the situations Ruth Rendell envisages, not even when it comes to a man's obsession with a dress-shop dummy, which leads him to act peculiarly in a basement. And why should there be, she might ask, when her theme is criminal derangement and the forms it takes – that, and the openings for depravity afforded by the modern world? Her new novel, under a new name, is equally chary of frivolity, but it also, by and large, cuts out the depiction of paranoia, which is very much a feature of the Rendell thrillers and detective novels alike. Vera Hillyard is not a woman in the grip of some revolting compulsion; it's an intolerable pressure that causes her to act as she does. Ordinary life, in this book, is eroded by a malignant strain, rather than harbouring some such quality. The effect of this shift in approach is to bring the book close to the requirements of serious, rather than "genre" fiction – a merger which the more accomplished among contemporary detective and thriller writers are always aiming to bring about.

P.D. James, who began by relishing the traditional features of the genre (the assembly of suspects and the interrelationship between them, the process of detecting, the surprises, subsidiary killings, twists of plot, and so on), and the constraints thereby imposed, seems to have reacted in some measure against the artifice inherent in any such prescribed plan of writing. (All along, it's true, she has set herself the task of seeing how much reality the essentially artificial framework will bear.) It's a naturalistic mode that engages her interest at present, even though her last novel, *The Skull Beneath the Skin* (1982), resorted to a whole range of gothic embellishments to achieve its effects. That book contains an epigraph and gains a title from the Eliot poem about Webster – a dramatist, like the author of detective fiction, much possessed by death. Friction and mystery, in a spot abundant in macabre associations, contribute to a full-blown atmosphere.

A flighty or insouciant view of death (an option available to the detective novelist as early as the mid-1920s, when Anthony Berkeley and others began to poke fun, often very effectively, at the more conspicuous accoutrements of crime fiction): this has never represented a serious temptation for P.D. James, who doesn't shirk the painful or distressing realities connected with dying. No one in the James novels larks about with arsenic or turns a funeral arrangement into a jape; no significant stockings, boiled corpses, poisoned caterpillars, demonic conjurors or disappearing tins of rat-bane ornament these works. The novels don't, however, exclude playfulness entirely. One in particular, *Unnatural Causes* (1967), is all but cast in the form of a parody, with the victim a novelist and creator of a figure – "an expert on wine, women, heraldry, the landed gentry, esoteric poisons and the finer points of the minor Elizabethan poets" – rather closely akin to Dorothy L. Sayers's Wimsey. Incidentally, P.D. James's own detective hero, Commander Adam Dalgleish, with his supplementary profession of poet, is sometimes singled out for acerbic comments by those to whom a literary policeman is a cause of exasperation: in the same way Wimsey, with his blue blood and prodigious assets, including sensitivity and unshakeable *savoir vivre*, got up the noses of a good many matter-of-fact readers. We may note that Dalgleish is now (*A Taste for Death*) afflicted with writers' block: perhaps the two activities, one involving practical and the other metaphysical elucidation, are incompatible after all.

Dalgliesh last made an appearance in 1977 in *Death of an Expert Witness*; the two P.D. James novels published between that and the current one are, respectively, a non-detective story, *Innocent Blood* (1980), and *The Skull Beneath the Skin*, starring Cordelia Gray, the young proprietor of a London detective agency, and heroine of an earlier adventure recounted in *An Unsuitable Job for a Woman* (1971). *Innocent Blood*, like Barbara Vine's *A Dark-Adapted Eye*, is centred on a bygone killing and its perpetrator (a woman sentenced to life imprisonment and eventually released), and doesn't derive its suspense from subterfuge; it's closer in feeling to the present James novel than it is to its successor, *The Skull Beneath the Skin* – though that book, for all its immoderate imaginings (bones, burial places, slit wrists, executioners' ropes, the whole charnel gallimaufry), manages to adumbrate some serious attitudes to death and dying, as well as having the admirable Cordelia Gray to keep us in touch with sanity and composure. Both *Innocent Blood* and *A Taste for Death* are set in London, a properly multifarious London, in which inherited grandeur is juxtaposed with various kinds of seediness and deprivation. (P.D. James, like her namesake M.R. James, and like *his* namesake Henry James, finds places "prolific in suggestion"). Both, as well, consider the destructive consequences following on from the initial act of violence: "Murder was the first destroyer of privacy as it was of so much else", thinks Dalgliesh at an early stage in his current case. And although *A Taste for Death* is in many ways a classic detective novel, it doesn't include the dumbfounding of the reader as a crucial part of its plan. The identity of the killer, once it's disclosed, probably won't come as much of a surprise to anyone.

The book conforms to a classic pattern by containing a victim who numbers a cutthroat among his closer acquaintances, and by causing the enquiry to focus on each of these in turn. The significant victim here is Sir Paul Berowne, whose recent resignation from his ministerial post may, or may not, be due to a mystical experience undergone by him in St Matthew's Church on the banks of the Grand Union Canal. The circumstances of the baronet's life are soon laid bare: the unsatisfactory second marriage, the cadging brother-in-law, the daughter entangled with would-be revolutionaries, the devoted mistress, the autocratic old mother, the deaths, while in his employment, of two young women. The ambience of nearly every person in the book, whether suspect, police worker or onlooker, is very carefully established, and everyone comes complete with his or her *curriculum vitae*. The resulting stories form an accompaniment to the main story, that of the murder, without necessarily being interconnected with it, or with each other. This arrangement wouldn't have suited the age of jigsaw detection, when the puzzle was paramount. It is, however, in keeping with the freer modes of the present – and besides, P.D. James understands the part played by digressions, and even loose ends, in conveying the sense of anxiety and disruption which co-exists in her books with the exhilarating tackling of a problem.

We find such items in *A Taste for Death* as an enlightening smudge of blood and the clue of a half-burned match; these hark back to an earlier variety of detective fiction, but they are only trifling decorations, inserted, perhaps, to remind us of the conventions, even while these are being more or less eschewed. Dalgliesh, whose character has been built up throughout the series, is notable for the bleakness, detachment and purpose-fulness of the way he goes about things: but he isn't incapable of unbending. He unbends, for example, on page 203, when he brings as a gift for a book-collecting woman friend a treasure entitled (as he has it) *Dulcy on the Game*. "Don't be naughty, Adam", comes his friend's response. "*Dulcy Plays the Game*. How lovely! ... This completes my pre-1930 Brazils." Unfortunately there is no pre- (or post-, for that matter) 1930 Angela Brazil story called *Dulcy Plays the Game*. *Margaret Plays the Game*, yes; but that's by a different author, Winifred Darch. Is this a slip, or is P.D. James playing games, testing the alertness of her readers? It's a moment of levity, in any case, and welcome in a book – albeit a continuously entertaining book – full of blood, malice, and other disquieting particulars.

Gladys Mitchell, who died in 1983, had a jollier and more idiosyncratic approach to crime writing. Her 66 detective novels (the last three published posthumously) all feature the same invincible investigator, Mrs Bradley (later Dame Beatrice), whom nothing nonplusses for long, neither the appearance of one body in the coffin of another, nor the apparent resurrection of a long-de-funct figure. *Speedy Death* (1929) was the opening novel of the series, and it was planned by the author with a male detective in mind. It was only in the course of writing that the pterodactyl-like lady, twice widowed, and a psychoanalyst by profession, came centre stage. Mrs Bradley – who is apt to provoke a suspect by giving him a good poke in the ribs – is nothing if not unorthodox in her investigative procedures.

The early Mitchell novels (some of which have been reappearing recently) are generally very high-spirited and blithe in tone, as well as being constructed on the thicket principle in detective writing: complications abound. *Dead Men's Morris* (1936) – reissued in the "Classic Collection" marking Michael Joseph's 50th anniversary – is quite untypically straightforward and subdued, though it isn't without its moments of ebullience. One of these occurs when the elderly detective, needing assistance to get her nephew Carey out of a predicament in the middle of the countryside in winter, throws off her outer clothing and pelts through a wood in her knickers. The book is set in a pig-farming community of Oxfordshire, at which Mrs Bradley arrives bearing (redundantly) a boar's head as a Christmas gift. She promptly encounters two local farmers – uncle and nephew – who are battering away at one another with, respectively, a blackthorn stick and a pig-bucket. One of these combatants later turns up gored by a boar, though not – as it turns out – the boar whose tracks surround the body. Mrs Bradley is there to ensure that no one gets the wrong pig by the ear. This is the second murder. Some time earlier, an elderly solicitor has gone out to meet a ghost (a headless Elizabethan priest, according to legend), and met his death instead.

Gladys Mitchell departs from her usual custom in this book by showing Mrs Bradley at a loss, albeit temporarily, and even allowing her to succumb to depression, a state not normally associated with a character who is famous for her disconcerting cackle. She's back on form in *Laurels are Poison* (1942), the book in which strapping Laura Menzies, later to become Mrs Bradley's secretary and assistant, first makes an appearance. Laura is a student at the Teacher Training College where Mrs B is acting as Warden and at the same time looking into the disappearance of her predecessor during an end-of-term revel. The unfortunate woman went off to pin up her back hair, and was never seen again. Before this matter is cleared up, the body of a cook has been retrieved from a local river, unaccountably separated from the corset that held it in place. It is left to Laura Menzies to bring this garment to light, which she does by going swimming in midwinter near the spot. Athletic behaviour is one of Laura's traits. Mrs Bradley, too, is shown acting characteristically in this novel. "Now, students, I am going to do some very curious things", she announces. "Open that window, Miss Menzies ...

I'm going to throw this student out." At one point she enlists the help of a visiting nephew – she has a lot of nephews – to carry a bag of bones along a gravel walk. Gladys Mitchell's novels quite often, and with considerable aplomb, occupy a dicey area between spoof and serious detective fiction.

She has been criticised for sometimes failing to make the motive fit the crime, and for allowing obfuscation to get out of hand: as Philip Larkin remarked in an *Observer* review, it's possible to finish a Mitchell novel without grasping the identity of the victim, let alone the murderer. Sometimes her plots run away with her – though not in either of the current reissues, and not in her 1945 *tour de force*, *The Rising of the Moon*. She is, however, consistently diverting, and possessed of an agile imagination when it comes to the devising and disposal of incidents. Mrs Bradley is among the most striking investigators in the business, as she goes about merrily abolishing all kinds of weird cupidity and wrongdoing.

In *Dido and Pa* – the latest in a series of "unhistorical" adventures for children which began in 1962 with *The Wolves of Willoughby Chase* – a stop is put once and for all, one imagines, to intrigues on the part of Hanoverians unhappy with the Scots succession which is posited with great gusto by the author, Joan Aiken. At the forefront of the foilers, once again, is one-time urchin Dido Twite, a splendid embodiment of lower-class London gumption, who thinks nothing of sliding down a slimy old buttress into the icy waters of the Thames, and never turns a hair in the face of rats, wolves, termagants and other menaces. These books are as decorative and inventive as the Kay Harker novels of John Masefield, which they sometimes resemble.

London Review of Books, 1986

MINOR UPHEAVALS

Alice Munro, *The Progress of Love*

In an early Munro story, "An Ounce of Cure" (1967), one phrase is singled out for emphasis: "the way things happened". The way things happened – this is what enthrals the narrator of that particular episode, recollecting an evening during her adolescence when things got farcically out of hand: "I felt that I had had a glimpse of the shameless, marvellous, shattering absurdity with which the plots of life, though not of fiction, are improvised."

We can take that as a declaration of policy. Such glimpses are the stuff of Alice Munro's fiction at any rate, part of an idiosyncratic approach which extends even to a continuous noting of the points at which transcription ends and transformation begins. Among the many things to savour in the work of this author is the playful disclosure, every now and then, of what she's up to. Take the story "Material" in the 1974 collection *Something I've Been Meaning to Tell You*. In this, the ex-wife of a novelist reads a story of her ex-husband's about a character once known to both of them, and sees in action the mustering of skills to give shape and permanence to certain oddments the memory won't let go of. These are skills to be respected – however, the story, characteristically ambivalent about the artifice inherent in re-creation, is written from the standpoint of someone well enough in the know to entertain, along with approval, a faint ironical objection to the process.

Similarly, in the last piece in that book, "The Ottawa Valley", we get a slightly tongue-in-cheek acknowledgement of failure, when the narrator, who had intended "to bring back all I could", looks at what she has done and compares it to a series of snapshots. This is both just and unjust. The snapshot method, in the hands of an author like Alice Munro, is among the subtlest and most illuminating of techniques.

The Progress of Love is her sixth collection of stories, and like the others it is set mainly in small towns and their outskirts in southern Ontario, Munro country, patchy and full-flavoured. The past looms large in all the stories, but the author isn't in the business of establishing a sense of continuity. She is interested rather in vicissitudes, oddities, the points at which somebody's future assumes one configuration rather than another.

Minor upheavals abound, and unaccountable behaviour. Wryness and resilience define her heroines. When young, they are apt to suffer comic misgivings about the way their personalities will unfold, but generally manage in the end to seem like anybody else, as one of them puts it.

Part of this author's method is to focus on a central and extreme aspect of someone's character. In the title story, a woman burns $3,000 in the kitchen stove – a legacy from her hated father. Her daughter recounts the incident: the point, she says, is her father's condoning of the act. "I call that love." Family matters, and ways of looking at things: these remain strong among Alice Munro's material. An early title, *The Lives of Girls and Women* (1967), denotes her inexhaustible subject matter. The current collection – 11 stories – stresses links between two or three generations, and resorts to a structure which is not so much loose as exceedingly pliable, to accommodate them. Children grow up to run women's centres, parents attach themselves to different partners, a decent farm becomes a hippy hangout. The past, as ever, is rifled for clues to certain eventualities.

What else do we find in *The Progress of Love*? The worst not happening ("Miles City, Montana"); violence ("Fits"); vindictiveness ("A Queer Streak"); women's resources, including sturdiness of outlook, adaptability and humour. Paradox comes into the book, with the evocation of moments both exceptional and ordinary, and the achieving of effects both artful and uncalculated. We gain an insight into the vividness of children's goings-on – "We were horses and riders both, screaming and neighing and bucking and waving whips of tree branches beside a little nameless river that flows into the Saugeen in southern Ontario" – alongside the hazardous and haphazard quality of the grown-up state, which sometimes makes for comedy, and sometimes disquiet.

Alice Munro is immersed to the full in the particulars of local life: gossip, reminiscence, family landmarks. There's a phrase in *The Progress of Love* which encapsulates the concerns of her entire body of work: "the stories, and griefs, the old puzzles you can't resist or solve."

The Sunday Times, 1987

THE ECCENTRIC
EMIGRANTS

Alice Munro, *The View from Castle Rock*

This new collection of stories by the incomparable
Alice Munro consists of two sections and an epilogue.
The first part, five stories gathered under the heading "No Advantages", is based on the author's delvings
into family history. A forward specifies the impulse to
recreate certain ancestral lives, "in a given setting that
[is] as truthful as our notion of the past can ever be".

The ancestors in question came from Scotland.
Alice Munro has already located a couple of stories in
this far country. "Hold Me Fast, Don't Let Me Pass",
for example, in the 1990 collection *Friend of My Youth*
opens with a Canadian woman in a chilly hotel room
making notes about William Wallace, Walter Scott, old
graveyards and grey stone buildings. Now, the notes

made by Alice Munro in connection with her investigations into the lives of her antecedents have blossomed into a sequence of pungent episodes concerning the Laidlaws of the Ettrick Valley (Alice Munro was born Alice Laidlaw): a backward place full of bad roads and ancient superstitions. The Laidlaws take shape as farmers, shepherds, heroes of local lore; and then as emigrants, survivors of hard crossings and strange environments.

Mention of the Ettrick Valley immediately focuses attention on the author of the *Confessions of a Justified Sinner*; and sure enough, James Hogg turns up as a figure in Alice Munro's distant background. (His grandfather was her five-times-great-grandfather.) Hogg's writings about his Laidlaw relations find their way into *The View from Castle Rock* – though only as spurs to set the author's imagination going. She has imagined, for example, the voyage from Leith to the New World undertaken in 1818 by old James Laidlaw and members of his family: a voyage rife with the usual shipboard privations, with enlightening encounters and roads not taken – and then the inevitable drift towards gravestones in a cemetery in Esquesing, Halton County, Canada.

The Laidlaws put down roots in Ontario, with scope to exercise their farming skills and Presbyterian severity. They led, on the whole, somewhat bleak, and in some cases eccentric lives. The final story in Part One, "Working for a Living", brings us into the twentieth century with Alice Munro's father Robert Laidlaw, who turned his back on the education to which his abilities entitled him, and opted instead for a life of trapping, care-taking at a local foundry, and eventual turkey-farming.

It is hard, nowadays, to envisage anything more miserable, barbarous and soul-destroying than fur-trapping or fox-farming; but at the time, the terrible occupation retained connotations of R.M. Ballantyne's novel *The Young Fur-Trappers*, the romance of the great outdoors and the pioneering spirit – a spirit woefully subdued in some descendants of the Laidlaw clan. "To think what their ancestors did," Robert Laidlaw muses. "The nerve it took, to pick up and cross the ocean. What was it quashed their spirits? So soon."

Fortunately, they weren't all quashed. The second part of the book contains six more-or-less autobiographical pieces, stretching from the author's doughty childhood to her present, seasoned incarnation in her seventies. These are all vigorous, engaging and resonant stories, and deeply attuned – as ever – to the life of rural Ontario. Alice Munro is celebrated for her wayward mode of perception, which comes out both in the way her stories are constructed, and in her faintly sardonic and compelling appraisals of the customs of the day.

You find a lot of upright stoical women in these pages, some wearing homemade dresses patterned with tiny flowers, along with men whose oddity or awfulness can reach heroic proportions ("If somebody told me that he was drowning in the river I would go and stand on the bank and cheer," one daughter says of her bullying father). All of them fit in to the fullest degree with the roles assigned to them. There are several outstanding stories in this great collection – "Lying Under the Apple Tree", for example, which gets an ambiguity into its title (it turns on an instance of sexual duplicity); and the title story, "The View from Castle Rock".

One day, some time around the turn of the nineteenth century, a Laidlaw patriarch leads his young son Andrew, along with a bunch of drinking companions fresh from the pub, up to the top of Castle Rock in Edinburgh. From this vantage point, a strip of coastline is visible in the distance. It is actually Fife, but he tells them they are looking at a portion of America.

It's unclear whether he truly believes this piece of nonsense, or is having them on. But what he is doing is akin to what the fiction writer does herself: magnifying reality, wilfully tampering with the facts to create a vivid impression.

Independent, 2006

SHINY FAMILIAR THINGS

Penelope Lively, *A House Unlocked*

The Hardy epigraph to Penelope Lively's children's
classic of 1974, *The House in Norham Gardens*, points
up a continual theme and preoccupation of this author.
"I see the hands of the generations", Hardy wrote (in
the poem "Old Furniture"), "That owned each shiny
familiar thing." Getting to grips with the passing of
time, and patterns of continuity, are bound up in the
most striking way with Penelope Lively's entire literary
impulse, whether she's writing for children or adults,
fiction or non-fiction. Now, following on from *Olean-
der, Jacaranda* – her engaging memoir concerning an
English upbringing in Cairo – comes *A House Unlocked*,
the house in question being Golsoncott in Somerset
(fictionalised as Medleycott in the novel *Going Back*),
which her grandparents had bought in 1923, and where
she came to live as an observant and faintly bemused
12-year-old in 1945.

Not an ancient house – it was built around 1908, in the style of Lutyens – Golsoncott is presented here as a kind of "signifier of the century", responding in its own way to social change and convulsion, secretly recording the things that impinge on it. Not all of these were expected. What, for instance, has sedate, upper-middle-class Golsoncott to do with the Russian Revolution, or with nit-infested urchins from London's East End?

As far as the latter are concerned – it was simply that the house became a billet for wartime evacuees, providing sanctuary for a group of city children who were given the run of the garden and had Beatrix Potter read to them after tea. Six of these children subsequently got worked into a sampler created in 1946 by Penelope Lively's needlewoman grandmother, adding a topical touch to an essentially old-fashioned undertaking. The Golsoncott sampler is one of the articles – Hardy's "shiny familiar things" – that carries a whole range of associations and implications, and thereby lends itself to creative deconstruction. Other objects "eerily charged with meaning" include a grand piano, along with such bewildering items of equipment as a knife rest and a pair of grape scissors. The emphasis falling on some significant heirlooms – "the Hall Chest, the Photograph Albums and the Picnic Rug" – gives a shape to the book, and enables the author to launch into a disquisition on domestic arrangements (say), on the redundant church building and its present uses, on gardening enthusiasm or on the British community in pre-Revolutionary Moscow. But it is, inevitably, the great, inexorable changes of the twentieth century that underpin the story of Golsoncott, with its ramifications, as social and family history converge. By the mid-century, for example, the unspoken social revolution had advanced sufficiently to allow "a girl from the southern gentry" to meet and marry a working-class boy, Jack Lively, from Newcastle-upon-Tyne.

The meeting-ground of this unlikely pair was Oxford, where "the clear blue air of higher education" had detached them, productively, from "the assumptions and expectations" of their respective backgrounds. But the backgrounds remain, to be scrutinised and analysed; and with them Golsoncott, like the house in Norham Gardens, "packed with events and experiences and conversations", reverberating back through all the years of the century. Always subtle and illuminating, *A House Unlocked* provides a further outlet for that highly developed "sense of relevance and connections" which informs all of Penelope Lively's work, and makes it so invaluable and intriguing.

The Irish Times, 2001

A TALE FASHIONED
FROM STURDY STRANDS

A.S. Byatt, *The Children's Book*

In the early months of 1903, the writer E. Nesbit visited
the British Museum in search of inspiration for her
next children's book. While she was there, she talked
at length to E. Wallis Budge, the Keeper of Assyrian
and Egyptian antiquities, and as a result *The Story of
the Amulet* was published in 1906 and dedicated to Dr.
Wallis Budge. *The Children's Book*, A.S. Byatt's compelling new novel, takes the British Museum visit as its
starting point, but relocates it to the South Kensington
Museum – not yet the V.&A. – moves it back some
years to 1895, and creates a distinctive character, Olive
Wellwood, to fit the Nesbit role. This is typical of the
way – the fascinating way – *The Children's Book* keeps
homing in on aspects of Nesbit's biography and then
sheering away from them into a densely imagined,
wholly fictional realm.

The novel opens in the South Kensington Museum. Two boys, not yet friends, are regarding with interest and a bit of self-righteousness the activities of a third, who appears to have entered the museum illicitly, and sits sketching gold and silver treasures in a glass case. The first boy is Tom, Olive Wellwood's son, the second is Julian, son of Major Prosper Cain, Special Keeper of Precious Metals, whom Olive is consulting in connection with her current researches, and the third, ragged boy is Philip Warren, a runaway from Burslem and potential potter of genius. Philip is the element in the novel that approximates most closely to a Nesbit plot, rather than to E. Nesbit's life. Just as a kind lady takes in Dickie from Deptford in *Harding's Luck* (1909) – or in the spirit of David Copperfield's arrival at Betsy Trotwood's, as A.S. Byatt has it – Philip is swept off by Olive Wellwood towards the sanctuary of her home, where a proper meal, clean clothes and a bath effect the beginnings of a transformation in the youthful vagrant.

The home to which Philip is transported is an old Kentish farmhouse named Todefright, tastefully modernised in an Arts and Crafts style. Like Nesbit's actual Well Hall, Todefright accommodates a houseful of adults and children whose relations with one another are not quite as straightforward as they seem. And A.S. Byatt has devised some additional complications to augment the original Well Hall set-up, the *ménage a trois* consisting of Nesbit, her husband Hubert Bland, and a friend named Alice Hoatson. (Their counterparts in the book are Olive, her non-monogamous husband Humphrey Wellwood, and her sister Violet.)

"Nothing was what it seemed", thinks one of Olive's daughters, Dorothy, at a critical moment in the narrative, sparking off an *Alice-Through-the-Looking-Glass* reflection as Byatt's recurring children's-book motif comes into play once more. Not only Alice, on the other side of the mirror or underground, but Lost Boys (and girls – e.g. Perdita), "aproned hedgehog-women" à la Beatrix Potter, Borrowers, Seekers, Mother Goose, Toad Hall and all add a decorative element to this long, clear-sighted, complex and evocative work of fiction. E. Nesbit herself is mentioned on page 398.

The Children's Book, though, is far from being a children's book. Beyond the playfulness, the idyllic midsummer gatherings of friends and relations, the masques and balls and little tree houses, the avant-garde arrangements, the impulses to do good to society and to individuals – beyond all these lurk darker issues, pervasive and often unspoken. War and poverty, the exploitation of workers, feminist disaffection, irresponsible seductions, all kinds of child abuse. Enchantment and wonder, yes, but also a flicker of an ambiance of *What Maisie Knew*; the best of times but also *Hard Times*.

A.S. Byatt has always been drawn to the novel of ideas, to a nineteenth-century expansiveness and formality, but filtered through a sensibility distinctly of the present; and in *The Children's Book* she marshals an impressive cast of characters and follows their interlocking stories with style and astuteness. At the same time, she gets to grips with plentiful anxieties and confusions of the age, with burgeoning ideologies such as Fabianism, Anarchism, Suffragism, women's education, with the Edwardian enthusiasm for varieties of antique Englishness and nostalgia for a Never Never Land.

With its vivid topical detail, its mingling of history and fiction, fantasy and documentation, allegory and actuality, biography and invention, allusion and innovation, *The Children's Book* is strenuously inclusive and tremendously enriching – an intricate tale, energetically fashioned from sturdy strands of material by "a spinning fairy in the attic", an indefatigable storyteller, which is never less than the real thing.

The Irish Times, 2009

A WORLD AWAY
FROM THE WAR

Owen Dudley Edwards,
British Children's Fiction in the Second World War

This is a remarkable book. It is cogent, intriguing and illuminating. It assesses the literary value of certain prominent children's authors – with some surprising parallels drawn and conclusions reached – and applauds unexalted juvenile fiction as an incomparable resource of children in wartime. "... One of the clearest images through the early months of the Second World War is the child sheltering behind its comic", the author notes. "Comics" are one thing, and they receive due attention in these pages – but the main drift of the book is to do right by popular authors in the genre, including Blyton, Brent-Dyer, Captain W.E. Johns, Richmal Crompton and so forth, whose achievements are substantially and sympathetically appraised. Owen Dudley Edwards politely challenges various kinds of received opinion, and his book should encourage misguided grown-ups to take a second look at fictional old favourites, before succumbing to condescension.

British Children's Fiction in the Second World War is, indeed, very far in spirit from an Arthur Marshall type of levity (though that has its pleasures too). The author has immersed himself in all manner of morale-boosting, spy-catching and squadron-leading works, and comes up with his gravity fairly unimpaired. He only gives way to a tongue-in-cheek impulse on page 684, when he cites A.J.P. Taylor's *Essays in English History* as a means of relaxing the mind "when self-exhausted by wrestling with textual problems of Enid Blyton and her fellow-sources". Well, by this stage, with all his chosen writers reinstated, placed in a historical context and given their due, he's entitled to a tiny frivolity.

Not that his book is without a high entertainment quotient throughout: his doughty and persuasive manner makes for lively reading. What he shows, above all, is that children's literature can be taken as childish, or quite the opposite ("Blyton produced ... a serious sociological reflection on Britain at the war's end: *The Put-Em-Rights*"); and he endorses what some of us have held to be true all along – that an appreciation of juvenile fiction isn't incompatible with an interest in the classics (say). Or, to put it another way, you can commend George Orwell *and* Frank Richards: even if, following the famous exchange between the two (Orwell's 1940 article on "Boys' Weeklies" in *Horizon*, and Richards's riposte), you come down on the side of the Bunter author.

Actually, Owen Dudley Edwards is very nearly unprecedented (but right) in singling out Frank Richards's "elegant ironies and classical comedies'" and in deploring the elevation of Billy Bunter, somewhat at the expense of the other Greyfriars characters, in the post-war books. (The cartoon Bunter in *Knockout*, nothing to do with Frank Richards, he rightly relegates to the trash can.)

Writing against the grain of conventionally limiting judgements, Dudley Edwards attributes a satirical purpose to the Greyfriars author, and praises the wartime feminist advancement of W.E. Johns (citing early titles in his "Worrals" series). Quoting Eileen Colwell's celebrated comment on Enid Blyton's *The Sea of Adventure* – "But what hope has a band of desperate men against four children?" (actually more wry than reproving) – he judges it to be both spot-on, and wide of the mark. Blyton, he says, was still – in 1948 – composing her fictions with Second World War presumptions in mind, "and a Britain in arms against Nazis at the height of their power had to believe the apparently absurd dream".

All this is interesting and stimulating. But the

most ingenious Dudley Edwards reappraisal concerns Malcolm Saville's novel for children, *Seven White Gates*. The wartime implications he reads into this novel are really striking. Black-bearded Uncle Micah personifies the UK, his estranged son Charles represents the US, "the unknown quarrel is the American Revolution, the injury during the process of return is Pearl Harbor ...". And it doesn't stop there. Even the perilous cable-car ride depicted on the dust-jacket, and Saville's plucky nine-year-old twins in the story, Mary and Dickie, have a place in Dudley Edwards's retrieved topical symbolism. Whether you go along with this or not – and whether it happened subconsciously on Malcolm Saville's part or not – this particular reading of the novel makes an impact.

The war was naturally at the forefront of everyone's consciousness, but some writers excluded it from their fiction altogether, or kept it firmly in the background, proffering stability, normality or fantasy instead, as a form of protection for children already distraught or dislocated by the effects of enemy action. Others, with considerable gusto, threw themselves, and their readers, into the war effort – the incomparable Richmal Crompton, for example, who, via William Brown, makes as merry a business of its exigencies as possible (though not without a sombre undertone or two, as Dudley Edwards reminds us).

It was a good time for adventures and excitements of all kinds. Evacuees and refugees, spies and double agents and airmen, and bombs and upheaval, and mysterious signals flashing in the middle of the night ... The war was, in some ways, a gift to those prepared to make the most of it. And *British Children's Fiction in the Second World War* provides the last word on all of them. It is a large book (a pity that its cost – £150.00 – will put it out of the range of many would-be buyers), and covers every conceivable topic from air operations to egalitarianism.

The present-day perspective enables Owen Dudley Edwards to consider, among other things, the question of how innocent or otherwise certain children's authors were, in relation to such matters as implied homosexuality, sleeping arrangements, quasi-erotic situations and so forth (he's alive to the humour in all of these). Certainly, a number of Blyton titles – *Mr Pinkwhistle Interferes*, the eponymous Mr Meddle and Mr Twiddle – might raise an eyebrow or two today. A poised and rational commentator such as Dudley Edwards can't help investigating byways such as these. He doesn't, however, go out of his way to apply contemporary strictures to works from a different era. He writes with the deepest understanding of children's literature and its vast contribution to the sum of human happiness. His book is a serious and scholarly undertaking, triumphantly carried out. I have nothing but admiration for it. But I can't resist tampering, for a moment, with Owen Dudley Edwards's authoritative tone, by bringing to mind an image of the renowned historian and man of letters poring over the antics of Desperate Dan, or getting to grips with the Chalet School old-girl network and the intricacies of Elinor Brent-Dyer's second-generation pupils' family connections.

The Irish Times, 2007

IN THE CHAMBER
OF SECRETS

Victor Watson (ed.),
The Cambridge Guide to Children's Books in English
Richard Abanes,
Harry Potter and the Bible:
The Menace Behind the Magick

The Cambridge Guide to Children's Books in English is
a vast and valiant undertaking. Victor Watson has
assembled an enormous team of contributors, many
of them academics from places as far apart as Cambridge itself and the University of Tasmania, whose
task is to assess the entire range of writing for children,
from Mother Goose to Michael Morpurgo. The *Guide*
is arranged alphabetically, and covers authors from
Aardema to Zwerger, outstanding titles, predominant
genres ("Camping and Tramping"; "Historical Fiction"),
major themes ("War Stories"; "Pony Stories"), and

even practicalities of book production ("Endpapers"; "Crosshatching"). Most of the entries are animated and efficient, a few seem unduly perfunctory, and one or two are positively buoyant: "a rag-and-bone man and his horse, Lightning, a scrap-heap dinosaur and a rampant, rearing lion ... make a visible-audible metaphor for a thunderstorm."

Metaphors aside, the concerns of children's literature have expanded in all directions in the last 30-odd years: upwards, into realms of elaborate and strongly realised fantasy; inwards, into all kinds of psychological defects and traumas; backwards, into the increasingly enticing mysteries of history. Indeed, the field has never been so rich — what with all the old imperishables, Bastables, Bunter, Ballet Shoes etc., available to new enthusiasts, and the ever more unflinching approach to social questions which contemporary taste demands.

Novels in the latter mode are mostly intended for older readers, and treat such topics as terminal illness, violence, disability and sexual abuse. But even some authors of books for five- and six-year-olds are now in the business of devising newer and newer varieties of anthropomorphic antics (*The Hare and His Disco Dance*), or confronting issues such as homosexuality (*Jenny Lives with Eric and Martin*).

No troublesome reality, it seems, is beyond the grasp of today's urbane young readers — as long as the tone is right. Keep the narrative encouraging and you can get away with anything, right down to alarming facts of life undreamt of in the world of Milly-Molly-Mandy or Rupert Bear.

All this is splendid, no doubt, though possibly one would wish to draw the line at some of the less engaging aspects of infancy, such as that suggested by the title of a 1986 picture book, "I Want My Potty". And it is slightly lowering to the spirits to contemplate all those "sensitive portraits of children living in present-day, urban, underclass neighbourhoods" – hundreds and hundreds of them, all deprived or depraved to varying degrees. But in the middle of all the grit and privation, up pops "a near-omnipotent millionaire elephant in a purple dressing-gown" to restore frivolity. Frivolity, gravity, intrepidity, unimpeachability: you can't complain about the variety of entertainment aimed at under-age readers these days.

Some surprising motifs are identified by the *Cambridge Guide* – "Nudity in Children's Books" is one example, though the drift of this is to show how the subject was more or less evaded before the 1970s, with even Tom in *The Water-Babes* getting himself covered in fish scales in the interests of modesty. Nudity leads on to "Sex", which is followed by "Sexton Blake" to make an intriguing juxtaposition.

Sex in teenage novels, again, only became a reality

in the 1970s, starting with Alan Garner's *Red Shift* – though the activity is tackled so obliquely here that you have to read between the lines – and continuing with Judy Blume's unsuggestive, brisk *Forever*, which reads like a handbook to defloration. As for Sexton Blake; he is one of those old-fashioned, upright, tremendous heroes, about whom commentators are often undecided whether to take a snooty tone, or consign to sociology.

The Cambridge Guide, on the whole, considers such figments of popular literature a bit beneath its dignity. It can't keep them or their creators out, but tends to give them rather short shrift, as in the case of Charles Hamilton ("Frank Richards"), who merits considerably less space than the American Virginia Hamilton. However, this latest guide to a fascinating branch of literature adds up to a treasure trove of appreciation and information. It contains, among other things, a good section on "Neglected Works", which goes some way towards reinstating such overlooked authors as Kitty Barne and Elinor Lyon. There are others, though, including the wonderful Katharine Tozer, creator and illustrator of the elephant Mumfie, and a couple of distinctive novelists of the 1970s, Geraldine Symons and Nina Beachcroft, who are now so neglected that they have vanished altogether ("For the Snark was a Boojum, you see").

In recent years, historians and critics out to identify some disgraceful tendency or other in writing for
children – mostly from the past – have had a field day.
This or that work, they thunder, will retard children's
mental development (Enid Blyton), foster all kinds of
prejudices (racial for Helen Bannerman; class for Eve
Garnett), or sanction the persecution of the obese (as
with Frank Richards's Billy Bunter).

There is, sometimes, some sense in this (though not
with regard to any of the above). No one in their right
mind, for example, could possibly excuse the Edwardian
author Kenneth Grahame's incessant sneering at "the
female sex ... and the reasons (speaking broadly) for
regarding it as dirt". But the practice can very easily
get out of hand. There are those, for instance, who
would censure the creator of Long John Silver for not
promoting a more positive image of the disabled (as
we learn from the section on "Bias" in *The Cambridge
Guide*).

The impulse to censor children's reading is not
new. It goes back to the aptly-named anti-fantasist Mrs
Trimmer, and beyond. At one point you even find Oliver
Goldsmith offering to bring "Dick Whittington" into
line with the eighteenth-century policy on storytelling
by cutting out the cat.

And still it continues. In Northern Ireland, where
I live, a toy shop manager has refused to stock Harry

Potter merchandise on the grounds that the J.K. Rowling series upholds "witchcraft and wizardry"; a local newspaper published a photograph of Harry Potter paperbacks set alight. Presbyterian fundamentalism, initiator of the campaign to "Save Ulster from Sodomy", is now going all out to save Ulster from sorcery.

There are other places where this ludicrous and disagreeable anti-Potter misapprehension has taken hold, among them Southern California. Here Richard Abanes, author of *Harry Potter and the Bible*, has worked, we're told, as a "minister/teacher, worship leader and Director of Creative Arts". Abanes's dismal study misses all the inventiveness, exuberance, *joie de vivre* and right thinking of the glorious Harry Potter books, and scrutinises them instead for evidence of a satanic subtext.

Abanes, the deluded author, goes so far as to suggest that "an unseen spiritual force of darkness" is a factor in the books' unprecedented impact. To respond to this in a proper spirit it's necessary to borrow the words of the magical nanny Mary Poppins who told Mr Twigley, "Ridiculous – that's what I call it!"

Independent Weekend Review, 2001

CHALLENGE, CHANGE
AND A CHORUS OF
DISAPPROVAL

Carol Dyhouse, *Girl Trouble:*
Panic and Progress in the History of Young Women

"Waves of anxiety, horror stories and panic ... have accompanied social change affecting women from Victorian times", claims Carol Dyhouse towards the end of her spirited analysis of attitudes towards young women over a period of roughly 120 years. (Young Englishwomen, that is: the special case of Ireland, with its additional burdens of religion and nationalism, is outside the scope of this study.) Girls en masse have constantly found themselves the focus of a lot of attention and apprehension as restrictions in one sphere after another were challenged, overthrown, and in some instances reinstated, albeit in a different form.

Trouble is the word, and it's considered here in all its varieties: asking for it, getting into it, being beset by it, stirring it up or trying to evade it. Trouble and social conditioning are intertwined, as new ideas surface, rebellion against old-style expectations breaks out and rearguard action is initiated in defence of the *status quo*. From about the 1880s onwards, "modern" girls outraged hidebound beholders by gadding about on bicycles, by appearing at Suffragette demonstrations, by driving ambulances, by affecting short skirts and cigarette holders, by going in for jazz and cocktails, by looking to Hollywood and the film industry as a source of inspiration in daily life, by gaining degrees from universities, by cocking a snook at supposed "womanly feeling and propriety". Some young women at any rate – those most strongly endowed with gumption, you might say – shocked society by engaging in all of the above or similar acts of defiance. The purpose of *Girl Trouble*, however, is not so much to single out the reasonable rebels against absurd social prescriptions, but to take the whole female population between the ages of 12 and 25 (say) and examine the ways in which it was held to constitute a social problem at different times.

There is plenty of contemporary material to draw on. Key accounts, such as Vera Brittain's *Testament of Youth*, let us know, for example, what clever Edwardian girls were up against. New women, revolting daughters, sweet (or not so sweet) girl graduates, wayward girls, athletic girls, delinquent girls, "poor girls weak in mind and character": all these were subjected, at one time or another, to approval, ridicule or abomination on the part of their elders, advocates or adversaries.

The whole thing started early. Once girls had ceased to sit acquiescently at home glueing seashells to boxes or crocheting pillow lace, the way was open for dire patriarchal predictions and gloomy forecasts about the future of the nation. If it wasn't the White Slave Trade getting a boost from girls on the loose – or loose girls – it was gynaecological deficiencies arising from too much reading. Conservative voices from every quarter joined in the dismal chorus of recrimination. A spate of terrible anti-feminist works of fiction appeared on the market, culminating in A.S.M. Hutchinson's *This Freedom* of 1922 which is surely a candidate for the worst novel of all time. As late as 1948, the educational writer John Newsom put forward a revised curriculum for girls' schools with cooking and housewifery at its centre. And, writes Dyhouse, such backward-looking strategies had an impact. Enter the *Woman's Home Journal*, frilly-petticoat-friendly 1950s.

Throughout the period covered by *Girl Trouble*, you find recurring chicken-and-egg situations. Was pioneering feminism a product of social change, or did social change result from feminism? Were girls unsettled by widening opportunities, or did widening opportunities derive from female perceptions of existing inequalities? Other questions exercised the minds of fearful prognosticators. Was it true that too much learning would rot the female brain? Where does sexual vulnerability end and sexual emancipation begin? Actually, critics of feminist advancement could never decide whether intensive education made girls undersexed or oversexed, or which was worse. What seems indisputable is that girls and their behaviour have always spread alarm among conservatives of an older generation, and that girls were in a special category as far as signs of the (declining) times were concerned.

By the 1970s – following on from the anarchic, up-for-it '60s decade, with its emphasis on hedonism and youth – "profound shifts in culture, language and social expectation" had occurred, spurred on by the new women's liberation movement and other forms of social agitation. As Dyhouse puts it, "strong girls were in fashion". Feisty girl heroines had begun to crop up frequently on cinema and television screens, she goes on, but she doesn't mention books, in particular girls' books, in which active and resilient heroines had always loomed large and worked a tremendous effect on juvenile readers – books enshrining a whole string of strong girls from Kate Crackernuts to Dido Twite, via Evadne Price's Jane Turpin.

Aside from this missing strand, though, *Girl Trouble* presents a well-nigh comprehensive, and timely, overview of change and challenge relating to the position of women in English society, coming right up to the present day and arriving at a cautiously optimistic conclusion: the outlook is favourable on the whole, despite "the ever-present possibilities of backlash, reaction and new oppressive forces".

If it's not entirely an original undertaking – many others have tackled the overthrow of female underdog status, from a variety of angles – *Girl Trouble* is uniquely succinct, informative and entertaining. On the question of what constitutes a feminist, for example, Dyhouse quotes Rebecca West's celebrated observation of 1913: "People call me a feminist whenever I express sentiments that differentiate me from a doormat." Fortunately, whatever setbacks should occur in the future, no one can doubt that the female doormat, long ago, went the way of the dodo.

The Irish Times, 2013

FIDDLESTICKS!

UNCLE MAX

Anthony Masters, *The Man Who Was M:*
The Life of Maxwell Knight
Nigel West, *Unreliable Witness:*
Espionage Myths of the Second World War
Nicholas Bethell, *The Great Betrayal:*
The Untold Story of Kim Philby's Biggest Coup

Like most biographers, Anthony Masters starts by
announcing his subject's date of birth. Unlike most
biographers, he gets it wrong. Charles Henry Maxwell
Knight was born on 9 July 1900, not 4 September, under
the sign of Cancer, not Virgo, however tempting it
may be, for reasons which become clear in the course
of the story, to assign him to the latter. Information
about Maxwell Knight is pretty scanty and unreliable
at most stages of his life, but a copy of his birth cer-
tificate may be obtained from the usual source, and

was surely worth looking at. It is also more precise about Knight's place of birth than Masters has chosen to be, specifying 199 Selhurst Road, South Norwood, Croydon, while he leaves it vaguely at Mitcham, Surrey.

Who was Maxwell Knight? Colleagues from MI5 still refer to him as a gifted and formidable intelligence officer, indefatigable in his efforts to suppress subversion on home ground, honourable, enigmatic, and addicted to intrigue. There is evidence to suggest that he contributed more than an initial to the "M" figure in the James Bond books: hence Masters' title. "M", true enough, was the office sobriquet of Maxwell Knight, though not his only extra appellation. His work made it necessary for him to have a pseudonym or two at his disposal – and so we find "Captain King" issuing instructions to his agents and arranging assignations in dubious hotels.

Masters resorts to speculation whenever the facts cannot be ascertained, showing, for example, an impossible familiarity with his subject's state of mind at fourteen. This was Knight's age when he enrolled as a cadet on the training-ship Worcester; no doubt he "entered this new world … with considerable trepidation", as Masters assures us more than once – still, we should like to know how he knows. It's the same when he comes to comment on Knight's unconsummated marriages: we find a succession of wives, and at least one would-be mistress, "living in hope" that ordinary sexual relations may eventually take place. Two wives, I suppose, were available to corroborate Masters's statement to this effect, but not the first, poor Gwladys Knight, who swallowed a quantity of barbiturates at the Overseas Club in 1935. "Tall, attractive and auburn-haired … with a passion for hunting and dogs", Gwladys Knight, in this account, seems to have strayed from the pages of *Woman's Home Journal*, rather than being a candidate for breakdown and suicide. Her achievement here is to inspire the most jejune pronouncement in the book, when Masters informs us that her marriage "was … one in name only".

A rather meagre tribute to Gwladys has been extracted by Masters from a one-time guest at the Exmoor pub once owned by Knight and his tall, auburn-haired wife: this forthcoming person "admired her enormously for her … determination to see that her guests had fun, apart from good food and good beds …". Masters does his best with Gwladys but she remains unreclaimable, existing merely as a detail in the disquieting persona being built up by Knight. Up until the outbreak of the Second World War, Knight was busy acquiring the notable background that gave him a certain *éclat* in intelligence circles. After leaving HMS Worcester in 1917, he spent the following year as a midshipman with the Royal Navy Reserve. He paid a visit to New York and was enchanted by it; he developed an enthusiasm for American jazz, returned to Putney and a spot of teaching, turned himself into an accomplished amateur naturalist, keeping grass snakes in the bath and parrots in the kitchen, and proved adroit enough to engage in exacting social activities on a rather poor income.

Recruitment to the Security Service came in 1924, after a happy meeting, at a dinner party, between Knight and its then Director-General Sir Vernon Kell – an event lushly described by Masters as having "opened a door into a completely new world for the restless and unfulfilled" prep schoolmaster. Marriage followed, causing further unfulfillment; the country pub was bought and run by Gwladys, with Knight putting in an appearance at weekends. (His appearances and disappearances caused some local people to take him for a werewolf, a detail not remarked by Masters.) He spent a lot of time on Exmoor instructing people in the techniques of fishing and lizard hunting. Less sportingly, he used to go on salmon-poaching expeditions (we learn from the biography), stuffing the fishy booty down his trousers. One way and another – what with dead fish, live insects and the nest of adder eggs he once hatched in a pyjama pocket – Knight seems to have considered his person a fit habitat for certain unlikeable animal species.

It all helped to gain him a reputation for eccentricity. This was certainly an asset in the devious world of MI5, where a lot depends on your ability to keep things dark, to impress your associates, and to spring surprises. It wasn't hard for Knight, with his unexpected areas of expertise – the occult was another of them – to get himself regarded favourably in the department. (His unorthodoxy eventually began to get up the noses of those in authority, but that was later.) A talent for the mechanics of counter-subversion was an asset too, even if it included a slightly romantic, mystifying tendency. Masters is surely right to stress his subject's affinity – especially in his own view – with the typical Buchan hero. There was always something rather dashing, in an old-fashioned way, in Knight's approach to security matters.

He practised an especial vigilance in the matter of Communist agitation. Reds, Jews and homosexuals were three groups towards whom Knight harboured a fair amount of hostility, though he was always willing to suspend his prejudice against the last two in individual cases. His stand against Communism brought about his first major success, and shows how patience is one of the qualities necessary in intelligence work. In 1930, Knight had picked out and trained an agent, Olga Grey, got her to become a Communist Party worker and ingratiate herself with certain Soviet sympathisers.

All went to plan, over the next eight years, with Olga Grey – a lapse or two apart – throwing herself willingly into the infiltrator's stressful role. As a result of her activities, a London spy ring was wound up. This business, highly gratifying for Knight, was labelled "The Woolwich Arsenal Case".

At the outbreak of war, Knight was running his own department within the "B" (counter-espionage) division of MI5: B5(b). He had married a second wife, Lois, whom he met in an Aldermaston pub and wooed according to his own peculiar ideas on the subject (he taught her to fish). Like her predecessor Gwladys, Lois, as Knight's wife, found herself taking second place to some rum creatures, including a bushbaby and a piping bullfinch. Masters tells us that one of her husband's pets, an Amazon parrot, took a personal dislike to Lois. It wasn't much of a life – despised by a parrot, kept sitting in the dark each evening while the animals slept, and married in name only. But better things were in store for Lois, who left London in 1940 to take up a post as secretary to the Chief Constable of Oxfordshire. The marriage between her and Knight was eventually annulled.

Masters's method as a biographer is somewhat odd. Instead of amassing all the available information and turning it into a coherent narrative, he tends to offer transcriptions, more or less verbatim, you feel, of all the tape-recorded interviews he was lucky enough to secure. You could call it the butcher-baker-candle-stick-maker method, with many peripheral figures – such as the Exmoor figure who remembered Gwladys affectionately – being brought in to deliver their comment, and then exiting from the story. It's a piecemeal way of going about things, and often digressive. The author is also at a loss to know exactly how much reliance to place on some of the testimonies he's got hold of: amnesia, ill-will or some less readily definable emotion may be a factor in any of them. He says as much, when he cautions the reader that the allegations of someone or other have to be seen in such-and-such a light. However, there are occasions when he displays altogether too much gullibility. More than once he accepts a particular version of events as the true one, when in fact it is nothing of the sort. Adequate checking and double-checking have not always been carried out. The chapter entitled "War: Joan Miller and Tyler Kent" illustrates the point. Joan Miller was a redoubtable young woman who found her way into the transport section of MI5 in September 1939, and attracted Knight's attention almost at once. It wasn't long before he had her transferred to the more glamorous "B" division.

Here I must declare an interest. In 1982, I was commissioned by Weidenfeld to "ghost" the memoirs of

Joan Miller; the book was duly completed and scheduled for publication in August of this year [1984], when the Government suddenly stepped in and banned it. [It was published under the title *One Girl's War* by Brandon Books in 1986.] By signing the Official Secrets Act in 1939, Joan Miller had effectively debarred herself from publishing her recollections of MI5 at any future date. Her book, which covers the war years, deals at some length with the period she spent as Maxwell Knight's colleague and ostensible mistress. It was not an easy alliance. She was captivated by Knight but also occasionally alarmed by his behaviour. He lavished attention on her, but also did some unaccountable things. He gave her a Himalayan monkey with a strong aversion to women.

At the time he met her, Knight was keeping an eye on a crypto-Fascist, anti-Semitic organisation known as the Right Club. It held its meetings on the first floor of a South Kensington restaurant called the Russian Tea Rooms. Among its luminaries was Anna Wolkoff, daughter of the tea rooms' expatriate proprietors. She and her fellow members were pledged to obstruct the war effort. Among other things, they used to go about in the black-out attaching "sticky back" notices to lamp-posts, telephone kiosks and so on. The notices informed passers-by that the war was a Jews' war. Parties of illicit bill-stickers would emerge in pairs from

Anna Wolkoff's flat, all of them *au fait* with the standard strategies for lessening the likelihood of arrest.

Knight had two agents on the spot, and through them he learnt that the Right Club was on the look-out for a War Office recruit. Joan Miller, he decided, would fit the bill. She was packed off to South Kensington with instructions to deliver herself audibly of Fascist views. "From then on," Masters writes, "she was invited to join the ... Right Club." (Why "from then on"? She was invited once and accepted, justifying Maxwell Knight's faith in her acting ability.) She didn't, contrary to what Masters says, become "involved in Anna's lampooning of news reels and fly-posting campaigns" – for the simple reason that the Right Club declined to expose its valuable War Office member to the risk of imprisonment.

A faulty version of what followed has become current, partly as a consequence of an interview given by Joan Miller to *The Sunday Times* journalist Barry Penrose (18 October 1981). Masters, sticking closely to the information contained in this piece, gives an unfair degree of credit to Joan Miller, while completely ignoring the contribution of another of Knight's agents, a Belgian girl named Helene de Monck. I don't think it was self-aggrandisement that led Joan Miller to place herself exclusively at the forefront of the action, but plain misrecollection after 40-odd years. When she read *The Sunday Times* article, she admitted that certain things were wrong; characteristically, she held the author of the piece to blame.

It was Helene de Monck, not Joan Miller, who ingeniously pretended to have access to the Rumanian diplomatic bag at a moment when Anna Wolkoff was eager to get off a communication to William Joyce (Lord Haw-Haw) at the Rundfunkhaus, Berlin. (Wolkoff's usual mailing route, via the Italian Embassy, was temporarily unavailable to her since her ally at the Embassy had become unwell.) A stratagem was thereby set in motion, with Wolkoff, whom Knight now suspected of rather more than run-of-the-mill subversion, as its object. And not only Wolkoff: a code and cipher clerk at the American Embassy named Tyler Kent came into the business too. MI5 was in possession of evidence suggesting that a highly confidential correspondence between Churchill and Roosevelt had fallen into the hands of the German Ambassador at Rome. It later emerged that a quantity of purloined telegrams, helpfully decoded, had reached Anna Wolkoff by way of Kent, and thence were dispatched in the Italian bag.

Joan Miller had a hand in the stopping of all this, but it wasn't as crucial a hand as certain recent commentators have suggested. Masters might have gained a clearer idea of what went on from a close reading of the Kent and Wolkoff chapters in the Earl Jowett's book

Some Were Spies (published in 1954, and not listed in Masters's bibliography, though he refers to it once in the text). Jowitt recounts the anti-Right Club activities of two MI5 agents whom he calls "Miss A" and "Miss B". It's only necessary to consult a typescript of the Tyler Kent trial to identify this pair as Marjorie Mackie and Helene de Monck. Joan Miller doesn't figure at all in this particular account. When Masters comes out with such statements as "Soon Joan discovered that Kent was showing the Churchill / Roosevelt correspondence ... to Wolkoff", and "Joan ... was able to unearth a considerable espionage operation", he is, quite simply, talking through his hat. Also, the entire Kent / Wolkoff conspiracy is more interesting and intricate than he seems to realise.

Masters, not a whale on dates, supplies a wrong one for the Tyler Kent trial, which actually took place *in camera* at the Old Bailey between 23 and 28 October 1940; the date he gives, 20 May, is the date of Kent's arrest. What else do we find? The author confirms that Maxwell Knight and John le Carré were acquainted with one another, but fails to add that le Carré – under his real name, David Cornwell – illustrated a couple of Knight's post-war publications (e.g. *Talking Birds*, 1961): a not uninteresting detail in a story that includes spies and intrigues among its ingredients, just as John le Carré's do. Then, there's an episode involving Joan Miller, later in the war, after her transfer from MI5 to PID (Political Intelligence Department). She hadn't been five minutes in her new job before spotting something dodgy under her nose. A Major Bell, with whom she shared an office, was jotting down the contents of all top-secret cables relating to the Middle East. The next minute Joan was on the blower to Maxwell Knight, and Major Bell was subsequently apprehended outside the PID headquarters, his pockets stuffed with incriminating papers. A link was established between him and the Communist Party of Great Britain.

The incident cries out for the keen investigation it doesn't get here. What was Major Bell's history? Why was his behaviour in the office so indiscreet? How did he escape prosecution? Why do we find him, after VE Day, turning up in Germany in the Control Commission? No explanations are offered by Masters, not even the circumspect surmise that Major Bell may have been treated leniently because his actions were undertaken on behalf of Russia, Britain's ally; at the moment of his arrest, England's survival was still dependent on the military effort of the Russian army. All we get is the barest outline, as Masters misses the opportunity to make a striking story of it. It isn't the only opportunity he misses. However, his work on the Benjamin Greene affair (to take that example) is thoroughly creditable. Greene, a cousin of the novelist, was wrongly arrested and interned in 1940 at the instigation of Knight's agent Harald Kurtz. It was an extraordinary blunder which reflected badly on Knight. His anti-Communist ideology didn't do him much good either at the time. His paper, "The Comintern is not dead", which predicted with great accuracy the developments in Russia's policy with regard to Britain after the war, was dismissed as "over-theoretical" by Roger Hollis, and various other Soviet experts considered it unimpressive.

The question of Knight's possible homosexuality isn't really tackled by Masters either. He neither confirms nor contradicts it. It was first mooted by Joan Miller, who endured Knight's unabated impotence between 1939 and 1943, and later attributed to her own naivety her failure to grasp the score. Was it not perfectly plain for all to see? Knight's abusive attitude to those not fully heterosexual becomes, in this reading, the act of one who protests too much. (Such a view suggests intriguing possibilities with to Knight's other bugbears, Jewishness and Communism: not to Masters, however.) On the other hand, Knight's third wife Susi utterly repudiated the allegation.

The errors contained in this book even extend to the publishers' handout, in which Knight is held to have become a television celebrity in the 1950s: he didn't. He became a radio naturalist who made occasional appearances on television. His new profession required a change of image: the mysterious "M" was turned into a figure of rather different provenance, Uncle Max. In his final chapter, which covers the post-MI5 period, Masters steps up the practice he's followed throughout. Many, many people are quoted, down to the headmistress of a school which once employed Knight's wife. When the author is driven back on his own words, he doesn't always trouble to make them illuminating or cogent. For example, our attention is drawn to the "instinctive bond of trust and understanding" existing between Knight, on the one hand, and children and animals, on the other. Has Masters got Uncle Max mixed up with Uncle Mac?

The MI5 historian "Nigel West" has written a book which aims to separate the actual from the apocryphal in the field of espionage stories. Two small examples from his own previous work illustrate how easily the unfounded assertion can get accepted as fact. First, we have his claim that Maxwell Knight's wife Gwladys "committed suicide after an occult experience with Aleister Crowley". I think Anthony Masters has the right of it here, when he denies any connection between the Knights and Crowley before Gwladys death. Masters, however, unreflectingly repeats a canard of Nigel West's. The German refugee and MI5 agent Harald Kurtz was not "distantly related" to the British royal family, as both authors aver. Both these figments originated with

Joan Miller: the first she'd got from goodness knows where; the second arose from a confusion between Kurtz himself and one of his sponsors when he came to England.

Unreliable Witness, though, on the whole, addresses its subject with shrewdness and animation. It rejects the supposition that Churchill might have rated the value of a code-breaking operation above the value of Coventry. Suspicions attaching to President Roosevelt, over the attack on Pearl Harbor and whether or not it took him altogether by surprise, are likewise cleared away. West has a buttonholing way of presenting his material, as well as a notably fair-minded approach, and his arguments convince. However, just to remind us of the impossibility of keeping small items of misinformation entirely at bay, the historian M.R.D. Foot has pointed out that three of West's five allusions to him contain an error.

The Great Betrayal gets off to a showy start, and continues as a strong tale exhilaratingly told. In the opening pages, an intrepid small group of anti-Stalin saboteurs is in a yacht approaching the coast of Albania. Those not concealed below deck are passing themselves off as innocent holiday-makers. The hidden passengers, dubbed "pixies" by the British (were they all very short?) are Albanian dissidents from the Hoxha regime, on the way to put into practice certain guerrilla tactics recently taught them at a base in Malta. This inspiriting episode, which rivets the attention straight away, was part of an ambitious joint enterprise on the part of the British and Americans, the aim of which was to undo the Communist takeover. Started in 1949, it wasn't relinquished until 1953, in spite of the greatest possible discouragement for its planners. Nearly all the Albanian infiltrators, hastily trained and inadequately equipped, were killed or captured very swiftly. There are many reasons for the failure of the operation, but the one from which the greatest irony can be extracted is the involvement in it of Kim Philby, at the time of its inception the MI6 representative at Washington.

London Review of Books, 1984

NOTIONAL DOUBLES

David Mure, *The Last Temptation*

At the start of David Mure's engrossing novel, the unnamed narrator, whom we may take to be the real-life Intelligence Officer Guy Liddell, experiences his own death as a kind of translation to the other side of the looking-glass. Characters called Alice, the Duchess and the Red King duly appear, the last, as in the original story, snoring his head off and possibly conjuring up the others as figments of his dream. Mure at this point appropriates bits of Lewis Carroll's dialogue, putting Tweedledee's lines in Alice's mouth, and Alice's in his hero's (it's as well to remember that the real-life Alice was also surnamed Liddell). A cliquish joke soon alerts us to the theme of the novel: espionage matters. "You know very well you're not real" (Alice remarks). "'Notional', murmured the Duchess, discreetly."

"There is ... the entirely fictitious double agent, the 'notional' double agent who never exists at all save in the minds or imagination of those who have invented him and those who believe him", J.C. Masterman says in his book *The Double-Cross System* (1972), a work on which David Mure's narrator has been indignantly ruminating, the looking-glass faculty for remembering forwards enabling him to get wind of its appearance (Guy Liddell died in 1958). He is aggrieved because he commissioned the Double-Cross report himself, back in 1945, on the understanding that to publish it would be in breach of the Official Secrets Act. He selected the author (who becomes "Tortoise" in the novel) for reasons not exactly flattering to him, the main one being that he hadn't noticed how Hitler's opponents within the Abwehr had contributed to the success of the cherished "double-cross" system, and therefore could be relied upon to give full credit to the Security Service, laying emphasis on the brilliance of its wartime recruits. It was necessary to get this view expressed in some official document or other, to obscure the suspicion that the Service had acquired a saboteur or two with its intake of accomplished civilians. Burgess, Philby, Maclean and Blunt were all on the spot, in one capacity or another.

Why, in fact, did Burgess and Co. so avidly take up spying, and why did the British Intelligence Service virtually give them *carte blanche* to get on with it? David Mure has set himself the task of accounting for these peculiarities, without going out of his way to discredit anyone. His novel, after its playful opening, settles down to simulate ordinary autobiography: we're not, in fact, being offered a Lewis Carroll parody, but a book which uses certain of Carroll's motifs to make a decorative framework for its serious concerns. The author, for example, attaches names from the Alice adventures to his own cast of characters: the Duchess and his Pig Baby are Burgess and Maclean, the Red Queen is Anthony Blunt, and so on. This device procures the appearance of fiction for what seems like a well-informed interpretation of the facts.

Mure's suppositions are striking. One of his aims is to show how self-effacement and loyalty to your employers can land you in the soup, or at least block your chance of promotion, given that the priorities of governments and intelligence outfits do not stand still. What was indubitably a right action in 1940, for example, can start to look very different once a new climate of opinion has set in. The experiences of the narrator illustrate the point. Born in "a Scotch mist", from which he eventually concludes he never emerged, the fictional Liddell, by the mid-1920s, has moved from the Special Branch where he started after the war (selflessly renouncing his ambition to be a professional cellist), to the "B" or Counter-Espionage Division of MI5, working under Brigadier Harker and Sir Vernon Kell ("Lion" in the novel). He has also, through his association with a girl called Alice — what else? — a student of Higher Mathematics and first president of the Cambridge University Communist Society, gained a certain understanding of the Marxist outlook, which at this point he equates with a sensible desire to reform society in a moderate way.

However, around the same time (October 1924) we have the affair of the Zinoviev letter. The narrator is more or less instructed to vouch for the genuineness of this dramatic communist document; though he knows perfectly well it's a forgery, his duty to the electorate must oblige him to take the opposite standpoint. He's fairly easily persuaded, and a Labour defeat at the polls is duly ensured.

Throughout the 1930s, Mure's narrator is busy consolidating his friendship with a young Cambridge don, the Red Queen, and a couple of undergraduates, the Duchess and the Red Knight (Philby). Two of the three he puts up successfully for membership of his club. Some time after war has broken out, we find the head of "B" Division (a post now occupied by the narrator) merrily allocating intelligence work to his leftist friends, and not only for private reasons; the need to get Russia into the war, he might have argued, surely put Soviet enthusiasts among the most valuable of MI5's recruits. The word "spying" isn't uttered until 1941, when the Driberg incident – the expulsion of this MI5 "mole" from the Communist Party – alerts at least one intelligence officer to the fact that a Soviet agent must be at work within the Security Service. Oddly enough, since it was he – Maxwell Knight (the "White Knight", a colleague of the narrator's and head of the sub-division known as B5(b) – who had Blunt suspended from an Intelligence course at the beginning of the war, this officer doesn't immediately put his finger on the Red Queen.

In fact, a good deal more might have been made of the White Knight's eccentricities, among which was an exorbitant distaste for Soviet Russia, an attitude he stuck to even when it wasn't entirely encouraged from above. Among the papers he kept writing on the topic of communism was one entitled "The Comintern is not Dead"; this was certainly submitted to Guy Liddell, who took its allegations no more seriously than anyone else. The author of this document finally destroyed it in an access of pique at its failure to make a suitable impression. If he'd waited until 1943, when a Soviet massacre of Polish officers came to light, he might have found an audience more receptive to his views.

Mure uses the Katyn massacre to account for the change of heart he attributes to the Red Queen;

according to this version of events, Blunt had repented of his spying by 1944, when he came clean to the narrator, assuring him of his intention to give it up: a promise which he kept. Blunt comes out of this story with his integrity intact. So does the central, Guy Liddell, figure in the book, who never subscribed to the extreme views held by his friends, and always acted to achieve the effect most dear to his employers at any given moment. His character, perhaps, suffers a certain diminution of steadfastness, as one political objective turns into another in looking-glass fashion; but what can he do? He needs to be as flexible as a slithy tove to keep pace with changing Security requirements. First Russia must be handled carefully, then America. After the war comes the Cold War. The conditions prevailing in 1951 make it necessary that Guy Burgess should be tacitly encouraged to scarper along with Maclean – the alternative being a very unwelcome spy trial, complete with disclosures that would certainly annoy the Americans.

The Last Temptation at this point departs from the facts as they are generally known. MI5 historian Nigel West, for example, records that Guy Liddell was "aghast" on 28 May 1951 to learn of the diplomats' departure. "Who warned Burgess?" West asks. "The trail went dead beyond Blunt ...". Mure's narrator refers to an incident in 1955, when Philby was named in the House of Commons as "the so-called Third Man who tipped off the Duchess and Pig Baby that the dogs were after them", and adds: "So far as I know, it was only the Red Queen and I who had rendered this service ..."; for purely patriotic reasons, naturally.

All of which makes fascinating reading. Judicious conjecture enlivens the historical and biographical materials of the story. Even if things didn't happen exactly as David Mure has it, his suppositions should outrage no one's sense of the believable.

Times Literary Supplement, 1984

SECRET SERVICE

Kate Atkinson, *Transcription*

Kate Atkinson is playing games again: this time, war games and games of deception. *Transcription* opens in 1981, with its principal character having been struck by a car while crossing Wigmore Street in central London, and finding herself lying on the pavement with the salient facts of her life running through her head. "What an odd thing existence was." The next minute we are into the story. The year 1981 acts simply as a framing device: it's the past that's important to Atkinson's narrative, the early post-war past (1950) when her protagonist Juliet Armstrong, then aged 28 or 29, is working as a producer of children's radio programmes at the BBC; and the slightly more distant past (1940), when the exigencies of wartime are imposing new ways of living and operating on the entire population.

Some of these ways are more cloak-and-dagger than others. Newly orphaned Juliet has secured employment as a typist with MI5, working from a converted cell in Wormwood Scrubs prison. From this tedious situation she is plucked by the dashing head of an ultra-secret division of the secret service, B5(b). "I need a girl", this person announces without preamble; and Juliet is it. Her new boss is the insouciant and enigmatic Perry Gibbons; and her new job, not very exciting to begin with, is to transcribe conversations overheard by means of a listening device, not always reliable ("'Bugger', Cyril said"), between a group of Fifth Columnists and their supposed leader, who is actually, of course, an agent of MI5. His name is Godfrey Toby – or it is not – and he is adept at dissolving his various identities in a fog of obfuscation (as well as receding, when necessary, into an actual fog: the London pea-souper works effectively here as an aid to apparent dematerialisation).

This is a novel about double-dealing, about honourable and dishonourable forms of duplicity, about multiple impersonations, about lies and secrets and their ultimate consequences. Juliet is soon provided with an alternative identity – Iris Carter-Jenkins is her bogus name – and sent to infiltrate a Fascist organisation known as the Right Club. This club holds its meetings in a flat above a cafe in South Kensington called the Russian Tea Rooms, which is run by an Admiral Wolkoff and his daughter Anna. The young transcriber has been upgraded to a full-blown MI5 agent, and adopts a mettlesome personality to go with her new role. "She had already decided that Iris Carter-Jenkins was a gutsy kind of girl." Gutsy enough to carry a small gun in her handbag, and keep her nerve in the face of imminent unmasking.

There's a touch of high jinks about Juliet's anti-Right-Club activities, and indeed about all her doings at this point, not excluding her romantic interest in her mentor Perry Gibbons, whom she fails to suspect of homosexual leanings, even when these are paraded under her nose. She feels at times as if she's been caught up in "a Girls' Own adventure" (actually, a *School Friend* adventure would be nearer the mark; the *Girls' Own Paper* was a rather staid publication); and Buchan and Erskine Childers are never far from her thoughts. What is paramount here is the blithe side of espionage, with such arresting details as a body in the coal hole of the Carlton Club, a death by strangulation with a Hermes scarf, a significant newspaper discarded on a park bench, to be picked up by prearrangement, and an over-crowded burial place. (*The Contents of the Coffin*, a 1928 detective novel by J.S. Fletcher, comes to mind here.) All tongue-in-cheek, of course, on the part of the author, and enormously diverting, even while the darker reality of blitz, annihilation, murder, machination and treachery is not eschewed.

As well as contributing to the spy, adventure and mystery genres, then, *Transcription* at one level keeps up a continuous commentary on the flavour and conventions of all of these. The effect is more subtle than parody, more in the line of deconstruction than homage (though homage comes into it too). Unspoken presences in the novel might include Edgar Wallace, Patricia Wentworth, Eric Ambler, Nancy Mitford, even Beryl Bainbridge (the Bainbridge of *The Bottle Factory Outing*, that is). Two works, however, are crucial to the Atkinson undertaking as a whole. One is Penelope Fitzgerald's sharp and engaging novel *Human Voices* (1980), dated precisely to 1940 and set in and around Broadcasting House in Langham Place ("The air seemed alive with urgency and worry.") The other ... but here I have to get personal and declare an interest, a considerable interest.

In 1982, I was commissioned by Weidenfeld & Nicholson to "ghost" the memoirs of a one-time MI5 agent, Joan Miller, to be published under the title *One Girl's War*. It did not prove to be a trouble-free project. Joan Miller had an interesting story to tell, but her recollection was imperfect, and her version of events not only included contradictory assertions, but often made no sense at all. Add to this difficulty a clash of personalities – hers and mine – and it seems a miracle that the book ever came into existence. (I am sorry to say that it might not have done so, had Joan Miller not died before it was completed. This allowed me the freedom to go back and try to rescue from chaos the areas of major interest in the narrative, as well as stopping up holes in the text.) However, I was intrigued by the bare bones of the story, as these were conveyed to me, by the overwhelming London atmosphere in wartime, and by Joan Miller's part in overturning the activities of the crypto-Fascist, anti-Semitic Right Club (among other things). I should add that Joan Miller had many good qualities. She could be entertaining and generous – she gave me the hat she had worn to the christening of her daughter Jonquil in 1947. She showed a considerable talent for subversion, and this was spotted and nurtured by a distinguished intelligence officer in the counter-espionage, or "B" division of MI5, the head of B5(b). His name was Maxwell Knight.

Like Kate Atkinson's heroine Juliet Armstrong, Joan Miller is rescued from routine work at the Scrubs, taken under the wing of Maxwell Knight, and after minimal training, sent out to ingratiate herself with Russian Tea Rooms habitués. As Atkinson says in the end notes to her novel, "Joan Miller is not Juliet Armstrong, but they have certainly shared some of the same experiences." (She also, with perhaps unconscious understatement, classifies Joan Miller as "not the most reliable of narrators"). Juliet is not Joan, indeed, being more agreeable, cleverer, more amusing, and possessed of a dry wit which the real-life agent lacked. For this and other reasons, *Transcription* is a much better book than *One Girl's War*. But at the same time, it is worth considering the extent to which Miller's and Armstrong's stories actually coincide, and why some names have been changed, but not others. (Really, they seem to have been changed or not changed at random.) Perry Gibbons, for example, is clearly Maxwell Knight with his idiosyncrasies and particulars intact, down to his skill as a naturalist ("'Kites,' he said") and a wife in his background dead by suicide (Perry's found hanged in a wardrobe, Knight's less colourfully dead from an overdose). Knight's advice to Joan – "If you're going to tell a lie, tell a good one and above all, stick to it" – is transferred verbatim to Perry Gibbons. When it comes to the Right Club – the founder of this obnoxious organisation, Captain Archibald Maule Ramsay, has as his stand-in in *Transcription* a Rear Admiral Ellory Scaife (in 1940, both of these are interned under Regulation 18B), while his wife, Mrs Ramsay/Scaife, is properly taken in, for the good of the country, by Joan/Juliet. Another agent, Mrs Amos, becomes, in the novel, a Mrs Ambrose who plays exactly the same part as the original; while a third, a Belgian recruit called Helene de Monck, is re-created as the glamorous and sexually active Giselle. These, Kate Atkinson says, were her "ghostly inspirations".

Then we have the affair of the code and cypher clerk at the American Embassy – Tyler Kent in reality, Chester Vanderkamp in the fictional account – who spends a lot of his time decoding highly confidential telegrams passing between Churchill and Roosevelt, and getting these into enemy hands via the Russian Tea Rooms conspirators. Juliet is conscripted to set a trap for the American Embassy traitor, just as Joan Miller was; and both stratagems result in a satisfactory outcome for the security service. Kate Atkinson, then, shows herself to be adept at creative appropriation; and the invigorating intermixture of invention and transcription (the title is well chosen) adds a touch of complexity and a self-mocking undertone to the plot. (It's not the first time a Joan Miller lookalike has featured in a work of fiction: one, called Diana Calthrop, makes an appearance in the 2007 *Stratton's War* by Laura Wilson; and Simon Gray's 1991 television drama "They Never Slept" was certainly inspired by the Joan Miller story, even if it departed quite radically from it in the end.)

What is baffling is that in her list of sources at the end of *Transcription*, Kate Atkinson dates the "original" publication of *One Girl's War* to 1945; I can assure her that this is not the case. It was first published in 1986 by Brandon Books in Ireland, and how that came about is another story. The completion of Joan Miller's memoir was not the end of the matter, as far as I was concerned. Indeed, during part of the three-year period it took to research and write the book, I felt I had somehow strayed into a world of clandestine activity, even while I was doing my best to bring an imaginative understanding to bear on the part of it connected to wartime. Strange things began to happen. By chance – I think – I met the MI6 historian and one-time SOE operative M.R.D. Foot at a party, and the very next day he turned up unannounced at my front door in Blackheath, which he "just happened" to be passing. We kept in touch thereafter, and I have to say the association proved beneficial, since he drove me on several occasions into the depths of the English countryside to visit long-retired security service personnel (from whom I might have gleaned some valuable information, had I known the right questions to ask). These old military / MI5 buffers must have wondered how an Irish girl living in London, with not the slightest experience of Intelligence circles, had got herself entangled in bygone counter-espionage business. It was something of a puzzle to me too. However, by immersing myself in the literature of the period, including all the security service histories and speculative tomes I could lay my hands on, and by talking to anyone willing to talk to me, I acquired a certain – temporary – expertise in what had previously been uncharted territory. (When I'd taken on the commission, I believed it would simply entail knocking into shape an already existing manuscript. As my grandmother might have put it, I didn't realise I was bringing an old house down on my head.)

Some time in 1985, I think, it became apparent that the process of publication was not going to run any more smoothly than the course of composition. The Joan Miller memoir was finished and delivered to Weidenfeld, who promptly reneged on the agreement. By signing the Official Secrets Act more than 40 years earlier, Joan Miller had effectively debarred herself from making any future disclosure relating to her wartime employment. The publisher was therefore hit by a governmental D-Notice forbidding publication. (Before this point, no one had mentioned the likelihood of such a thing happening.) Quite laughably, *One Girl's War* was held to constitute a danger to national security – or at least, the ban was enforced to discourage others (which it didn't). The book was then taken on by Steve McDonogh of Brandon Books and published in 1986, whereupon the British Attorney General Sir Michael Havers attempted to block its distribution in Ireland, as well as in England. The attempt failed when a High

Court judge in Dublin ruled in favour of Brandon; but the UK ban remained in force.

What has the publishing history of *One Girl's War* to do with *Transcription*? Nothing, indeed, but I believe it's worth recounting here to set the record straight, and also because the latter could not have been written without the former. However, after the central MI5 events in Kate Atkinson's novel, the two part company altogether. (There's an interesting twist in the novel's tail.) The integrity of *Transcription* transcends its elements derived from different sources – and the sources are conscientiously listed. (An aside. When Kate Atkinson mentions in her endnotes "the spectres of the Cambridge spies" which have lodged in her consciousness and played a tiny role, I can't help remarking that the Co Antrim house I have lived in for 20 years was the birthplace, in 1855, of Donald Maclean's grandmother Jane Morrison.) The author has praise, for example, for the aforementioned *Human Voices*, which has minimally affected the quirky BBC atmosphere enveloping Juliet Armstrong after the war. This, in the novel, is a time of repercussions following on from the wartime imbroglios: mysterious threatening communications arriving for Juliet ("You will pay for what you did"), and the apparent resurrection of people long thought to be dead, are not the half of it. All the enticing subterfuge and intricacy of the plot is handled with a knowing authorial alacrity and a light touch – like the "light and heartless hand", perhaps, beloved of Fleur Talbot in Muriel Spark's novel *Loitering with Intent*, the events of which take place in the winter of 1949/50. *Transcription*, alert to every nuance of subversion and counter-subversion, goes on its way rejoicing in the freedom to mix and match exuberantly, to tamper with tones, traditions and angles of vision, and to keep through it all a sparkling effect.

Dublin Review of Books, 2018

FIDDLESTICKS!

Norman Iles, *Who Really Killed Cock Robin?*

Who really killed Cock Robin? Norman Iles has the answer: the bowdlerisers who turned him into a figure fit for the nursery. The unadulterated version, he assures us, was far from being childhood fare. Nursery rhymes, in fact, are nothing of the sort, once we get down to the primary images and what they stood for.

Norman Iles enlists imagination and common sense in his project to uncover the original import of lines which are now read as jingles. Charming and exuberant nonsense, we may have thought them, with their agile cows jumping over the moon, and the continuous collapse and re-erection of London Bridge. However, they had a meaning, and a plain enough one, according to Iles, before the purifiers got their hands on them. How did the latter go about the business of emasculation? By encouraging readers to take the metaphorical details literally, adding aberrant material and going out of their way to distort the actions evoked. The tone, though, stays the same; hence the sportiveness of the surviving verses.

Sometimes, fortunately, the prettifiers didn't carry out their work with sufficient thoroughness, leaving clues to the true meaning of their picturesque fabrications. We don't have to look too closely at the little nut trees, fiddlesticks, choppers, horns and so on, to grasp what's being alluded to. "The King of Spain's daughter / Came to visit me, / And all for the sake / Of my little nut tree!" With "Oranges and Lemons" the message of the bells is pretty brazen, while "Cock A Doodle Doo" laments with due innuendo and merriment a temporary failure of potency. To call a naughty girl a black sheep, as in "Baa, baa …", isn't to pull the wool over anyone's eyes, least of all Norman Iles's. "Jack and Jill"? Some moralist of the eighteenth century, it's clear to him, has turned the actions of this pair upside down; it's Jill (of course) who falls on her back, though the line, "Up Jack got, and home did trot" can stay as we find it without sacrificing the double entendre. As for the business with vinegar and brown paper – that's inserted just to throw us off the scent. Paper plaster indeed! It's no infantile mishap that's recounted here.

Neither, we learn, does "A Ring, A Ring O' Roses" refer to the Black Death; that misbelief has been foisted on us in defiance of the medical facts, says Norman Iles, who sees the composition for what it is: a wedding song. When these characters fall down (as Jill did), they don't lie still. So it goes on. After restoring 26 nursery rhymes to their original state, or as close as he can manage it (many of his amendments are really quite ingenious), the intrepid author turns his attention to certain carols which got themselves subjected to the same watering-down process, and restores these too. If his expositions are not as scholarly as the Opies' – say – he has enormous fun with his retrieval and celebration of bawdy England and its hidden outlets in so-called "nursery" verse. The point is to see how far he can go with his recreations (all the way to Babylon, it seems, candlelight and all); and one effect of his engaging book will be to send us back to our nursery rhyme collections in a more alert and knowing frame of mind. What are we to make, for example, of Polly Flinders playing with fire, Wee Willie Winkie ready for bed, Little Boy Blue receiving an instruction with regard to his horn – not to mention the lady gaily mounted on a cock horse? Iles (an Oxford friend of Philip Larkin, Kingsley Amis, Bruce Montgomery *et al*) doesn't hesitate to put us right on these and other matters: and if the word "Fiddlesticks!" occasionally springs to mind as he presents some striking interpretations of this or that "nonsense" line – well, he is often convincing, and always diverting, with his bold and sparkling exercises in reinstatement.

New Society, 1986

THE CORPSE
IN THE COPSE

Gladys Mitchell, *The Whispering Knights*

"I have heard of your work ... More: I have read your books. Utter rubbish. How do you do?" Mrs Bradley, Gladys Mitchell's detective, and the person to whom this remark is addressed (in the 1930 novel *The Longer Bodies*), is not in the least put out by its outspokenness. Nor does she seem at all discomposed when another character points out her resemblance to a serpent or a crocodile (she is undecided which). Add to this the fact that *The Longer Bodies* contains an old Scottish cook who counters every order from her mistress with the phrase, "I'll see masel' drooned first", and it should be plain that we are dealing with a form very difficult to carry off successfully, the humorous detective novel.

It's a form that Gladys Mitchell handled with great conviction, for as long as it engaged her interest. But in fact her crime fiction has undergone quite a few changes since it began with *Speedy Death* in 1929, even though each of her novels features the same central character, the redoubtable Mrs Bradley (later Dame Beatrice). For most of the 1930s, her objective was at least partly to satirise the conventions of the detective genre, and this resulted in a number of splendid comic works, including *Death at the Opera*. *The Saltmarsh Murders*, praised by C. Day-Lewis in 1942, is rather more serious in effect, but composed with an equal amount of gusto. In the early 1940s, the author seems to have lost direction for a while, turning out works of almost impenetrable complexity (*Hangman's Curfew*, *My Father Sleeps* and *Here Comes a Chopper* are three examples). Interspersed with these, however, were admirable novels such as *St Peter's Finger*, *Laurels are Poison* ("It is a sound instinct", noted W.H. Auden, "that has made so many detective writers choose a college as a setting") and the semi-autobiographical *The Rising of the Moon*, which is saturated in a dingy, tarnished, small-town atmosphere, and is quite distinct in feeling from the other books.

The Dancing Druids in 1948 marked the end of Gladys Mitchell's middle and least successful phase, but we still find unnecessary convolution in plot-making as late as 1962 (*My Bones Will Keep*); and quite often the disclosure of the murderer's identity fails to provide a proper resolution, usually because the motive for the killing is ludicrously inadequate. Only in the early comic novels is this defect turned on its head, as the author exploits the discrepancy between something preposterously trivial and its outcome: in one instance, a piece of bad acting sparks off a murderous impulse in an elderly perfectionist. Two at least of Gladys Mitchell's villains are "absolutely unhinged on the subject of sexual relationships", going in for wholesale slaughter as a warning to wantons. Once the spoof element disappears from the books, though, the murderers' motives will not often stand up to scrutiny. When the time for explanations arrives, the author is often obliged to diagnose lunacy.

By 1950 the details of the killings have become less gory, with never a putrefying head, a boiled body, a bloody ear or a hacked-off hand in sight: nothing but a neat corpse lying inoffensively with its face in a gorse bush. Dame Beatrice, too, is rather more restrained in manner, and minor quirks like her taste in dress are toned down (no more tartan ties worn with orange and purple jumpers). In the latest group of novels, dry retorts have begun to replace the disconcerting cackle which used to represent the detective's method of dealing with the recalcitrant. Only the statutory gathering of impostors, dissemblers, intriguers and adventurers remains, to test the investigator's powers as she returns each time to the scene of a murder. If she rents a castle, as in *The Croaking Raven* (1966), she is sure to find its owners lurking on or near the premises, concealing their true relations with one another and cheerfully embarking on wrongdoing when they think they can get away with it. (The fateful entrance of Dame B. and her party under their battlements is, of course, the beginning of the process of exposure.)

In the formal construction of her stories (especially from the 1978 offering *Wraiths and Changelings* on) and in the articulate sedateness of her dialogues, Gladys Mitchell's work is coming more and more to resemble that of Ivy Compton-Burnett, a writer whom she admires. The influence is quite overt. "'So we await the judgement of Paris', said Owen in the manner of Ivy Compton-Burnett", is a sentence which occurs halfway through her new novel, *The Whispering Knights*. Like Compton-Burnett, too, she refuses to differentiate between comedy and tragedy; this is one reason why her books are so memorable.

But Gladys Mitchell's traits are all her own; she's a writer who can absorb influences without being overwhelmed by them. Literary allusions, jokes, ambiguities, unexpected twists and tricks are just a few of the devices she employs to fill the gaps caused by necessarily incomplete characterisation. She possesses the kind of wit that sees a connection between the subject of an epitaph written by Ben Jonson and a murder victim in one of her own books, resulting in the naming of the character Salathiel Pavy. She can't resist calling one of her murderers' houses Weston Pipers, so that this may be changed, in the course of the story, to the very appropriate Nest of Vipers (the title of her last novel but two). And in *The Whispering Knights* the usual process of separating the sheep from the goats is complicated by the name of the girl who is to some extent the focus of interest: Capella, meaning "a stinking she-goat".

The Whispering Knights, like the Dancing Druids, form a group of standing stones to which myth and superstition readily attach, providing an apt location for the re-enactment of a sacrifice to a god (the modern god is the usual one of cupidity). Gladys Mitchell has made a thorough study of the prehistoric circles mentioned in her novel, in particular the Rollright Stones, Clava and Callanash; and the information she's inserted unobtrusively into the text makes a bonus for the reader. No stone circle can fail to make an impression on anyone in the least susceptible; and the party depicted in this enthralling novel contains at least two young women who "see things".

The most prominent member of the sight-seeing group in *The Whispering Knights* is Dame Beatrice, whose presence gives rise to some speculation: has she or has she not been asked along to keep an eye on someone thought to be mentally unstable? (She is, as addicts will know, a psychiatrist attached to the Home Office.) And if so, is the person liable to run amok? Whatever the truth of this matter, we can be sure that some interesting occurrences will take place. What's even more surprising than the rate at which Gladys Mitchell's novels are coming out (two a year for the past three years), is the fact that their store of wit, learning, assurance, vigour and stylishness is actually increasing. Julian Symons, in *Bloody Murder*, placed her among those writers of the "Golden Age" whose work is now seldom discussed. Perhaps it's time for a reappraisal.

Times Literary Supplement, 1980

CHARNEL CHARM

Michael Cox (ed.),

The Oxford Book of Twentieth-Century Ghost Stories

The ghost story continues to enthral, and the possibilities for new combinations and regroupings seem endless. Women's ghost stories, Victorian ghost stories, English ghost stories ... so it goes on. Now Michael Cox has put together a handsome twentieth-century collection featuring all kinds of insubstantialities and shades of darkness. It has often been remarked that the ghost, as a literary figment, might have been expected to vanish with the coming of electric light, whereas, in fact, a host of authors rose splendidly to the challenge of insinuating their wraiths into the most unghostlike of settings. By the 1920s, indeed, it had become *de rigueur* for ghost-story writers to combine their eerie effects with an unromantic or up-to-date location. The impact of the story depended partly on an incongruity – the incongruity between ordinary, natural life as depicted by the author, and a spookish occurrence. The idea was to start off as temperately as possible, and gradually increase the sense of something awry, before arriving at a flesh-creeping climax. M.R. James had set the tone: sedate and subtle, in contrast to the graveyard gallimaufry of an earlier generation. His stories cut more ice, when it came to chilling the blood, than those of Vernon Lee (say) and others whom prosaic settings left cold. The Victorian ghost story risked getting fatally entangled in its own grisly trappings. Its characters were apt to wake in the night as frightful old women emerged from the wainscot, or find themselves overwhelmingly in touch with displaced and terrible emotions. With the new century came a new approach: among other things, ghosts were not slow to latch on to the telephone as a means of getting through. Hotel rooms, library stacks and the cabins of passenger liners were all commandeered by resolute revenants at one time or another. Anything at all, it soon became plain, from a dubious kit-bag to a saucepan on a stove, may suffer a spectral infestation.

Ghost stories are all about seeing or sensing "things" and the story-teller's business is to usher in the ineffable in such a way that it makes sense, as well as making the hair stand on end. Some writers, it is true, get bogged down in the device itself, which can either scupper the narrative altogether, or turn it into something different: an exercise in ingenuity. It is possible, I think, to isolate a few exemplary ghost stories, all replete with charnel charge, against which all others may be measured – "Oh, Whistle and I'll Come to You, My Lad", by M.R. James, for example; "The Empty House", by Algernon Blackwood, or Edith Wharton's "Afterward". These are timeless – however, as we approach the present, we may note how certain preoccupations of modern life are easily accommodated within the supernatural framework, from Fay Weldon's enticing feminist case-histories, to (a current commonplace) psychological damage incurred in childhood. *The Oxford Book of Twentieth-Century Ghost Stories* finds room for both of these, along with Penelope Lively's entertaining "Revenant as Typewriter", which treats a haunting ironically. In this cheerful piece, a woman of some precision and elegance finds herself requisitioned by a force which isn't only uncanny but also uncouth. Not too much horror is transmitted here, it's true, but in compensation the Lively approach eliminates tedium. Elizabeth Bowen, with "The Cheery Soul" (included here), about a dead drunken cook who goes on leaving rude notes for her employers in the fish-kettle, had already shown that spirits didn't have to be dispiriting.

These stories are unforgettable, along with others such as "The Meeting House" by Jane Gardam (wonderfully plain and stark), the atmospheric tale by Robert

Aickman about waking the dead ("Ringing the Changes"), or "Three Miles Up" by Elizabeth Jane Howard, which imagines a kind of transposed Charon's Ferry. Others tend to blur in the mind, so that it becomes difficult to separate "The Tower" from "The Roaring Tower", or to differentiate between night-fears (L.P. Hartley) and all those night nurses who suffer them. (See, for example, "The Shadowy Third" by Ellen Glasgow.) One or two of Cox's choices have a whiff of the pot-boiler, rather than the blood-curdler, about them; this is the case, oddly enough, with the F. Scott Fitzgerald story ("A Short Trip Home"), in which a pretty, popular girl gets into the clutches of a rotter and con-man – who happens to be dead. And "The Highboy" by Alison Lurie, about a piece of antique furniture with a mind of its own, lacks a frisson of the sinister to offset its whimsicality.

The protagonists of the stories assembled here are all especially vulnerable to psychic impressions, whether it's a matter of being pursued by a sack, or experiencing death as a spiral staircase going down and down into the dark for ever. Michael Cox is a clear-headed editor, and this is an intriguing collection which takes in a good range of tones, from the decorum of M.R. James to the opulence of Angela Carter – and comes pleasantly imbued with a proper unearthly light.

Times Literary Supplement, 1996

LIGHT RELIEF

John Gross (ed.), *The Oxford Book of Comic Verse*

"But comedy shall get its round of claps too", W.H. Auden decreed in his "Letter to Lord Byron"; and indeed, applause for this winning branch of English poetry is indicated in the numbers of anthologies devoted to the subject. John Gross's *Oxford Book of Comic Verse* comes in the wake of Kingsley Amis's *New Oxford Book of Light Verse*, which itself followed on from Auden's light verse anthology of 1938; and Michael Roberts and Gavin Ewart have had a hand in defining the genre too.

Definition is important: there is broad general agreement about what constitutes a "comic", or a "light", or a "humorous" poem (and these terms are more or less interchangeable); but different anthologists draw the line at different places. Ewart, for example, shows more of a tendency to include blue verse under the heading of "light" or "comic" than the others do – while his sticking-point comes at unwitting, or McGonagallesque, funniness. (Well, this is more or less true of all of them.) Amis isn't fearfully keen on "Anon'" or Lear, or on epigrams. John Gross admits to a distaste for the more extreme versions of licentious songs such as "The One-Eyed Riley". However, where Gross departs from his predecessors is in aiming for comprehensiveness, and pretty well achieving it.

Comprehensiveness of range, at any rate; his approach is, he says, "firmly (or … weakly) eclectic", and he doesn't exclude such items as the advertising jingle, or the anonymous quatrain entitled "Examination Question" which must have raised the spirits of more than one generation of ex-pupils:

O Cuckoo! shall I call thee Bird
Or but a wandering voice?
State the alternative preferred
With reasons for your choice.

Many enjoyable trifles of this sort are interspersed with the wordier, more socially illuminating or polemical poems which are cast in a comic mode: that is, at as far a remove as possible from density and intensity. John Gross, indeed, has found a place for everything: "The Vicar of Bray" and his unabashed expediency, Pope's wonderfully funny "Imitation of Chaucer", Lear's (uncompleted) sequel to one of his better-known efforts, which opens with the enticing lines, "Our mother was the Pussy-Cat, our father was the Owl,/So we are partly little beasts and partly little fowl".

Not everything in the book produces so bracing an effect. However, since it's all chosen to exemplify some aspect of the English comic tradition in verse (not excluding the rest of Britain, or America), it is possible to swallow even those contributions which display – to our taste – an excessive blandness or facile tone, such as Millikin's "The Groves of Blarney"; or make an exasperating ado about a small event, like R.H. Barham's "The Jackdaw of Rheims". These defects, perhaps, are peculiar to the past; but the present is not without comparable pitfalls. What's essential to the comic poem of any era is aplomb; but once this quality gets touched with modish self-regard or whimsy, the thing is apt to turn completely jejune. We can see this happening with nearly everything by Roger McGough, for example, or in George MacBeth's bit of piffle entitled "The Orange Poem". "The Orange Poem" lacks appeal.

"The best comic verse ... has been the work of serious poets". If you leave aside such light-verse specialists as Lear and Calverley (say), you can take John

Gross's comment on the situation prevailing over the last 60-odd years, and extend it backwards indefinitely (well, to Chaucer, which is as far as he goes). Certainly to Byron, whom Kingsley Amis praised for inventing "the most flexible and expressive style ever devised for light verse", and who referred forthrightly to a poem of Wordsworth's as being "Writ in a manner which is my aversion". Byron, Burns, Goldsmith, Jonson, Johnson, Swift ... there's plenty of ballast in *The Oxford Book of Comic Verse* to offset the airiness associated with the pure nonsense rhyme, the delectable piece of word-play or the parody (all of which are present in abundance). There are, as well, many unfamiliar voices to enlarge our sense of what's admissible under the "comic verse" tag. With the Gross anthology – and this is a rarity – you may even hold the odd omission to be creative. In place of Louis MacNeice's ubiquitous "Bagpipe Music", for example, we get a splendid chunk of "Autumn Journal", all sardonic social comment and self-mockery.

It's only with those contributors born after 1932 that a slight falling-off occurs. True, Paul Durcan and Fuller/Fenton are always admirable; and Wendy Cope (for example) is an adroit parodist. But you can't help feeling that more, and funnier, material ought to have been available. On the other hard – it is hard to voice any complaint whatever about an anthology so replete with riches – one, moreover, upholding the idea of humour as a by-product of an idiosyncratic vision, with ease-of-manner resulting from cast-iron control. True comic verse, as we find here, is inseparable from comic verve.

The Spectator, 1994

COUNTRY MATTERS

Karl Miller, *Tretower to Clyro: Essays*

A new collection of essays by Karl Miller is a cause for jubilation, and this one comes with a bonus: a 31-page preface, or companion piece, by Andrew O'Hagan. O'Hagan's foreword, "The Excursions", sets the scene for what's in store. It features a series of literary jaunts, undertaken in a spirit of homage and exuberance, by three friends, distinguished fellow-Celts, all endowed with the strongest instinct for assessment and allusion. ("Karl and Seamus sat on a bench and argued about the Latin on Vaughan's grave.") A Scotsman, a Scots-Irishman and an Irishman. They are Karl Miller, Andrew O'Hagan and Seamus Heaney, and the places they visit include the Scottish Borders, the Welsh Marches, the Aran Islands and Abergavenny. These were chosen for their rich associations: with local poets, national poets, diarists, novelists, biographers and so on. And more and more literary figures got drawn into their environs, as the lively-minded trio allowed free rein to their collective capacity for evocation and recall. Hence Thomas Hardy is invoked in a church in Scotland, and T.S. Eliot has a showing near the River Usk in Wales.

A country theme predominates throughout the sixteen invigorating essays by Karl Miller, ushered in by "The Excursions" (and presided over in some sense by Miller's two travelling companions). The opening article, "Country Writers", considers Kilvert, Raymond Williams, Flora Thompson, Ronald Blythe and others, and touches, astutely and entertainingly, on the Stella Gibbons/Mary Webb conjunction. You find a Scottish theme, too, running through the book, with riveting commentaries on James Hogg (for example), best known for his *Confessions of a Justified Sinner*; on Hogg's collateral descendant, the resonant and engaging Canadian short-story writer Alice Munro; and on afflicted Candia McWilliam, of the "memoir of blindness", *What to Look for in Winter* (among other books).

Ireland has a place in *Tretower to Clyro*, as well, with praise by Miller for John McGahern's subtlety and veracity, and for steadfast Heaney – the Heaney of *Stepping Stones*, the quasi-autobiographical, question-and-answer compilation put together by Dennis O'Driscoll ("poet, senior tax inspector, strict questioner"). The poet's generosity of spirit, immense achievement and "disciplined coolness" are justly applauded. What else do we find in this outstanding collection? We're treated to a close scrutiny of John McNeillie (Ian Niall) getting to grips with the landscape of Galloway, and Francis Kilvert observing every aspect of Clyro life in the 1870s (Clyro, incidentally, has the same meaning as Heaney's Anahorish, "Clear Water").

You have to say that Miller's versions of pastoral – like William Empson's – are not all rural (with pieces on Ian McEwan and Irvine Welsh) and not at all countrified. The country matters, though, with all its ancestral implications and enduring effect on the literary imagination. Miller is consistently alert to every nuance of his subjects' preoccupations, and his observations are shaped by a quirky eloquence which accommodates both charm – of an austere, Scottish variety, indeed – and cogency. Words applied by James Hogg, the Ettrick Shepherd, to an ancestor of his, Will o' Phaup – frolic, agility and strength – can be applied to Karl Miller in his critical persona too.

Independent, 2011

HARRISON ENTIRE

Tony Harrison, *A Cold Coming*
Neil Astley (ed.), *Tony Harrison*

Maybe it takes one to know one: "the remarkable Tony Harrison", wrote Derek Mahon a year or two ago, "one of the finest poets in England today." Other commentators aren't quite so sure, or at least their praise is modified by hesitations or misgivings. Is Harrison a proletarian poet, and if so, what does he mean by displaying all the resources of language and scholarship traditionally denied to the working class? Is his purpose to restore to the verse-drama all the vitality that went out of it earlier in the [twentieth] century, and if it is, why does he allow himself to get diverted into sonnet sequences and the like? Such demurs denote an ill-conceived approach to a body of work that cries out to be considered in its entirety, not partitioned under separate tags. (We have the author's word for it that his output is all of a piece: "Poetry is all I write", he says, "whether for books, or readings, or for the National Theatre, or for the opera house and concert hall, or even for TV"). One of the great merits of Neil Astley's *Tony Harrison* – the first in a proposed series of Bloodaxe Critical Anthologies – is that it directs our attention to the ways in which this unifying impulse operates. It also provides enough evidence to bear out Mahon's judgement (though an alert reading of almost any Harrison poem ought to have the same effect).

Not that there aren't anomalies even here. The Astley book is made up of articles, reviews, interviews, and a preface or two; and its contributors (more than forty of them, including Harrison himself) sometimes prove to be at odds with one another. Even the simple matter of registering a few ingredients of Harrison's *School of Eloquence* sonnets isn't as clear-cut as you might think. Certain features of a Northern working-class childhood during the 1940s – street life, sweet shops, comics, the cinema, pubs, coal fires, allotments, bowling greens and the schoolboy's experience of the Second World War – are absent from the sequence as far as one critic is concerned, and abundantly present in the eyes of another. The odd thing is, there's a sense in which both are right: that is, when such details occur, they are detached from any association with "local colour", and hence fall into an unexpected configuration.

Harrison isn't out to encompass anything so banal as heart-warming evocation: his more exacting intention is to fuse together a lot of complex feelings about the past (his own past, that is, and also that aspect of the past in general which consists of a whole stifled under-class: "the dumb go down in history and disappear") with all its ironies and intensities. The result is a work of astonishing resonance and coherence.

John Haffenden, in an interview with Harrison originally published in 1984, puts his finger on a driving force behind the poetry: "In most ways you gratify that sector of society which is educated to read literature," he says, "but at the same time you disabuse it of its expectations." Harrison, indeed, can be called subversive, wayward or refractory. He engages in conscious acts of unsettlement, and enlists his immense technical expertise to this end. He's effectively opposed to anything glib or facile, and always on the side of sanity and order (as filtered through a decent radical consciousness). His work is "political" to the extent that it gets to grips with all kinds of social delinquencies and abuses. But among the arguments for taking it whole, as it were, is the fact that a piecemeal reading may encourage a disputable verdict. The word "populist", for example, occurs in the Bloodaxe anthology, only to be contradicted (rightly) by Douglas Dunn, for whom Harrison's poetry is "sometimes demotic, but never populist". What else? If he's rated "immediate and accessible", somehow this implies a Betjeman-like figure a bit further up north and down the social scale, while "colloquial" – another common tag – has its own quotidian connotations, quite misplaced. (Harrison, it's true, has perfected a poetic language from which local quirks are conspicuously not excluded – an alternative strategy to Eliot's "purify[ing] the dialect of the tribe" – but that is something different.) If you grant him accessibility, you have to add that it comes with an edge of idiosyncrasy, which raises it to an altogether craftier level. (And of course we have the case of Harrison's *V* which ought to have been accessible but clearly wasn't, since a lot of dunderheads read, or heard, the "V" as "F" and thought it was directed at them.)

In Harrison's poetry, the aesthetic, political and personal all work together to produce a vibrant effect. Nothing seems outside the range of this poet – from the "sex and history" (his description) of *The Loiners* (1971) to the sparkling urbanities of his version of Molière's *Misanthrope*. Critics who complain about a certain northern bleakness of outlook miss the element of self-mockery which accompanies the note of protestation in poems such as the well-known "Them and [Uz]". Those, on the other hand, who relish the seriousness of Harrison's outcries against oppression and exploitation, may find themselves taken aback, and therefore in the wrong mood, to encounter the virtuosity of a rich and luminous poem like "A Kumquat for John Keats":

> As strong sun burns away the dawn's grey haze
> I pick a kumquat and the branches spray
> Cold dew in my face to start the day.
> The dawn's molasses make the citrus gleam
> still in the orchards of the groves of dream.
> The limes, like Galway after weeks of rain,
> glow with a greenness that is close to pain,
> the dew-cooled surfaces of fruit that spent
> all last night flaming in the firmament ...

The latest Harrison publication, *A Cold Coming* (two Gulf War poems), also seems to have attracted some hasty reactions – yes, fine, the argument might go, let's applaud the poet for dashing this off in a fine old anti-war rage, going all out for an exorbitant topicality. In fact, the hard-hitting and ferociously specific "A Cold Coming" and its more intricate companion-poem, "Initial Illumination", demand to be considered in the context of Harrison's unceasing concern with the whole spectrum of twentieth-century darkness, atrocity and malaise. He has never balked at harrowing his readers, if any artistic or catalytic purpose may be served thereby. (A recent poem, "The Mother of the Muses", contains images relating to the bombing of Dresden which are very hard to take.) "A Cold Coming" is a fierce and sardonic poem about the procreative precautions of canny Americans – "Three wise soldiers from Seattle / who banked their sperm before the battle". "Initial Illumination" triumphantly modulates from the cormorant-figurations of seventh-century manuscripts to the oil-soaked casualties of the recent war – true to the principle enunciated in "Lines to My Grandfathers": "I strive to keep my lines direct and straight, / And try to make connections where I can." But whether it presents itself as indomitable or intoxicating, Harrison's poetry is fuelled by the strongest feeling and most exhilarating erudition, and attains a quite remarkable singularity.

It's true that it doesn't always yield up its riches easily – and this is one reason why an assortment of appraisals such as those assembled by Neil Astley comes in useful. The drift of the book is cheering, it offers a lot of information and a good many insights, and contains valuable contributions from Harrison himself, including the text of his cogent and imaginative defence of Salman Rushdie, "The Blasphemers' Banquet", and a spirited presidential address to the Classical Association entitled "Facing Up to the Muses". The Muses, indeed, aren't all that Tony Harrison has faced up to – but he goes on countering apocalyptic possibilities with the surest appreciation of the here-and-now, as in the marvellous recent poem "The Pomegranates of Patmos". Bloodaxe deserves great credit for providing an intelligent introduction to the work of this distinguished, and distinctive, poet.

Times Literary Supplement, 1991

WILD CHILD WHO
TAUGHT US TO COOK

Lisa Chaney, *Elizabeth David: A Mediterranean Passion*

Elizabeth David was 20 before she knew how to make a cup of tea, and at about the same time her first attempt to cook lunch for herself resulted in a plateful of burnt onions. This was not surprising. Born in 1913, she possessed the kind of English upper-middle-class family background which had relied on generations of kitchen staff, and for most of whose members cookery was a closed book.

The way to the kitchen, for those not themselves from the serving classes, was paved with social qualms. David's achievement was to change all that – partly in an access of outrage occasioned by the terrible food of her childhood ("mutton and beef ... boiled potatoes ... slippery and slimy ... greasy ... stodgy"), and partly as a consequence of certain upheavals of the mid-century, including the Second World War.

It took some time before Elizabeth David lighted on her metier; but it was plain from the start that this spirited second daughter of a Conservative MP named Rupert Gwynne and a titled lady from Northumberland was destined to make a mark in one of the professions. Among her inherited traits were a streak of aristocratic eccentricity and a full measure of Gwynne-Ridley pig-headedness. Thwarted in her ambition to be an actress (she wasn't good enough), she followed her star to the South of France, setting sail in 1939 in a boat called "the Evelyn Hope", with her then lover Charles Gibson Cowan – a flamboyant actor, writer and one-time tramp, about whom her family took a predictably snooty tone. Truly, it was not an auspicious moment to leave the country. War broke out and the pair were stranded for a time on the Riviera, before making their escape via Corsica, Italy (where a night's imprisonment awaited them), and a Greek island, and ending up in Cairo.

There Elizabeth David found employment as a librarian with the Ministry of Information. By the end of the war she had met and fallen under the spell of her mentor, Norman Douglas, enjoyed the expatriate sociability of Egypt and married an Army Officer named Tony David, spending time with her new husband in India before returning to England ripe for the new gospel of gourmet eating. A culinary prodigy was about to be born.

There's an Auden line about the drift of "pallid" northerners, gastronomic ignoramuses, "southwards into a sunburnt otherwhere". A Mediterranean abundance and Epicureanism seemed the perfect antidote to listless post-war England with its food rationing and other deprivations. Elizabeth David's earliest writings capitalised on the glamour of a garlic, olive and aubergine, sun-drenched repertoire. There is no doubt that she almost single-handedly revolutionised concepts of cooking and eating in the middle of the [twentieth] century, first by lauding the dishes of France and Italy with their enticing piquancy and exotic ingredients, and then by rediscovering an all but lost English tradition of wholesomeness and seasonal variation.

It wasn't only her recipes that got an entire generation of would-be culinary sophisticates scurrying about in search of fresh wild thyme or black truffles, but her whole evocative, erudite and urbane approach to the cookery business. Even those, like the late Angela Carter, who allowed David's "magisterial hauteur" to get up their noses, acknowledge her primacy among cuisine commentators. Just when it looked as though it might be discarded altogether, as "convenience" foods became widely available, she reinstated the middle-class stove.

About half-way through this exuberant biography of Elizabeth David, the life story takes a back seat. The culinary accomplishments, the journalism, the *Book of Mediterranean Food, French Provincial Cooking,* the establishment of – and quarrels over – the Elizabeth David shops, and so on, all take over. Lisa Chaney goes about her work in a capable, rather showy manner, cramming in as much social and historical detail as she can muster. A pity, though, that she allows so many prominent figures in the David story to remain shadowy and vague.

It's a colourful life, indeed, what with its enlightened hedonism, sexual escapades, pioneering itineraries and strength of will, but it looks as though we shall have to wait for the authorised version by Artemis Cooper (due next September) to have a few of the outlines filled in. One thing we do learn: if Elizabeth David had a reputation for being a bit high-handed, it wasn't necessarily deserved. It may be traced back to a misprint in her first book, published in an era of paucity and austerity. What should have read as a simple instruction – "Take two to three eggs" – appeared in print as "Take twenty-three eggs", no doubt to the alarm of its earliest readers.

Independent, 1998

A LONG LOOK
THROUGH HER LENS

Julian Cox and Colin Ford,
Julia Margaret Cameron: The Complete Photographs
Victoria Olsen, *From Life:*
Julia Margaret Cameron and Victorian Photography

Virginia Woolf's play *Freshwater*, put on to entertain her friends and relatives at her sister Vanessa Bell's studio in 1935, was a kind of parody of their own Bloomsbury group with all its intimacies and absurdities. The play, subtitled *A Comedy*, features a forerunner of Bloomsbury itself.

Freshwater (on the Isle of Wight) denotes a no less dazzling assembly of friends, fellow-artists and personages, all luminaries of the Victorian age. Tennyson, with his wife and sons, was the first to settle at Freshwater Bay; and around him gathered an illustrious entourage: poets, scholars, famous female beauties, churchmen, artists and whatnot. Among them was Woolf's great-aunt Julia Margaret Cameron, renowned for her eccentricities and her expertise, who photographed the lot of them.

Cameron's eccentricities were well to the fore in the biographical essay, also by Woolf, which accompanied the selection of her work issued in 1926 under the title *Victorian Photographs of Famous Men and Fair Women*. "She had little respect ... for the conventions of Putney", her great-niece wrote. "Dressed in robes of flowing red velvet, she walked with her friends, stirring a cup of tea as she walked, half-way to the railway station in hot summer weather." Red velvet, indeed, does not seem suitable for the time of year; however, Cameron was used to much greater heat than that of Putney. Born in 1815 in an affluent suburb of Calcutta, Julia Margaret Pattle (as she then was), one of several remarkable sisters, had married Charles Hay Cameron, a Benthamite jurist on the Supreme Council of India, and 20 years her senior, in 1838. Once he had retired, and the colonial Camerons had returned to England, the bulk of their income came from his coffee plantations in Ceylon, and it wasn't adequate. They were plagued by money worries for the rest of their lives.

Nevertheless, in 1860, Julia Margaret managed to scrape up the funds to acquire two adjacent houses on the Isle of Wight, near her friend the Poet Laureate's

Farringford. Three years later – the story goes – the gift of a camera from her daughter and son-in-law set her off on the course which would make her name.

Actually, as Virginia Olsen's illuminating new biography shows, her interest in the budding art of photography did not occur as suddenly as all that. However, the felicitous present certainly activated her creative impulse to the fullest degree. A coalhouse was quickly converted into a dark-room and a chicken coop turned into a photographic studio ("The hens were liberated, I hope and believe not eaten"). And then, in 1864, came a breakthrough. "Annie – my first success" is a slightly out-of-focus, but vividly alive impression of a bright-eyed eight-year-old with untidy hair and wearing a buttoned-up sealskin coat.

Photography was not an easy business at the time, either for the practitioner or the sitter. The technical process involved a heavy glass plate, coated in collodion, which was placed in a camera resting on a tripod and exposed for up to five minutes. During this time Cameron, by sheer force of will, imposed immobility on her suffering subjects. No one enjoyed being photographed, but most potential sitters were caught up in the photographer's overwhelming enthusiasm.

There were exceptions. Occasionally Julia Margaret's dramatic gestures misfired. She failed to capture one visiting statesman (Garibaldi) who, as she fell to her knees raising filthy hands to implore him to sit for her, mistook her for a beggarwoman and brushed her aside. Often she was driven to lurking near her doorway, ready to pounce on any likely-looking subject who might pass by.

The anecdotes multiplied, but so – fortunately – did the photographs. This was no flibbertigibbet but a dedicated professional and innovator whose work survives as a testimony to her artistry and assiduity. Her series of hieratic portraits – of Tennyson, Darwin, Longfellow, Browning, Carlyle, Sir John William Frederick Herschel and so on – achieves an almost hypnotic density, making their images archaic and modern at the same time. These famous men had their counterparts in the radiant women, pre-Raphaelite in their 1860s picturesqueness, conscripted as models: maidservants Mary Hillier and Mary Ryan; young relatives including May Prinsep, Julia Jackson Duckworth (later to be the mother of Virginia Woolf) and Katie and Lizzie Keown; Ellen Terry. Even the posed tableaux, illustrating such works as Tennyson's *Idylls of the King*, with their tinsel and draperies smacking of amateur theatricals, for which Cameron was persistently derided ("childish trivialities", Shaw called them) – even these distill, for viewers of the present, a sense of enchanted artifice.

It was time for a reassessment of Julia Margaret Cameron, and the Olsen biography, with its painstaking detail and sound historical sense, helps to bring its subject more sharply into focus, with all her passionate energy and endearing imperiousness. But it is *The Complete Photographs* which will enhance her reputation for many years to come. In the preface to her book, Virginia Olsen pays tribute to the pioneering researches of Julian Cox and Colin Ford, to whom, indeed, all Cameron enthusiasts must be indebted. Their magnificent catalogue raisonné, which contains over thirteen hundred illustrations, many full-page and some in duo-tone, is a breathtaking work of scholarship and appreciation.

Now, at last, we can marvel at the full range of Julia Margaret Cameron's photographic feats. Both books, the biography and *The Complete Photographs*, are published to coincide with the current Cameron exhibition at the National Portrait Gallery in London, curated by Colin Ford, who is also responsible for the accompanying catalogue (*Julia Margaret Cameron: The First Great Woman Photographer*). As a visual experience, the effect is stunning – a perfect encapsulation of the light of other days.

The Irish Times, 2003

MISERY GUTTED

Anthony Thwaite (ed.),
The Selected Letters of Philip Larkin 1940–1985

"Ends in themselves, my letters plot no change;/They carry nothing dutiable; they won't/Aspire, astound, establish or estrange./Why write them then? …".

Well, to let off steam, for one thing; to provide an outlet for the vivid phrase or simply to delight the recipient. Philip Larkin was an inspired and inspiriting letter-writer: "To the end, a glimpse of the Hull postmark brought that familiar tiny tingle of excitement and optimism", writes Kingsley Amis in his *Memoirs*. Through all the changes of mood and tone recorded in this volume, a vigorous diffuseness is kept up. If his poems were more and more severely rationed as time went on, until the supply dried up altogether, Larkin's correspondence continued unabated.

It's not that disgruntlement doesn't loom large. The famous Larkin irascibility wasn't mooted without cause. But the letters start off boisterously, at any rate ("I'm all for beer & plenty of it"), full of undergraduate joviality and relish for the robust phrase: "Faint heart never fucked the pig". Larkin is in favour of Auden, Yeats and D.H. Lawrence at this fairly innocent stage in his life. He wants to be a novelist (unlike his friend Kingsley Amis, who wants to be a poet), and sees no reason to keep his angst or his lust to himself, or to gloss over his consequent difficulties with girls.

Girls are a problem: indeed, Larkin seems to have held a low opinion of women up until the early 1950s and his removal to Belfast, where an enhancing affair with the wife of a colleague altered his attitude somewhat. But an element of resentment lingers on. Women impose too many restrictions, they are deficient in give-and-take, they create disorder. The thought of marriage scares him stiff. The rueful poem, "Letter to a Friend about Girls", unpublished during Larkin's lifetime, furnishes a clue or two. Enlightened, uninhibited women only come the way of those possessing the first requirement of a Lothario, i.e. good looks. Everyone else, including Larkin, has to make do with those who base their code of behaviour on *Woman's Own*. "I have to pay for two women at the pub and the flicks instead of one and I don't get my cock into either of them, ever."

Larkin's anti-feminism was part of a pose that burgeoned later to include not only the half-comic, testy conservatism which became something of a stock-in-trade, but also the insufferable pronouncements for which he has rightly been upbraided – the bits alluding to wogs and niggers and so forth. Does he only do it to annoy, because he knows it teases? It's hard to say. Perhaps it's best to regard this side of Larkin as the unattractive aspect of what Barbara Everett has identified as "a principled philistinism" – and an essentially English philistinism – in the work of Larkin and Amis: that is, a steely rejection of bullshit. Or horse shit, if you like: washing his hands of the whole of British poetry after 1960, Larkin lumped it all together under this unabashed heading. And when it comes to individual poets ... well, we've already had quite a few samples in the press of Larkin's choicest epithets, with Heaney dubbed "the gombeen man" (why on earth, when the phrase refers to an unprincipled moneylender?), and poor Ted Hughes coming in for the lion's share of denigration: "not a single solitary bit of good."

All very striking and amusing, no doubt; but is it really fair to print these private insults out of context, or to print them at all? Anthony Thwaite has carried out quite a bit of censoring, but the frequent ellipses only leave you wondering about the omissions. What on earth was said about Charles Causley that had to be deleted … ? And even with all the excisions, a feeling of prying persists. We knew that Larkin's English reticence was covering something … but a taste for naughty magazines featuring spanking? His exchanges with Robert Conquest on this topic ("the porn shops aren't what they were") make uneasy reading. And what starts off as ribald high spirits (in the letters to Amis, for example) turns rather more seedy with the onset of glumness and middle age.

It's his male friends and contemporaries who elicit the most unbuttoned observations. The letters to women are more decorous, and those to the novelist Barbara Pym in particular are positively respectful. Clearly something about her mannerly imbroglios struck a chord with Larkin, though it didn't stop him composing the following limerick (included in a letter to Gavin Ewart): "The chances are certainly slim/Of finding in Barbara Pym/(I speak with all deference)/The faintest of reference/To what in our youth we called quim."

As well as Pym, we find him merrily reading Billy Bunter, before Dick Francis came on the scene to bowl him over. This resolutely low-brow orientation is all of a piece with his egregious conservatism – that is, part joke, part front: "My political opinions are really no more than gouts of bile."

After Belfast and the library at Queen's, which he seems to have enjoyed, things kept on getting grimmer for Larkin — according to his correspondence, that is. He spent a few years hating Hull, where he moved in 1955 to take up the post of university librarian. From then on, it's a catalogue of anxieties: about his job, his reputation, his talent, his entanglements with women, his rivalries with fellow-authors, his health, his gregariousness versus his need for solitude, his mother, money, drink, moving house ... all ebulliently presented, but never quite excluding the darker undertone.

The letters don't conceal either despondency or despair; but for all that, Larkin's capacity to rivet the attention never falters. It's a matter of judging continuously the demands of the recipient — and, added to that, a knack of amusing. Once, complaining to Robert Conquest about someone having sent him a book, "c/o" an unreliable publisher, he comments: "which is like sending me a saucer of cream c/o the cat". For all his quarrels and querulousness and other shortcomings, you have to judge him in the end as a letter-writer more captivating than captious.

New Statesman and Society, 1992

PUSS IN BOOKS

Clare Boylan (ed.), *The Literary Companion to Cats*

It's incumbent on cat anthologists to disclaim a dewy-eyed approach to the topic, and Clare Boylan duly begins by repudiating the word "puss". This is a sop to those who believe the term degrades author and animal alike, and also possibly a ploy to win over others for whom the whole business of cat appreciation smacks of whimsy. "Puss", indeed, underscores the problem with writing about cats: finding a felicitous tone. Get the tone wrong, and the effect can be disastrous. The subject seems to require some decided idiosyncrasy (Christopher Smart, Stevie Smith) or astringency or charm – and it's the last, of course, that so easily topples over into kittenishness.

However, a number of recent anthologies – Boylan's among them – testify to an abundance of material, much of which is inspiriting or intriguing. It's true that, with all the classics of cat literature, and all the secondary sources to which compilers must turn, a good deal of overlap occurs with these collections. Francis Wheen's *Chatto Book of Cats*, for instance, which came out just over a year ago, duplicates quite a few of Clare Boylan's selections. This is not a problem. It would have been idiotic of either anthologist to over-look the most obvious things that spring to mind in relation to cats, from "Pangur Ban" onwards. And aside from these – "My Cat Jeoffrey", "Bustopher Jones", etc. – the *Literary Companion* comes up with a good variety of more obscure and wayward pieces, from Edward Topsell's *A Historie of Four-Footed Beastes* (for example) to an incidental image of Florence Nightingale mer-rily setting out on her travels with an entourage of 60 Persians. There's the cat as accessory (Elinor Glyn once created an effect by appearing in public with one draped around her neck); as symbol, as curiosity, as companion, as object of aversion. Some cats are better endowed than others with distinctiveness or grace or amiability, and these are often the ones we find in anthologies. However, it is hard to disagree with Clare Boylan's singling-out of a five-line poem by Francis Scarfe as the quintessential cat-piece:

Those who love cats which do not even purr,
Or which are thin and tired and very old,
Bend down to them in the street and stroke
                              their fur,
And rub their ears and smooth their breast,
                              and hold
Their paws, and gaze into their eyes of gold.

This is one discovery; there are others, some from Ireland — it is good, for example, to come across an extract from Mervyn Wall's comedy of mediaeval monasticism, *The Unfortunate Fursey* ("'Forgive me', said the sexton, 'I have neglected to make the usual introductions. This is Tibbikins, my familiar.' The cat nodded cheerily and favoured Fursey with [a] grin"), alongside Flann O'Brien ("'What you heard last night was the Sea-Cat! The Sea-Cat!!' The blood drained from my face when I heard that evil name ...".) Some inclusions are less satisfactory, among them Wendy Cope's unengaging epigram ("My cat is dead,/but I have decided not to make a big tragedy out of it"), which bristles with self-satisfaction; and Kathleen Hale's Orlando without the pictures, which nearly makes as little sense as having captions from Korky the Kat. And banality is supplied by two of the Liverpool poets — Patten and McGough. These are minor annoyances, though, in a collection which alerts us to

471

the riches of the genre, and gains our assent far more often than not.

Times Literary Supplement, 1994

WHETHER FOR DUSK, DAWN, NIGHT OR LIGHT, EVERY WORD HAS ITS PLACE

Robert Macfarlane, *Landmarks*

In his 1883 publication *Nature Near London*, Richard Jefferies has a vibrant passage enumerating all the wild flowers he encounters on a single roadside verge. Conspicuous among them are buttercups, cowslips and dandelions. The Jefferies passage is quoted late on by Robert Macfarlane in his compelling new study, *Landmarks*, and it ties in poignantly with a turn of events he has cited earlier. These words – buttercups, etc. – he tells us, along with others such as ash, acorn, bluebell, otter, kingfisher and heron, were deliberately excised from the 2007 edition of the *Oxford Junior Dictionary*.

They were deemed to be no longer relevant to children's experience. In contemporary life, it's out with willow and heather, and in with blog, broadband and chatroom. It is not, Macfarlane says, a question of either/or: both sets of nouns and what they signify have a place in the world of today. But life is unquestionably impoverished if you do away with bluebells, conkers, larks and other common words denoting nature and natural forces.

Landmarks is a book about words, among other things, words for features of the landscape, for ice and snow, for dusk, dawn, night and light. Each of its eleven chapters, with one exception, comes with a glossary containing words peculiar to different regions of these islands, from Connemara to Carloway on the Isle of Lewis: intriguing, expressive and eccentric words. (The exception is the final chapter, whose glossary is left blank to accommodate future coinages.)

A nab, for example, is the summit of a hill in Sussex; a Cumbrian sheep stranded on its back is a riggwelter. If you found yourself in a blinding snowstorm in Shetland, you might say you'd been caught in a moorie caavie. The author includes a selection of Irish and Northern Irish words among the indigenous terms for this or that sight, sensation or event – sliabh, bearna gaoithe, skiff, skite, hirple – though I was sorry not to see "foundered", meaning "perished with cold" (as in "The Foundered Farmer", a 1790s poem by James Orr), and still in common Ulster usage. But, as Robert Macfarlane says, his glossaries here are inevitably going to be very selective. They serve as an indication, no more, of endangered riches in the field of place-language and local linguistic particularities.

Macfarlane has won acclaim in recent years for his elegant and invigorating engagement with country matters, with language, continuity, lore, tradition, all kinds of fieldwork. He began with *Mountains of the Mind* in 2003, and went on to write *The Wild Places, The Old Ways* and *Holloway*, all of whose titles make explicit his fascination with unpopulated environments and unbeaten tracks. His books are original and illuminating, but they're not without predecessors; and *Landmarks* is, in part, a tribute to literary, as well as literal or physical, landmarks, and to those writers whose expertise in observation and evocation has affected his own approach and enlarged his outlook. Custodians of languages and runes, of ancient hedges and ditches, indefatigable walkers and explorers, inhabitants of enchanted places: these, in Macfarlane's book, are trailblazers and exemplars. Nan Shepherd falling under the spell of the Cairngorms (*The Living Mountain*); J.A. Baker getting as close as anyone can to predatory bird-nature (*The Peregrine*); Roger Deakin viewing Britain's landscape from a swimming perspective (*Waterlog*): these and others endorse and enhance

Macfarlane's preoccupations. They are salty, clear-eyed, strenuous commentators, with never a pastoral prettifier among them.

Wildwood enthusiasts and word conservationists contribute to a general sense of urgency and apprehension about the countryside and what may become of it. "O let them be left, wildness and wet", urged Gerald Manley Hopkins, in prescient mode. "Long live the wet and the wilderness yet." It isn't only the wilderness, however, but also indeterminate territories, edgelands, tail ends of cities and their accoutrements, that captivate Macfarlane. He eschews a narrow view of Earth and its attributes. "I am an edgelander", he declares at one point in the engaging autobiographical strand that runs through his narrative like a path through the woods. Alongside such suburban saving graces as field-paths, beech trees and the odd hedgerow, are raw ingredients of an inescapably bleak terrain. But if haulage depots, gravel pits, arc lights, litter-strewn canal banks and so forth can't be ignored, they may in some sense almost be relished, by adjusting one's attitude to aesthetics. In this respect, Richard Mabey and Iain Sinclair are names that spring to mind.

Landmarks covers a good deal of ground, from the Arctic north to the Sierra Nevada, while homing in continually on distinctive British chosen grounds, all abundant in imagery and implications, social, moral and regenerative implications. Some of the writers considered in depth by Robert Macfarlane get to grips with the landscape, and draw sustenance from it, by lying down on top of it; and there are other ways of experiencing nature to the full, even without going as far as one John Muir who, in the 1870s, flung himself headlong into a Yosemite avalanche ("Gloriously exciting", was his verdict). You can, for example, immerse yourself in woods and water, or head for the mountains to gather cloudberries and blueberries. Keeping the country in good heart by celebrating the countryside in all its aspects, in all its moods and seasonal variations: this is one of Robert Macfarlane's aims, and it's wonderfully achieved. He knows its mountains, lakes, forests, wildlife, fields and hedges in all their glory and singularity, and understands their need to be cherished. As far as conservation is concerned, he has found no need to make a mynydd out of a wonty-tump.

The Irish Times, 2015